GOOD ENOUGH TO EAT
A CONSUMERS' GUIDE

Warning: EATING CAN SERIOUSLY DAMAGE YOUR HEALTH

GOOD ENOUGH TO EAT

A CONSUMERS' GUIDE

MICHAEL BATEMAN

SINCLAIR~STEVENSON LTD

FOR
DANIEL, PAUL, SIMON, SARAH,
ALEXANDER, GEORGIA-MAY AND FAY

First published in Great Britain by
Sinclair-Stevenson Limited
7/8 Kendrick Mews
London SW7 3HG, England

Copyright © Michael Bateman 1991

British Library Cataloguing in Publication Data
A CIP catalogue record for this book is available from the British Library.
ISBN: 1 85619 090 0

Typeset by Butler & Tanner Ltd, Frome and London
Printed and bound in Great Britain by
Butler & Tanner Ltd, Frome and London

Contents

AUTHOR'S
ACKNOWLEDGEMENTS

I'd like to thank the very many people who have made this book possible, in particular those experts who have allowed me to quote them at length and who have advised me.

They include Professor Philip James, Professor Richard Lacey, Professor John Yudkin, Professor Alan Holmes, Professor Michael Crawford, Professor Brian Spencer, Dr John Burnett, Dr Magnus Pyke, Dr Richard Pugh, Dr David Player, Dr Erik Millstone, Dr Maurice Hanssen, Dr Gerald Solomon, Dr Norman Chamberlain, David MacLean MP, Sir Richard Body MP, Derek Cooper, Geoffrey Cannon, Egon Ronay, Drew Smith, Colin Spencer, Alan Long, the late Jane Grigson, Peter Bazalgette, Richard Guy, Henrietta Green, Miriam Polunin, Philip Diamond, Sue Dibb, Professor John Garrow, the late Professor Hugh Sinclair, Dr Reg Sayner, Dr Mark Holmes, James Erlichman.

The press offices of many organisations have kindly answered enquiries or given permission to quote from published material. They include: the Flora Project for Heart Disease Prevention, the Butter Information Council, the Health Education Authority, the Sugar Bureau, the British Nutrition Foundation, the World Health Organisation, Food From Britain, the Flour, Milling and Baking Research Association, Chorleywood, the Meat and Livestock Commission, the Ministry of Agriculture, Fisheries and Food, the Department of Health, Marks & Spencer, Sainsbury, Tesco, Safeway, Parents for Safe Food, the London Food Commission (now the Food Commission), Chickens' Lib, the Soil Association, the Seafish Industry Authority, the Lord Rank Research Institute, High Wycombe, Alcohol Concern, the Food Manufacturing Industries Research Association, Leatherhead, the Rowett Research Institute, Aberdeen, and Health Today.

In particular, I owe a special debt to Penelope Hoare, editorial director of Sinclair-Stevenson, for her guidance and support. And Sue Ramus and Jenny McLaren for research assistance.

AUTHOR'S INTRODUCTION

Britain's food technology is in advance of most countries in the world. So why doesn't our food taste better?

Our farmers produce more grain per acre than any in the world. So why don't we have better bread?

Our farmers are more efficient at producing beef, pork, chicken and eggs than most other countries, yet their expertise has been harnessed to the efficient production of cheap and highly processed food, food which lacks quality, is unhealthy, and sometimes unsafe.

Yet we have become complacent about the standard of our food, bombarded as we are with television commercials, often more entertaining than the programmes they interrupt. In supermarkets we are overwhelmed by food piled high, thanks to the most imaginative advertising agencies and creative marketing and packaging people in the world.

But the reality is that every few months we are faced with a new food scare: salmonella food poisoning from factory eggs and chickens; listeria in cheeses; brain disease transferring from sheep to cattle. We are advised by nutritionists that the high level of heart disease in this country, and cancers too, are due to an unsatisfactory diet. We are anxious about additives, yet food irradiation has been pressed upon us against our will.

If it's true that we have got our priorities badly wrong, the arrival of the Single European Market in 1992 will come as a shock to our food producers. At present our imports exceed exports by £5 billion in our annual £70 billion food bill. But our deficit could increase dramatically.

Stop the first dozen people you meet in the street, and ask them about British food today: many will voice suspicion and concern.

Who can we turn to for reassurance when there is a crisis of confidence? When Government, the Ministries, the food scientists, the food industry, farmers and growers, seem to have failed us?

In an attempt to establish the truth about the food we eat today, I set out to talk to those people in all facets of the world of food whose concern this is. They include directors of scientific research stations, professors of nutrition, Government Ministers, pressure groups and campaigners, social historians, food writers and broadcasters. Although in this book they have largely related their views in their own words, I must take responsibility for the emphasis given to them.

Talking to experts in each field, I discovered fifteen major areas of concern (the titles of the following chapters) and came to the following broad conclusions.

Technology. We produce too much processed food. On the grounds of taste, value, health, nutrition and safety our food technology must serve the ideal of producing more fresh food, not creating substitutes for it.

Meat. Never a country to inquire too closely into how meat is produced, we've been shocked by what we've seen as a result of the BSE scare. We must find ways of ensuring that we have better, safer meat.

Fish. Fish consumption is dropping, at a time when we discover that fish is a better protein for us than meat, that the oil in fish thins the blood and relieves heart disease. At the same time, we discover the extent to which our seas, rivers and estuaries are polluted. We should eat more fish and to do this we must ensure that our waterways are cleaned up and made safe.

Protein. Notions that the world might run out of food are premature. We need never go short of protein if we switch resources from animals to plants. Textured vegetable proteins are only the beginning. We need more research and resources in this area.

Nutrition. In spite of public disagreement among the giants who retail rival foods, there is little disagreement among the world's nutritionists. They unanimously agree about the need for nutritional training in schools, universities and colleges. All teachers, medics and hospital staff should be able to communicate basics to those who need to know.

Health. The healthy have as much right to continue to enjoy good health as the ill and infirm need to rediscover it. National Health Service bills could be considerably reduced if society as a whole was made aware of the dangers of obesity; the effect on the heart of eating too much saturated fat; the effect of salt on blood pressure; the fact that sugar overloads the metabolism with unnecessary work by providing energy without nutrients; the effects of smoking and excess alcohol consumption. Full health education should be taught to every level of society and the subject should be established in the national curriculum.

Additives. A focal point of attention in the 1980s. Not as dangerous as food phobics would have, but not as harmless as the confectionery industry would want us to believe. We must ensure that they are used only to good effect and prevent them from being added to poor quality ingredients, simply to give cosmetic appeal and a longer shelf life.

Irradiation. If this had been classed as an additive, every chemical component affected by food irradiation would have to have undergone stringent tests for carcinogenicity. It has been classed as a food process and has nevertheless undergone extensive tests. But we must ensure that irradiation, together with all other new processes, really does carry an advantage to the consumer and is not simply being used to make money for the food industry, at the expense of the consumer.

Food safety. The consumer has been lulled into complacency about the food he or she brings into the home. In grandmother's day, potential hazards in food were recognised and strict controls were observed: the washing of hands, raw chicken not being stored beside cooked meat, and so on. Nowadays, chilled food, conveyed through the food chain to the supermarket, must also make its way safely from the store to the home, to the fridge or freezer and onto the stove. We need food education relevant to today's needs.

Real food. Why should there by any kind other than real food? Why not fresh food for all? Food is too important to be left to market forces, for the supermarkets and the food industry to manage. We need a Ministry of Food, responsible for food only, and not lumped in with the often contradictory interests of agriculture and fisheries. We need the Ministry to be responsible for quality, health and safety.

Food of superb quality is still available in Britain, mostly in specialist or expensive shops. But for many people the supermarket is the powerful voice of the 1990s; supermarkets have put to flight the traditional high street grocer, greengrocer, butcher, baker and fishmonger. The big chains now sell 70 per cent of all food sold. If we want better produce, it is largely to them that we must address ourselves.

Changes can and do take place when consumers identify problems, when they speak and act in unison. For example, the shopper has forced supermarkets to restrict the use of additives such as colourings and preservatives, and to provide nutritional labelling. And consumers are now demanding, and getting, more produce farmed organically, in protest against herbicides and pesticides sprayed on crops, fruit and vegetables.

In Britain today we continue to breed the finest beef and lamb and pork in the world, and those of our rivers still unpolluted yield fine salmon and trout. Our shores provide oysters, scallops, lobsters. The moors provide woodcock, pheasant, partridge and grouse; the glens give up their venison. Dairy farms are beginning to provide a superb range of indigenous cheeses; we have the craftsmanship to smoke haddock and kippers and eel and mackerel. We can make fine beers, ciders, whiskies (and even some white wines) as well as any in the world. Yet we haven't learnt to prize our own fresh produce as it deserves. It needs all the support we can give it, and now, before it is too late.

In writing this book I have been motivated by a wish to see only the best, the most tasty and healthy food on display in the shops we use every day. To help me achieve this end, I interviewed and consulted very many people. I am extremely grateful to them for their wholehearted support. I cannot thank them enough. I hope that in sharing their expertise and concern, you too will be able to ensure that the food you serve to family and friends will always be Good Enough to Eat.

Michael Bateman, 1991

1

THE FOOD WORLD

As we approach a new millenium, we should be anticipating a Golden Age of Food.

Our farming and agricultural skills have been advancing as never before: doubling in efficiency in a matter of twenty years. Our food science and technology are dazzling, and a few thousand machines make all the bread that in our own lifetime once took tens of thousands of ill-paid bakers, working long unsocial hours, to produce.

In a few decades, we have lived through the most extraordinary changes in our food supply and production that we have experienced in our whole history. Less than 150 years ago these islands experienced real famine, as bad as anything endured in the Sudan today, when potato blight destroyed Ireland's staple crop and half a million people starved to death. And we only have to look back half a century to find people suffering from malnutrition, notably in the north of England, on a diet of bread, margarine, jam and tea.

If we choose to look back to the Good Old Days of our childhoods, let us not forget the grocers and fishmongers and butchers where food went bad because it wasn't chilled or preserved effectively; the apples with spots; the cabbages and pea-pods and lettuces crawling with caterpillars and slugs; the 'real beer' that went sour and cloudy.

What we might look back upon with sentimental regret – and rightly so – is the way that farming and agriculture, food products and cooking, have passed from expert craftsmen to food technologists, so that tender loving care has been exchanged for impersonal efficiency. A Golden Age won't arrive until the benefits of science are applied to quality as energetically as they have been applied to achieving profits.

In the 1990s we should be basking in the glory of our achievements, but the fact is that we are not.

In the 1950s we struggled out of the hardship of post-War austerity and the loss of cheap food supplies from the Empire. We set a target of self sufficiency in the 1960s – and achieved it. We launched food technology and in the 1970s started to reap its benefits; supermarkets began to promise a shoppers' paradise. By the 1980s we'd not only achieved sufficiency, we had a surfeit.

The modern supermarkets which sell 70 per cent of all food in Britain are Aladdin's caves, piled with rich treasures in brightly lit and colourful avenues, not just satisfying needs, but making seductive advances, soliciting for business with their garish promises. Pleasant canned music tinkles in the background as shoppers load their trolleys until they resemble overflowing cornucopias on wheels. Every shopping day is a holiday for the children whose clamour for the brightly packed sweets and snacks and cereals cannot be refused. And if any doubts at all are harboured, there are signs on all sides assuring customers of the company's commitment to nursing the planet with environmentally friendly sprays and washing-up liquids, to reducing additives to the absolute minimum, to healthy eating initiatives and complete nutritional labelling. Whatever your anxieties, they seem to have anticipated them.

The goodness of our food is emphasised daily, on our television screens, in glossy magazines, its quality apparently magical in its ability to enhance our lifestyles. It is a picture of a glamorous and exciting world, the world of food today.

And it is amazing. Thirty years ago we did not have the freezer displays which offer a wealth of gleaming white dairy products or nourishing packs of red meat, nor the packaging skills to bring out-of-season exotic fruits and vegetables from across the world. We didn't have the microwave cooker to convert ready-made chilled recipe dishes in a matter of moments. Now, everything we might want is there, done for us: fish is gutted, filleted and packed in windowed boxes for the chill-units, saving us the distasteful business of preparing it; even salad leaves have been washed, selected, and sold in peak condition. It's easy to forget how recently this has all come about. The previous generation was not brought up on fish fingers, frozen produce, and chickens as cheap and freely available as they are now.

Food technology has created for us a kind of Garden of Eden where everything from all over the world is available all the year round: at any other time in history, an unimaginable dream.

We should be grateful, but we're not. If you consult health experts, nutritionists and so on, they will probably each voice a concern about the food they are eating: whether it is safe, healthy, free of insect sprays or additives; if it's beef, pig or chicken, how it is reared, whether it is injected with hormones; whether the waters fish and shellfish come from are polluted.

Expressing concern is, of course, a luxury enjoyed by those of us living in the affluent West. In large parts of Africa, Asia and the Americas the obsession is real, simply because there isn't enough food to keep people alive. Painfully, we expect thousands to die of famine in Africa, sooner rather than later. We know that millions in India are seriously undernourished, and have a pitifully short life expectancy compared to our own.

It is an embarrassment that we have a life of choice and abundance and can do so little, in spite of our twenty-first century technology, to help those who need it most; it is also an embarrassment that the Western world manages to make itself ill through its affluence, literally ill, through diseases related to excess. In Britain one person dies every three minutes of premature heart disease due to a diet high in saturated fats. Cancer is often considered to be diet-related, too.

The more that comes out into the open about the nature of the British diet, the food supply, food production, and food handling, the more people begin to feel concern, shame, disgust and occasionally outrage. Inevitably it falls to Government to explain.

Ministers of Agriculture, Fisheries and Food have in turn taken the hot seat and, instead of fighting Britain's battles in Brussels, find themselves fighting in the trenches in a consumers' civil war against their own people. We are being panicked into alarm about intensive farming methods which seem to incubate disease; about weak links in the food chain, about chilling cabinets which nurse listeria instead of inhibiting it, about microwave ovens which have cold spots where salmonella will not be killed. Other consumers are agitated about the use of colours derived from coal tar and azo dyes which are associated with hyperactivity in children who are most exposed to them (in sweets and cola drinks in particular). These and other additives are banned in some countries, but not ours, and we want to know why we should be put at risk at all.

A general suspicion falls on the food industry as a whole, which tends to be judged by its worst practitioners rather than its best – as when we discover that it's considered fair trading to add water to bulk up bread, increase the weight of ham, bacon, frozen poultry, fish, and to 'glaze' prawns with a heavy film of ice; or when additives are used as cosmetics to disguise poor quality ingredients.

But the area of greatest concern, which has been concealed in the shadows until now, is the question of the balance of the British diet itself. It has seemed hardly possible to the generation which emerged from the shortages of the War and post-War years that the bounties of the good life – plentiful meat, cheese, butter and cream – would set a time bomb ticking in the hearts of people so obviously full of good protein, vitamins and nutrients. But now excessive fat in our diet has been spotlighted as the major cause of heart disease, the biggest single cause of death in Britain, higher here than in any other country in the world. Other diseases are associated with our diet – cancers of the colon, diverticulitis. And others are attributed to the 'refined' foods we eat: white flour (in biscuits, cakes and pastries in particular) and the vast amount of refined white sugar we consume in many forms (dissolved in coke drinks, squashes, in ice creams, even in savoury foods such as baked beans and tomato sauce).

We now question our lack of cereals, fresh fruit and vegetables, which are thought to give protection against cancers.

It is difficult to know where the ordinary consumer can turn for balanced advice. Who can arbitrate on issues such as the relative merits of saturated, polyunsaturated, mono-unsaturated fats, when the eloquent voices of persuasion are ranged on opposite sides of the debating chamber, ready to spend many thousands of pounds to press their case through advertising? Take the merits of butter and margarine.

The Flora people spend £6 million a year advertising their margarine which is on the crest of a healthy eating wave. It is made with sunflower oil, which is unsaturated, unlike butter which is saturated fat. They also finance the Flora Project for Heart Disease Prevention, which energetically seeks out certain parts of the national unconscious and spreads a more potent message than is permitted in paid advertisements. It is a very successful strategy and margarine now outsells butter for the first time in 150 years.

In direct competition, the butter people spend £7 million a year on advertising, and they fund the Butter Information Council which promotes an image of butter as 'traditional food'. It conducts a sniping campaign against margarine, often ready to cast doubts on its merits (might polyunsaturated oils provoke free radicals, those agents of cancer? they ask). But chiefly, like an advocate in court, they seek to show their client in a rosy light, minimising the role of butter in the 'fat story'. For example, they point out that butter represents 7.1 per cent of our average fat consumption, compared with 11.8 per cent from cream and milk, and 25.6 per cent from meat and meat products. Their conclusion is soothing: 'Butter lovers can still enjoy this natural food, as they have for thousands of years, as long as they eat it in moderate amounts and keep an eye on their total fat and energy intake.'

Sugar is another case in point. For twenty years, at least since Professor John Yudkin wrote his famous attack on the industry, *Pure, White and Deadly*, sugar has been under pressure because sugar damages children's teeth, because it is associated with getting fat, and because obesity can lead to heart disease.

In 1990 the sugar industry launched a £12 million campaign to promote its image. The television advertisements were glorious: a parade of wildlife was evocatively summoned up, closing with a sensational shot of a humming bird poised to suck nectar. In Chapter Eight you'll see how convincingly and entertainingly the case for sugar is put. Sugar doesn't damage your teeth, they assure you, it's the acid released by bacteria in the mouth, so brush your teeth and the bacteria will starve. Sugar doesn't make you fat. Except when you eat too much of it.

The loudest voices have the most money to spread their message. The food industry spends around £700 million a year advertising its goods. In contrast, the voice of moderation and caution, the Health Education Authority has had a comparitively modest budget of £2 million to advertise its message, *Look After Your Heart*.

Chocolate, that irresistibly delicious mixture of sugar, vegetable oil and milk powder, accounts for the largest advertising budget – over £80 million. Cereals are next with over £60 million – those bland, sweetened flattened flakes of maize, and exploded rice grains, and denatured wheat, whose most beneficial contribution to our nutritional well-being is the milk we put on them.

The next big budget is some £50 million for powdered coffee, our daily pick-me-up, those shots of caffeine which make us so alive, so appealing and, if we are to believe the commercials, so sexy. Salad creams, sauces and pickles are next with around £30 million; then margarine, tea, frozen meals. Crisps weigh in with a staggering £20 million advertising budget, matched by children's sweets and biscuits.

All are pleasant, tasty foods, of course, colourful strands which weave the fabric of our society. But all of them are manufactured foods which depend on the added glamour that advertising confers on them, and most of them are the products of a few enormous and influential companies, such as Unilever who market margarine and ice cream, sausages and processed meats, soups and ready-made meals (they declared £1,454 million profits in 1989); Tate and Lyle – sugar (£300 million profits in 1990); Rank Hovis McDougal (bread and cakes); Cadbury Schweppes (chocolates and soft drinks); Rowntree Nestlé (chocolates and biscuits); Beecham and Reckitt and Colman (soft drinks); United Biscuits and Nabisco (biscuits); Allied-Lyons (cakes) and Mars (chocolates). Naturally, they take a firm stance against accusations that their own products in any way contribute to the country's poor health.

The food industry has an ally in the British Nutrition Foundation, whose director, Dr David Conning, has openly attacked some critics of the food industry, blaming them for starting scares. 'Food and nutrition are becoming a national obsession. Self-publicists are undermining the reputation of basic foods such as meat, milk and eggs. Their warnings should be taken with a pinch of salt.' And salt too, he adds, is the subject of persistent arguments. Some scientists say it is a cause of hypertension, while others say reduced salt could lead to kidney damage. Some reports link polyunsaturated oil to cancer, others say exactly the opposite. 'Every time we read that coffee, for example, is dangerous, we are guaranteed to read days later that it is actually good for us,' said Dr Conning.

Many people think we should be able to look to a Government agency to lead in these matters. But the Government position has become increasingly difficult, not least for historical reasons.

Food issues touch every aspect of the national life; on the one hand, food is agriculture, industry and Big Business; on the other, it is an essential part of the national welfare, our health and nutritional standards, for mothers, children, the elderly and the sick, as well as the active. One Ministry, the Department of Health, is responsible for some aspects, another, the Ministry of Agriculture, Fisheries and Food (MAFF) is responsible for the others. A conflict might therefore be expected, say, between the interests of the farmers, those of the supermarkets, those of the food industry and those of the consumer.

In other decades the role of the Minister was clear-cut. In the last War, Lord Woolton, as Minister of Food, was second only to Sir Winston Churchill in persona, managing the food economy in order to lead us from the brink of starvation (even lending his own name to a substantial parsnip and potato pie). Each Minister assumes the mantle that history throws on him: initiating a research programme to Make Britain Self-Sufficient, or leading the Navy into a Cod War with Iceland, or battling for our farmers in the conference rooms of Brussels, headquarters of the Common Market.

In the 1990s, the Minister will be required to restore consumer confidence in the food chain which was rocked by a series of crises, salmonella in eggs and chickens, listeria in cheese, and mad cow disease in beef herds. To this end in 1989 the Minister of Agriculture, Fisheries and Food, John Gummer, appointed Food Safety Minister, David MacLean.

David MacLean is a young politician in his mid-thirties, an Inverness farmer's son who trained in law, and worked for Securicor before turning to politics. He firmly believes the Ministry shouldn't be dictating what people should eat, since the food industry amply fulfils market demands. Government should be the policeman who administers law and order, and where necessary apprehends the villains and sees off the rascals.

'Until very recently the agricultural departments of every country in the world have had the traditional role of trying to feed their starving people, and that went for Britain too, just after the War. We still have a role in the European Community in this overall department, fighting for British farmers' interests, fighting to increase our share of the food supply and food subsidies. But we're no longer going to "sponsor" the food industry, to use an old word. We're not going to champion them, right or wrong.'

He's extremely happy about the way the big food companies have

been leading the way in the 1970s and 1980s, and thinks it's good
that the power should be in their hands. 'Ordinary farmers complain
about the power of the supermarkets and multiples, but they are
using their power to reduce colourings and additives, to bring in
organic foods, to produce more humanely reared meat, setting standards for free-range chickens, the conditions pigs are kept in. They
will continue to impose standards according to what they perceive
to be the demands of the housewife.'

He says it's not the Government's role to make initiatives or push
a specific line. 'There's no problem about feeding our people any
more. We see our policy as being more neutral. Arbitrating on safety,
labelling, letting consumers have choice. We're not going to do
the supermarkets' job. And we're not going to do the chemical
companies' job. It's not our job to develop foods without additives,
but it is our job to tighten up and control. We have announced bans
on dozens of colourings, and restrictions on the rest.'

On safety he is extremely confident. 'We take advice from a
large number of scientists and independent committees, as well as
Government agencies, like the World Health Organisation and the
American Food and Drugs Administration. In the end we can be
the only independent arbiter. You can't look at medical associations,
because they have their bias. The British Nutrition Foundation is
funded by certain companies. The London Food Commission was
sponsored by left-wing councils. Various institutes, university professors and journalists have their axes to grind.'

But does the free economy best serve the interests of the whole
nation? The well-informed and the better-off will always be able
to buy tasty, healthy, nutritious food and we hope that the
Government's law and order will ensure that everyone gets safe
food. But couldn't we do better in providing a balanced, varied,
affordable diet for all?

Consumer awareness of good eating is improving, but any change
on a major scale would have to be achieved by a political initiative
affecting the roots of our society. This is the well-expressed view of
Drew Smith, a former editor of the *Good Food Guide* who forcefully
backed restaurants which sought out good, fresh local ingredients
instead of slipping into the easy, profitable but ultimately self-
defeating convenience packs so readily supplied by catering companies.

Drew Smith, author of *Modern Cooking* and a campaigner against irradiation in food, believes that politicians should not be allowed to evade their responsibility for the future of our food, its quality rather than safety (safety, in any case, ought to be taken for granted in the world of the 1990s).

'Government got a taste for power during the last War when it introduced rationing to make it possible to feed ourselves. Since then successive Governments have dictated agricultural policy, especially as far as yield is concerned. They have looked on the excess as a nice means of helping underdeveloped countries. We dumped all this stuff on them. Mass agriculture produces food which we may or may not want.'

But does Britain produce enough food of the right sort? 'No, the figures are frightening. Since 1972 the EEC imports from France are nine times more than we export to her. Five times more than we export to Holland, Spain and Denmark. We are not making any money on our food economy. We are buying it in with money we've got from elsewhere. We seem to trust the multinational companies. They are now more powerful than the Government which is no longer our representative. Britain as a food-producing nation is bankrupt.'

Drew Smith says we've lost our way in every sense. Nutritionally, culturally, economically. 'The food we are providing is patently not in the interests of the ordinary people of this country. We are eating foods which we know we shouldn't be eating, which the doctors say we shouldn't be eating, such as chocolates and biscuits. In most supermarkets they have fresh food for 10 per cent of their customers; that is serious for the remaining 90 per cent.'

Why is it so bad? 'It's because we've lost the local control. Look at the food in schools. It's disgusting. They have a centralised buying policy, so eventually you get the money from Government going to a multinational company which produces baked beans or chocolate bars or crisps, as opposed to a localised policy where all the money would have gone to local suppliers. The fishmonger, greengrocer and butcher would have actually counted on that as part of his weekly income. Now he's gone out of business. And as a result of this policy we have no local shops. People say: Well, you know, we can still get what we like. But they can't. They don't get a genuine choice. The area of crafts in the food industry is no longer there. When local suppliers move out, people have to go to large super-

markets. The fishmongers, delicatessens and greengrocers are vanishing, and the market gardens, too. Look at the economics of it. We
have an unemployment problem, and we've lost jobs in all the food
crafts. We had 11,000 fishmongers in 1952. There are only 2,500
now. It's the same for other tradesmen.'

If we leave it to the multinational companies, we are selling out.
'The money will not stay in Britain. It just goes. It dissipates into
somebody's pocket. If you control it in some way by keeping some
form of local identity and local support, then the money stays within
your local orbit, and you have a chance. The only way to survive in
the marketplace is to create quality. That means choice. To have
choice you have to have your local premium product there on the
shelf, so, when the stuff comes from New Zealand and Canada,
you've then got a choice of not one or two, but three items.

'We British have sold out around the world, whereas we should
have held on to what is the French approach. Compare French wine
and English beer. A hundred years ago, Monsieur Petrus would look
at his vineyard in Bordeaux and say: I'd better be careful about
this – one century from now my great grandsons will be able to
sell a bottle of wine for £20 or even £200 if it's Chateau Petrus. The
French build in local identity as a mark of special quality, and make
a selling point of its source and origin. They say, they won't allow
it to be adulterated and then it will have an identity, and they
will keep their identity. In international trade French wine is of
significance. You don't get that with English beer. But it's equally
unique. Real ale is to keg beer what champagne is to carbonated
white wine. Basically our companies are not interested in premium,
locally made, high quality beers – instead we are advocating lager,
which is an international product which has steamrollered the entire
business.'

The French continue to provide good examples of managing their
food to the maximum benefit of everyone. 'If you go somewhere like
Toulouse, you'll find they have a green belt area designated round
the city, where farms have been given to people as a cooperative. As
part of getting that farm they have the obligation of sending food to
market so that Toulouse people get fresh food which fulfils the
criteria of good nutrition and good taste. If it doesn't sell in Toulouse
in the morning it goes across the road to the national market at
Rintjes in Paris on the bus. It's all good business. It may not be the
most profitable business in terms of money. But in terms of the role

of food in society, the quality of society, of holding society together, it's actually very functional.'

France is three times bigger than Britain, an agricultural nation, and they protect their producers. 'Instead of bringing in more mangoes from Colombia and turning Colombia into a cash crop economy, we should be concentrating on specialist, premium value goods, for our own use, which have an identity. Take Cheddar. Cheddar was originally an identifiable cheese which we made for ourselves. We ruined it, because we industrialised it so effectively that it also works very well for Canada and New Zealand, Holland and any other Tom, Dick or Harry around the world who wants to build a factory to do it.' By making cheese on this big scale, we have devalued the product itself.

The argument for increasing the scale and volume of food production is that it is more efficient. 'Being more efficient is a political belief. It also means putting people out of work more efficiently, and giving people worse things to eat more efficiently. Governments do not know how to look after communities. 'When you centralise food processes, you run out of food. You see it in Soviet Russia and in Eastern Europe. In Ethiopia, they've gone beserk. They no longer know how to look after their own communities. Ten million people are dying and we in Britain, a frontier nation, a First World country, can't do anything about it. We can't airdrop McDonalds ready-made hamburgers on them.'

2

TECHNOLOGY

In the 1990s it has become fashionable to despise food technology. As we come to realise that there's almost nothing we can eat which has not been modified or processed as the result of intervention by plant geneticists and food scientists, a feeling of resentment sets in and, with it, a nostalgia for places where it is different and times when it was better.

But it never was better. Food and travel writers may enthuse over the country markets of Europe, the fish markets of the Mediterranean ports, the exotic tropical delights of Bangkok, Bali and Burma, but the truth is that it is the British high street which is exotic.

Today the average high street supermarket is a cornucopia of plenty. We have short memories. We take it for granted in the West that we can avail ourselves of almost any kind of foodstuff the world can produce, at almost any time of the year, and in an extremely good condition when we get it. Yet somehow we think it was better on our Mediterranean holidays when we went to the fish markets, and we remember the glistening metallic shine of so much freshly landed seafood: hake, red mullet, sardines, anchovies, squid, octopus. We remember the souks of North Africa, the vegetable markets of Italy, Spain and Greece with so many highly coloured ripe vegetables, fruits, herbs and spices imparting their rich scent under the hot sun.

Equally we look back to the Good Old Days, the days before our own food was highly processed, when chickens tasted of chicken.

The Good Old Days were good for the privileged – the only people who got to eat a good old chicken. In the Good Old Days food was marvellous only when it was fresh. The average grocer's shop in the 1930s had no refrigeration, although meat would have come from cold stores. Out the back there would be a pungent aroma of stale cheese and smelly bacon and ham, and each day the worst pieces, turning green, would be cut off and discarded. The housewife ignored at her peril the message of her nose and eyes, identifying fish smelling of ammonia, clammy and limp with dull eyes, or stinking sausages or sour kidneys. It might be proof of freshness that cabbages still retained their complement of insects, pea-pods their caterpillars, lettuces their slugs. In the Good Old Days most of the fruit in the greengrocer's shop was deteriorating at a fair old rate. But it still got sold, and there are still a few 'traditional' greengrocers observing the good old rules, serving bad produce with the fresh, such as apples, carrots or potatoes in a bag which includes one good one, two average ones, and one or two diseased, damaged, bruised or rotten ones. The good stuff was arranged artistically at the front of the stall; what you got was from a bin under the counter. You most certainly couldn't test fruit to see if it was ripe, and fruits were even aggressively labelled *Do not touch me till I am yours*.

Post-War food technology mastered the problems of food spoilage and put an end to an era it is convenient to remember selectively. The benefits of food technology were quickly taken for granted.

What angers the critics of food technology is the way that the food industry has used it to exploit the consumers for profit, offering no longer a choice of either excellent or indifferent, as in the Good Old Days, but a choice of utterly average, ordinary, dull, bland, tasteless, watery products, calling upon food technology to make them seem something which they are not. Food technology has been harnessed to make inferior, low grade products; it is still waiting to be put to the service of the Good New Days. But even to contemplate this, many would say, is an extraordinary luxury.

Even in our own memories, efforts to feed ourselves adequately have been a relentless struggle against Nature. Until recently the food on our tables has been completely seasonal. Eggs would be hard to come by in winter, over-abundant in the spring. The first salads, vegetables and fruits would appear in early summer; and by October most of the harvest would have been taken, to be dry stored, dried and smoked, salted or preserved as best as possible.

We have done more to ensure the planet's food supply in our generation than at any time in its 5,000 million years of existence, or since life emerged ten million years ago, or in our two million years as hunters and gatherers.

Early man seems to have led a nomadic life, killing animals and birds, catching fish, eating fruit, berries, nuts, roots, seeds, and, if he was lucky, honey. One can only guess at the hardships of trial and error as the tribes chose their foods, distinguished safe from poisonous, beneficial from harmful, and suffered from disease, malnutrition and starvation, and resorted to cannibalism, as we know, when all else failed.

The first technology was the use of simple tools which enabled man to settle, dig land to plant grass for the seeds which seemed so nourishing, which they would one day learn to crush and make into edible pastes, and eventually bake into bread.

When man first settled, about 8,000 years ago, he gathered scavenging animals around him, feeding them on scraps; they were the fore-runners of our cows, pigs, sheep and chickens. As a species, we seem to have settled for a compromise between the ferocious carnivores, the cat family, and the mild herbivores, our cousins the apes.

The discovery of fire was the greatest tool of technology, enabling indigestible foods to be broken down and in the process killing harmful bacteria. How the boiling of foods became an art form is recorded in the history of the Chinese people who to this day employ more subtle and sophisticated ways of using the world's food resources than any other people; and in the court cooking of the Persian empire, and later the Roman Empire, and later in the courts of the Kings of France, and later still in the Austrian–Hungarian Empire.

For those not of elevated status, food has simply been a matter of survival. From the eighth to the fourteenth century in Europe food shortages were a matter of sheer desperation. Men ate anything at all that could be digested. In Germany bread was made from grass, seeds and roots; in Sweden of 90 per cent bark and straw; in France of acorns – a slight but not enormous improvement. Much of Europe was in an almost continual state of war which made agriculture impossible to sustain.

The search for food supplies motivated wars, but it was also responsible for the exploration of a wider world. Precious spices, for example, could be traded at almost their weight in gold. Marco Polo had opened up a spice route from China by land, and it was the lure

of financial reward which caused investors to buy and fit out fleets
of vessels. Thus Christopher Columbus found America in error
when he was looking for a shorter spice route to the Far East.

Europe benefited from the import of unusual fruit and vegetables,
such as the tomato and of course the potato, which came to supplement grain and reduce dependence on corn crops and the terrible
consequences of failure of grain harvest.

But in spite of additions to the food supply, the poor of Britain
continued to eat an extremely meagre diet right up to the middle of
the nineteenth century – when the Industrial Revolution served as
a blessing and a curse. The population surged in size. London tripled
to three million in the first sixty years of the nineteenth century, and
soon three-quarters of the population had migrated to the cities. It
was to sustain the people in the towns that food technology in Britain
developed.

Early man's food science had concentrated on preservation. Fish
was dried in the sun, as it still is in the Far East; or salted and dried
(Portuguese bacalão – salt cod – was dried by their fishing fleets as
far away as Newfoundland); or dried over smoke to give us our
characteristic smoked salmon, haddock, kippers, red herring, bloaters. Meat, which had been dried out, could be carried by horsemen
and reconstituted into a stew over a camp fire, the origin of the
goulash in Hungary, the Biltong which is eaten by cattle ranchers,
and Pemmican which was used by Red Indians. Technology in the
form of tools aided agriculture. The invention of the watermill in
Greece in 450 BC was harnessed 500 years later by the Romans to
turn stone querns to crush wheat; just as the windmill, invented in
Persia in 600 AD, was later turned to milling wheat also.

It wasn't until the eighteenth century in Britain that science
was effectively applied to agriculture. Farming benefited from the
invention, by Jethro Tull, of the seed drill which was applied to the
sowing of grain in East Anglia – where the soil had wrongly been
thought unsuitable for wheat. Norfolk soon became the 'Granary
of England'. Other discoveries made it possible to feed animals
effectively throughout the winter; Charles ('Turnip') Townsend
introduced root crops as a winter food, and processes were evolved
to produce linseed and rapeseed oil cake for animal feeds.

The greatest scientific contribution to agriculture was made in the
mid-nineteenth century by the German Justus von Liebig, who
found that carbon was derived almost entirely from carbon dioxide

in the atmosphere, and that nitrogen was absorbed by the roots in the form of ammonia, thus establishing the basis of fertiliser as ammonium salts (nitrates), potassium salts and phosphates, a discovery that revolutionised agriculture.

The nineteenth century saw the birth of many new processes. Canning was mastered at the beginning of the century, the result of work by a Frenchman, Nicholas Appert, who discovered how to seal food hermetically in glass jars, after standing them in hot water to expel air. A Briton, Robert Durand, very effectively applied the principle to iron containers, and the process was at first exclusively used to furnish the Royal Navy. At its worst the process was subject to abuse, and some of the bad cuts of meat, gristle and fat, which were preserved and served in this way, gave rise among sailors to the expression Sweet Fanny Adams – the name of an unfortunate murder victim of the day who'd been cut up into small pieces. It wasn't until the end of the century that canning really took off in the States. In 1905 Mr H.J. Heinz's tinned baked beans were introduced to Britain. The 1914–18 War was the stimulus that was needed to jog British canning technology: factories that sprang up to provide bully beef for the Forces went on to produce tinned vegetables and fruit after the War. In the 1920s and 1930s Britain became a major importer of American canned food, particularly peaches, pears and pineapple, and jams from Australia. The major British breakthrough was the canned pea, introduced by Smedley's, made with dried peas and dyed a garish glaring emerald green.

Canned meat and fish, soups, vegetables and fruits made a valuable contribution to the British storecupboard, and even now, when they are not essential, they have established a cosy niche for themselves, not only tins of the enduring baked beans, but canned salmon and tuna and sardines and mackerel, which are stock items in every home.

Convenience foods arrived in the early years of the century, and nothing could be more convenient than Alfred Bird's instant custard. Alfred Bird was a Birmingham chemist whose wife was fond of custard but allergic to eggs, and he evolved a mixture of cornflour, colours and flavours, which could be reconstituted by the addition of milk. He marketed it brilliantly, and in that way evolved the idea of branding.

The 1860s saw farmhouse crafts like cheese-making passing to factories and, once we'd got a taste for it, factory cheese became a major staple of the working class diet, much of it imported from Australia and America. It developed in parallel with margarine, the poor man's butter (called Butterine until the diary industry forced it to withdraw this name).

Technology brought many 'luxury' goods within reach of working people. In Britain the metal roller mills of the 1870s had dramatically brought down the price of the white loaf, which until then had been an extravagance for the well-to-do. As the roller mills had made it possible to extract white flour cheaply (the fine bolted white flour had always been reserved for the masters) so sugar was easily processed by machines, to be combined with milk powder and cocoa flavouring to produce chocolate (in the seventeenth century the ultimate luxury, when it was known as a drink – Dr Samuel Johnson frequented coffee-houses which sold it). Cadbury's was the first company to produce a milk chocolate bar on a mass scale; In the First World War its nutritional value and good keeping qualities won it a place in emergency rations.

The biscuit, which had been another aristocratic luxury, was revolutionised by factory technology. By the turn of the century many companies had made their name by mechanising this subtle kitchen craft, such as William Crawfords, Carr's of Carlisle and Huntley and Palmer's of Reading. The biscuit is such a convenient product, half snack, half food, with excellent keeping qualities, that it has come to be seen as a staple of the diet of most of the population, and a company like Tesco will sell 200 different brands today in its superstores.

Another expensive luxury, ice cream, was mechanised. Technology was applied to sugar, milk powder and fat to bring it within reach of the ordinary person's purse. The fat used initially was lard, for the company which made the breakthrough was Thomas Wall and Sons, sausage manufacturers, and ice cream manufacture was undertaken to utilise labour which otherwise would have been laid off in the summer months when demand for sausages dropped. They were joined by J. Lyons, who virtually monopolised the market in the 1930s, establishing the importance of advertising and promotion as the tool of technological food – a form of added value.

The Second World War gave a huge impetus to food technology, and the post-War years saw the development of freezing. It was one of the oldest techniques known to mankind but had proved expensive to duplicate by man-made means. The Chinese used ice-houses to store fish and fruit several thousand years ago. The sixteenth century philosopher, Francis Bacon, stumbled on the principle of frozen chicken by stuffing snow round a freshly killed bird – but he died a few weeks afterwards from a cold he contracted as a result of his experiment. In Britain it wasn't until the eighteenth century that the big landowners started to have ice-houses built on their estates to preserve meat and fruit; but the idea extended to the salmon rivers as a means of keeping the catch fresh, and eventually to fishing fleets taking ice with them on their expeditions. Ice had to be cut from lakes in winter months to be preserved and insulated with straw below ground.

The freezing process was discovered in the early 1800s and the first ice-making machines appeared in the 1850s. For thirty years vast sums were invested in fitting out ships with freezer systems to export meat from Australia and Argentina, and there were many fortunes lost before it was successfully achieved.

The emphasis of world trade shifted. No longer do local producers bring in frequent fresh supplies; instead international trading giants use their power to direct the economy of whole countries. A banana republic is a country depending on single crops which are so sensitive that, if the bananas are not collected within a day of being picked, and packed into freezer containers, they pass their saleable point, go mouldy and rot by the roadside.

Freezing individual items for the home was Clarence Birdseye's idea. He was an American chemist who set up the first freezer factory in New York in 1923 after visiting Labrador in Canada and seeing fish frozen hard as planks, which thawed out into excellent food for the table. He evolved the process of quick-freezing which doesn't allow time for large ice crystals to form, which would lead to deterioration in quality and texture. He invented a way of freezing food between metal plates. It was introduced to Britain just before the last War, but didn't take off until after it, when Unilever, the multinational corporation, bought Birdseye and brilliantly created a market for its products.

It was not only a matter of producing the new frozen foods, but of creating customer demand for them through advertising; stimulating the sales of fridges and freezers; and putting pressure on shopkeepers to invest in adequate refrigeration capacity by persuading them what increased profits would be possible. Unilever set a benchmark for quality and efficiency which is reflected today in the massive array of chill cabinets which line our major super-markets – and it gave us, too, a new generation of easy foods to take home: not only cuts of meats, whole chickens, fish, vegetables and fruit, but convenience products with no waste: burgers and breaded fish which go straight under the grill. The fish finger, introduced in 1955, pointed to a revolution in customer expectations – the house-wife was handed the right to give her family fresh, appetising and nutritious food without having any tiresome and time-consuming preparation beforehand. From frozen foods it was a short step to frozen meals, and finally to the development of tasty cook-chill recipe dishes.

Modern British food and drink technology, instead of bringing us a range of ever more wonderful beers and lagers (like those of every city, town and village in Germany) or breads (like those in other European countries) or vegetables and fruit (think of our own tasty apples on the trees), gives us fizzy carbonated keg beer, limp wrapped sliced bread, and pears and tomatoes with no taste at all. These foods grew *not* out of customer preferences, but the needs and requirements of a mechanised food factory handed over to robots, commanded by computer panels. Henry Ford introduced the prin-ciple of mass production and it works only if every product is identical. What the food (and drink) technologist is called upon to achieve is uniformity – the very principle which confounds the artist craftsman.

Bread, our staple food, the very staff of life, is the most obvious example. It happens not to matter to me that ice cream, burgers, sausages, biscuits and extruded snacks are often of miserable quality. But I find it depressing that the world's finest wheat, flour, milling and baking scientists should produce something of such manifestly insignificant quality, flavour, taste and character. The question of nutrition is debatable, but it is a fact that a lot of the goodness of the wheat berry has to be knocked out in order for the machines to get to work on the gluten, that element which inflates so airily when filled with gas bubbles, which, aided by additives, so effectively holds water as well as air. How did bread come to be so boring? You must ask the plant geneticists and food scientists.

The quality of bread used to depend on high protein wheat which used to be imported from Canada; but when the Government of the 1960s and 1970s set out to make Britain more self-sufficient for food supplies, the brief to the plant geneticists was to develop home-grown grain which would give high yields. John Bingham, head of the Plant Breeding Institute at Cambridge, was responsible for bringing in many new strains of wheat. He could boast that he'd enabled the British farmer to double his yield in the space of twenty years, partly by introducing new varieties, partly by directing how the land could be farmed more intensively. 'We get more out of an acre than anyone else in the world,' says Bingham. 'In Canada they only get three-quarters of a ton an acre, but that's partly because their wheat is spring sown. It could not endure the Canadian winters. And Canadian wheat is given a lower nitrogen feed.

'The average per acre in Britain is nearly two-and-a-half tons, 2.35 tons to be exact. You can't do that with 'muck and magic'. You've got to use artificial fertilisers to get high yields. The British Government requested us to reduce the level of food imports. Thirty years ago we produced only two-and-a-half million tons of wheat. Today we produce over eight million tons, only two million tons short of our needs.

'Making bread is just a physical process,' says Bingham. 'It depends on the protein. The quality of the protein is decided by its genetic make-up, so the aim has been to produce a wheat with high quality protein, strong resistance to disease, and good lodging (that means short straw, so that it won't be beaten down by wind). It needs early ripening qualities, bearing in mind the erratic British summer. And to make it profitable for farmers, it needs to give a high yield, and therefore respond to large doses of artificial fertiliser.'

Protein level, not taste, is the yardstick by which wheat is judged, and this can be put down to the European Community standards which guarantee farmers a minimum price for wheat – if the market price is lower they pay 'intervention', but only if the flour is judged to have a required level of protein – around 11 per cent, which can be judged by the stickiness of the dough. The head of the Flour, Milling and Bakery Research Association at Chorleywood, Herts, Professor Brian Spencer, arbitrates on behalf of the EC. 'The obvious test for flour is a baking test,' he says, 'but the Common Market partners can't agree on what that might be. So the tests are just machinability tests.'

Professor Spencer took over at Chorleywood from Dr George Elton, under whom the famous Chorleywood Breadmaking Process (CBP) was created in 1960. CBP utilises a fast dough mixer, and uses much more yeast and higher temperatures than conventional bread-making. It can cut back the first 'bulk fermentation' period from three hours to a few minutes. Brilliant technology, except that it is the slow fermentation which gives bread its special texture and flavour.

By trial and error they had evolved a system which did not depend on the craft of skilled individual bakers. 'We were trying to help bakers with tolerance,' says Professor Spencer. 'A craft baker can still work little tricks, produce a good loaf, but he needs tolerance so his bread won't be ruined if he takes his eyes off it for four or five minutes.' They had removed the elements of doubt due to variables such as the quality of the flour, weight of yeast, proving temperature, the heat of the oven, and changes caused by adding fat and additives.

And, in creating the Lowest Common Denominator, a bread that any old 'machine' can make, they said goodbye to the Highest Common Factor, the excellence achieved by artist craftsmen working with materials they knew through years of experience.

'What else could we do?' asks Professor Spencer. 'The muffin man doesn't come round any more. Where were people going to buy their bread? In 1918 there were 24,000 independent bakers in Britain. Today there are about 4,500. Without factory bread there wouldn't be enough bread.' 4,500 bakeries can't produce the fifteen million loaves which Britons buy each day.

He's not sentimental about the disappearance of the old-fashioned loaf. He thinks the public don't want it.

'It's not our job to dictate to the public what sort of bread they should buy. We took the advice of marketing people who said that the housewife wanted bread which stayed fresh longer and didn't stale quickly.' The CBP method produces a bread with a long life. This suits supermarkets too, giving it a longer shelf life; but when bread tasted good people ate it, they didn't leave it on the shelf.

When the mood swung to wholemeal and brown bread in the early 1980s, Chorleywood provided the technology, so that machines could put out wholemeal loaves which met the consumer's idea of palatability. But they still have no taste. Whereas the craft bakers' wholemeal can have a rich, nutty, chewy, satisfying taste and texture, the factory wholemeal is taken apart and put together again cockeyed, satisfying the customer's expectation in name only.

Professor Spencer would argue that's what people want. 'What-ever people want to buy, the commercial people will make. Don't underestimate these commercial boys. They are highly competitive. They try to get better bread than the rest. If they can make an honest penny, they will. If people want bread which is black and blue with green stripes, they'll make it.'

It's not striped bread we want from our food technologists. Instead they must address themselves to texture and taste, quality and value, freshness and goodness. High Quality technology is forever being put to the service of Low Quality performance. Why?

High Quality food technology brings us tingling fresh garden peas, pearls captured in their emerald beauty to be frozen at the moment of picking; Low Quality food technology means that the variety of pea grown is one of the most boring and tasteless.

High Quality food technology gives fish fingers bursting with cod, as fresh as the moment it was dragged from the net off Dogger Bank; Low Quality food technology means that it is stretched by the addition of low-cost rusk crumbs and batter and oil, with the result that the pure beauty of the cod is masked to such a degree that it must now suffer the humiliation of having flavour enhancer, Monosodium Glutamate, added.

High Quality food technology gives us free range chicken, bred by natural selection, fed on highest grade feeds and priced to match, sometimes a sheer flavour sensation (at the gourmet end, the famous blue-legged Poulet de Bresse). Low Quality food technology gives us the broiler fowl, bred in a space no bigger than itself, because activity uses up energy, and energy is feed, and feed is money, and money is profit; it tastes of blotting paper (for a generation who never experienced blotting paper, let's say wet cardboard, but not as distinctively flavoured, for this chicken has *no* flavour).

High Quality food is a Bradenham or Kersey ham from Suffolk, dark and succulent, matured in a rich brine (Asda does hams of this quality because the company owns a bacon business). Low Quality ham is a damp plastic-wrapped pink slab with sodden fat which splutters if it goes into a frying pan; it's cheaper because the makers have used the food scientists to replace ham weight with water, which is done by dissolving polyphosphates, a gelling agent, in the liquid.

The food industry likes it this way. They say the customers like it this way. The only way they can be proved wrong is if it affects their pockets. Only then will they jump to it and give you what you want.

3

MEAT

Eating meat is central to the social systems of the West. Providing sufficient meat of the right quality within the family is a symbol of your standing. It is as much a matter of pride to the working family to have meat on the table every day, as it is for the international executive to select exquisite and rare meat dishes from the menus of the most expensive restaurants, where cost and value are added by means of rare garnishes such as truffles.

The question of the actual taste is secondary at a social function. The host will make a positive statement by presenting a whole, large joint of beef or lamb; if this statement is too crude, then the beef, the most expensive fillet, of course, may be served on a duxelles of sautéed chopped shallots and mushrooms and wrapped in puff pastry, baked as Boeuf Wellington; with if required knobs on, knobs of foie gras.

The serving of meat is a clear social message, and so is not serving it. Alan Long, scientific adviser to the Vegetarian Society, remembers that as recently as the 1950s the people who didn't eat meat were virtually social outcasts. 'If you were a vegetarian in the Civil Service it was something you'd hide as surely as concealing homosexuality.'

In many societies sheer personal size and stature has been an indicator of status and wealth and, as soon as they can afford it, people will eat meat, even to excess. The Japanese who have eaten a diet of rice, fish and vegetables for many centuries (the poor man's bowl of rice is a symbol of poverty in Japanese literature) now ostentatiously pay more for their fillets of beef than anyone in the

world, as cheerfully as their company heads or chiefs part with
fortunes for cultural symbols of the West, such as Van Gogh's
Sunflowers. But as the Japanese increase their consumption of meat,
so their high levels of good health start to fall; and heart disease
becomes more common.

We live in an age of affluence, and on all sides we are tempted to
excess. Meat, the ultimate symbol of affluence, is too readily available
at absurdly cheap prices. Earlier this century those who couldn't
afford roast beef might have to settle for sausages. But not any more:
the 1990s burger gives you all the meat you can eat, compactly
prepared and packed in such a way that you can eat it even on the
run. It's classless, it's meat for all. Its image, thanks to advertising,
promotes a lifestyle as thrilling and exciting as any highly promoted
cola drink is able to.

But how long will meat stay fashionable? Sales of butchers' meat
have been declining, as people begin to take seriously the need to
cut down on animal fat in the diet for the sake of their hearts. And
now the way we feed animals in captivity has been called into
question, suggesting it may be the cause of the spread of the Mad
Cow Disease, Bovine Spongiform Encephalopathy.

It is easy to see how meat won its significant place in our lives. In
earliest times meat would not be the basis of the daily diet, but a
once-in-a-very-long-while treat, when the hunters had the good luck
or skill to bring in something from the wild. This is still the case
today in the few remote tribes of the rain forests who have not been
driven to extinction. Man has hunted animals for fifteen million
years, but it was not until about 10,000 years ago he settled down
to domesticating animals around permanent and semi-permanent
encampments, animals which could feed on grasses such as sheep,
goats, cattle and horses; or scavengers such as pigs, dogs and chickens. But almost at no time in history were any of these meats eaten
in any more than very modest quantities, except perhaps by the very
few. It has been determined that in Europe in the seventeenth and
eighteenth centuries meat made up some 10 per cent of the calorie
intake of most people, and seldom more than 25 per cent. It wasn't
until the nineteenth century that scientific principles, especially
winter feeding, were applied to increasing yields effectively.

Meat, it seems, has instinctively been understood to be nutritious,
clearly being of the same composition as our own bodies. Perhaps

for this reason man does not shrink from cannibalism at times of hardship; it is even held by some tribes that you will acquire the brains or balls of an adversary by eating them. Indeed a link into the investigation of the mysterious Mad Cow Disease in cattle, where the diseased brain comes to resemble a sponge, was discovered among a cannibalistic tribe.

On the basis that a little is good, so a lot more must be better, Western society has stepped up its consumption of meat to the level of unthinkable excess. Not only in quantity, but in quality. In the wild, lean meat accounts for 75 per cent of the animal, and its fat only 4 per cent. In farmed animals, the lean meat represents 50 per cent, and the fat is 25 per cent. In terms of calories the difference is even more marked, as, by weight, there are more calories in fat than in the protein of lean meat. Measured by calories, the farmed animal produces ten times as many calories from its fat content than the wild animal – and it's fat we don't want, since the object of eating meat is to benefit from the nutritious and useful protein. So, in domesticating animals from the wild, in feeding them well to increase body weight, in limiting their power of movement to keep up this body weight, we have, in an upside-down Alice-in-Wonderland way, turned logic inside-out.

In the past, such animals which were complementary to man, the cattle and sheep grazed pasture and moor which had no other use, the pigs and poultry were fed off household scraps and farm gluts, such as windfall apples and root crops. Now the country's best land is set aside for them, not to be grazed by them, but to grow the crops to feed them. Half of our grain crop is earmarked for farm animals. Apart from the ecologists' arguments that this land could yield crops which would provide better, cheaper nutrition, the result does not even give us satisfactory meat, that is, meat with good taste, or meat which is healthy and nutritious, because of the high level of 'saturated' animal fat it contributes to our diets. Fat represents 40 per cent of the average calorie intake of everyone in the country and is associated with 300,000 deaths from heart disease every year, and very many deaths from cancer (particularly breast cancer and cancer of the colon). These epidemics of degenerate disease sound out a warning that Western society has changed its diet for the worse, and unless this is recognised quickly the West will drag other countries along the same path. European 'harmonisation' in 1992 offers the opportunity for Northern Europeans to adopt the healthy eating

diets of the Mediterranean countries. Or, dangerously, will it mean
the spread of Northern Europe's unhealthy diet, excessive in animal
fat?

It has taken a series of crises in farming to bring the subject of
animal husbandry into focus.

The Salmonella crisis in 1988 was the first warning that things
were not all right with our farming methods and controls were
slipping. News of a wholesale disaster was shyly revealed in a press
hand-out that August, when the Department of Health warned
against eating raw eggs in mayonnaise, tartare sauce, milk shakes,
mousses or ice cream. The *Lancet* then pointed out that the Salmonella bacteria would not be destroyed unless yolks were cooked
solid, so fried, scrambled and soft-boiled eggs were considered to be
unsafe. By December, the Ministry of Agriculture was admitting
that a quarter of the plants which processed protein for chicken-feed
were contaminated with Salmonella, leading to the admission a
few days later by the Junior Health Minister, Edwina Currie, that
'most of the egg production in this country is, sadly, now infected
with salmonella,' although the admission was later contradicted
by John MacGregor, the Minister of Agriculture. Sales of eggs –
which run at thirty million a day, dropped dramatically, and one
million birds in the egg-laying flocks were slaughtered and egg
consumption dropped by 50 per cent. But it returned to almost
normal a year later, and so did the consumption of chickens,
ten pence or so a pound more, due to the scarcity which followed
the scare.

If it hadn't been for the Salmonella and BSE crises, we might
never have had cause to look so closely at our animal husbandry
practices. But having looked, we don't like what we see. We eat
about five million tons of meat a year, a business turnover of some
£10,000 million. Any idyllic notions of black and white cows
mooning at trains as we speed by their pastures, or pigs rolling in
clover, are soon shattered by the discovery that of the 170 million
farm animals in the country (three for every man, woman and child)
over 100 million of them will never graze in a field. In darkened
pens, instead, they will gobble up concentrated meals of cereal, half
Britain's grain crop.

Much has been written about the conditions in which battery hens
live. There are some thirty-seven million chickens laying eggs for
us, and 90 per cent of them are housed in conditions so cramped

they can barely turn round. Many are debeaked to reduce damage from pecking.

The Government lays down the minimum space a battery chicken must be allowed, 0.55 square feet, a living space about the size of the page you are reading now, twenty-one centimetres by twenty-one centimetres. Two Oxford University researchers have shown that a bird needs double that space merely to preen its feathers, and four times as much to flap its wings. This kind of imprisonment produces fowls which are highly stressed, and very weak. When the birds, known as a 'crop', are gathered up for slaughter, their bones are easily and often broken – at one estimate 30 per cent go to slaughter with broken bones.

To give chickens better lodging, say the chicken industry, would raise production costs by 5 per cent (for a 560 square centimetre living space) or 15 per cent (for a 750 square centimetre living space). In the interests of cheap eggs it is not done.

The broiler chicken, designed for the table, is a poor dispirited thing. There are 400 million broiler chickens in Britain, and most of them are housed, from 20,000 to 100,000 at a time, in hot, windowless sheds, for their abrupt forty-nine-day life, or the time it takes them to reach four and a half pounds – a time of slaughter computed on a graph where 'rate of growth' and 'cost of feed and keep' show highest financial gain. To sustain them in this breakneck race, they are heavily drugged to make them immune from diseases which would otherwise spread quickly in these conditions.

There is nothing to say about the flavour of these birds for the table, as there is none, and the texture is poor.

The sight of the great chef Albert Roux holding up one such poor specimen on television in his cookery series, comparing it with a fully-grown fowl, full of flavour and texture, was a convincing argument for any who saw it that these poor things are not worth having *at any price*. It would be better to have something else. No wonder the success story of the last few years in the supermarkets has been a wave of Chicken Tikka and Indian spiced chicken recipes. To think that these spices, which in hot countries come to the rescue of meat going-off in the intense heat where there is no refrigeration, should have their role to play in adding some taste to the 1990s' dinner menu! Chef Marja Lesnik of Claridges Hotel, where the aristocracy stays, served Poulet de Bresse, that aristocrat of French poultry, each with its own identity number of authenticity. His less than knowledgeable diners sent it back. 'They said they didn't think that's how chicken ought to taste!' In a period of twenty years enjoyment of the taste of chicken has been bred out of customers!

Pigs fare no better. They might have been designed for our exploitation, because they obligingly suffer every indignity we can devise. The males are castrated without anaesthetic, the tails of the young pigs are cut off; they are kept in overcrowded conditions without straw. There is no way they can indulge their rooting instincts or exercise or play (for pigs are friendly, playful animals). The sows are kept chained, in permanent restraint, in stalls, close to each other, stamping in each other's urine and excrement, infecting each other. Their litters are removed at three weeks and the piglets are then put on to an intensely rich protein feed which will boost them to one hundred pounds within fourteen to twenty-two weeks, when they will be slaughtered. The agreeable sow will produce two-and-a-half litters a year, until she is spent at five years, when her life of service to man, mercifully, is terminated.

In comparative tasting panels, you'll find that the intensively reared pigs provide tasteless, over-fatty meat of poor texture. Meat from pigs that have grazed outdoors has a marvellous flavour, a flavour which is lodged so far back in our unconscious that those of us who did know it, have forgotten it.

Beef cattle usually spend some time at grass, but increasingly more time indoors under unnatural conditions. Calves are separated from their mothers within a week of birth, and then reared on substitute milk, which is often medicated. Veal production is well known to be deeply distressing to animal welfare groups and many people will buy none of it on moral grounds. The animals are kept in confined, dark spaces in so-called Dutch crates, five feet long by two feet wide, for their miserable twelve weeks of life. Because any exercise at all would toughen the muscles and reduce the milky soft tastelessness that veal is bought for, the calf when it is released for slaughter can barely stand, let alone walk. Of course, the classical chef regards its lack of taste and delicate texture as the ideal vehicle for his subtle sauces, and veal bones sell at a very good price to restaurants, making the best glutinous and delicate stocks – the fonds de cuisine on which haute cuisine is built.

Only sheep, those admirably low in-put animals, which thrive on grass, escape contamination and exploitation, as long as the grass hasn't been sprayed with pesticides. Lamb fat is saturated, like any other animal fat, but you can cut off or pour away a lot of it.

If you are what you eat, as the great gourmet philosopher and lawyer Jean-Anthelme Brillat-Savarin put it, we are eating what the pigs and cows and chickens have eaten: petro-chemical residues, ground-up bones, animal and chicken excrement, all go into the pot under the heading of protein. A chemist for a chicken company told me how she had tested in the laboratory a feed which contained chicken excrement. ('It was disgusting, but we couldn't complain because we didn't want to lose our jobs.') She passed it as biologically safe and free from toxicity, and it was duly fed to the flocks. 'They all got diarrhoea, so the experiment had to be dropped,' she said. A case of commonsense triumphing over exploitation by 'science'.

You need a stong constitution to stomach tales from the abattoirs, but the handling of meat has never been a pretty business at any time in history, or in any place in the world. In Leningrad, where winter temperatures drop from minus 17°F to minus 40°F, you may see open trucks piled high with meat carcasses being driven to the city meat shops. 'Butchered' would be too refined a word to describe the way the frozen meat pieces are hacked, regardless of which part of the animal they come from. In this crude operation the customer is protected from disease by the local climate, colder than any domestic refrigerator. Far more disturbing is a visit nearer the equator to a Bolivian market, where carcasses are hung from rails in the outdoor market, protected from the direct rays of the sun by awnings; the slightest movement releases a black cloud of large flies, which immediately resettle.

Critics say that these extreme examples are harmless, as the customer is aware of what's been done, and will render the meat safe at home in the preparation and cooking. It is what they cannot see and don't know about which is insidious.

In Britain some companies choose not to export to Europe rather than improve their conditions, believing the profits will be outweighed by investment in cleaning up their premises. James Erlichman, the consumer affairs correspondent, wrote in the *Guardian* that at the beginning of 1989 conditions in British slaughterhouses were such that 90 per cent of them did not qualify for EC meat exporting licences. He reported that EC inspectors had encountered contaminated meat tumbling out of bins, bad drains, cleavers and knives which had not been properly sterilised. Meat was smeared with faeces because the intestines had burst open during slaughter.

Workers hosed down meat in an attempt to clean it. On the other hand reports from some Common Market countries are no more cheerful. A spokesman for New Zealand meat told me how he'd been shocked to find in an EC approved abattoir in Antwerp men smoking and building site labourers trundling barrows of wet cement through it. And the inhumane aspect of French farmers burning alive lorry loads of British sheep appals us.

In Britain handling meat is hardly regarded as a fine craft, so the disappearance of the expert butcher and his direct access to a local abattoir where animals from the fields around it are killed, means that our trust will be transferred more and more to the big super-market chains who set their prices by quality, and can therefore enforce vigorous inspection at all times. But their control may extend no further than an insistence on hygiene. In the interests of cheap meat, they do not interfere in the factory farming processes.

Britain's 1,000 or so slaughterhouses will have to be brought into line with EC standards by 1993 – or close down. This means huge capital investment, equipping abattoirs with air-conditioning and sealed doors. Many will go to the wall, leaving giant meat companies in command.

Achieving cheap meat has been aided by cheap feeds. Companies like J. Bibby, Dalgety, British Petroleum and Unilever are the traditional suppliers, and some of the waste material from other activities, such as processing oils from cotton seed and palm kernels yield protein-rich animal feed. Until the United States' soya bean crops failed, we had imported soya cake, and this we substituted with fishmeal, another excellent protein source. It must have seemed a stroke of genius when someone came up with the idea of ground-up sheep's remains as animal protein. There could be no reason to think that a disease of sheep's brains, called Scrapie, could be passed to cattle in this way – especially as the feeds were boiled for a long time at a temperature it was assumed would kill any bacteria or disease. But the active principal of BSE, although still unknown, is found to survive these high temperatures. When the epidemic of BSE was revealed in 1989 the outcry was enormous, and it swept through television and the press like a crackling forest fire. Amazingly, it was then revealed that the authorities had known all about it from the early 1980s and had done nothing about it. Half compensation was given to farmers to slaughter infected animals, but when it became clear this wasn't adequate incentive, full compensation was offered, and soon animals were being slaughtered at the rate of a thousand a month. The Ministries made it clear, however, that there was no danger to humans from eating meat which had been infected. At least, that's what their advisers told them.

It was the death of a Bristol cat called Max in May 1990 which brought anxiety to its peak. After it died, from a shaking illness similar to that of BSE infected cattle, its brain showed the tell-tale sponge pattern. It had been fed butcher's meat and the inference was that the disease could certainly jump from one species to another. Was it because of eating meat? It was enough for the popular press. The newspaper *Today* went on record with: 'Scientific proof: Mad Cow link to humans'. Minister of Agriculture, Fisheries and Food, John Gummer, backed his scientists and said not only was British beef safe to eat, but he would continue to eat it, and he would feed it to his family, arranging a celebrated photo-call in which he fed his small daughter, Cordelia, a beefburger. While he quoted his own Government scientists, others were homing in on the consequences of feeding herbivores, like cows, meat protein (the rendered remains of sheep carcasses). Dr Mark Holmes of the Cambridge Veterinary School summed up the consensus of opinion: 'It takes little thought to work out that if you feed a grass-eating animal meat, something is bound to go wrong. Cows have evolved defences against diseases they are likely to catch through eating grass. They have not evolved defences against diseases they get from eating sheep's brains.'

Having been visited by Salmonella, this new plague threatened to open up even more disastrous consequences. Yet by the end of the summer a House of Commons Select Committee had sat and heard expert evidence (some of the proceedings were shown live on television which gave the viewers an unrivalled opportunity to assess for themselves which witness they might most trust) and its conclusion was that beef was now safe. Infected cows were being slaughtered as they were found to have contracted the disease, the feed had been adjusted to exclude animal protein. There was nothing to worry about any more.

The scientists went away, with their £12 million, to study spongiform diseases more carefully.

A postscript was provided by the food writer Derek Cooper, presenting a late-night Channel 4 programme called *The Mad Cow*

Mystery, which revealed many more pieces in the world jigsaw. It started with a study of the Kuru tribe in the Eastern Highlands of Papua, New Guinea, which lies immediately to the north of Queensland, Australia. An investigation by an Australian into thousands of deaths among the womenfolk and children, but never the men, failed to find any explanation until American anthropologists discovered the unlikely cause: because the male hunters forbade their wives and children to eat any of the meat they brought back from their hunting expeditions, the women thoughtfully supplemented their protein by eating choice parts of the members of the tribe who passed away, removing them as they prepared the corpses for burial. The organs, such as the liver and kidneys, were found to be nutritious and the brains also, and these easily digestible parts were also fed to the children. The illnesses they developed led to partial paralysis and a lack of physical control which caused it to be called the 'Trembling Disease'. The brains were studied by scientists, but it was not until 1959 that they noted similarities to a brain disease in sheep, Scrapie, so called because the infected animals rub themselves against fences to relieve itching discomfort. Over the last thirty years, as more evidence came to light, it was shown that a concentrate made from the brains of infected animal species could be injected in another, and pass the disease, which makes tiny holes in the brain tissue, like a sponge, giving it its scientific name 'Spongiform'. In laboratories in Bethesda, New York, scientists showed that it was possible to pass the disease to chimpanzees and many of the fifty-four which had been injected died within two years.

This led to making the association with a brain disease in humans, CJD, Creutzfeldt Jacob Disease. Laboratory experiments involving mice, goats and marmoset monkeys, confirmed that it could easily be transferred across species. Eventually, in each case they identified an abnormal protein which shows up under the microscope as fibrils, which are like a cluster of small broken twigs. This is the concrete sign of the transmissible disease, and it resists destruction by heat, so it is quite possible that it has been passed from infected sheep into the food chain. It is probably in some of the fertilising bone meals we buy for the garden – and indeed the journalist daughter of an English doctor who died of CJD associated her mother's death with the fact that she was a keen gardener who used a lot of bone meal, and could easily have rubbed her eyes with a poisonous dose of the concentrate. But this is what science regards as anecdotal evidence.

Scientist Iain Pattison, working at the Compton Animal Disease Centre in Berkshire, was the first in this country to warn that the disease could be contagious and would not be detected, because it only developed after a four-year incubation period. His work showed that the disease can inhabit all cellular tissues, with the most likely concentration in the brain and spinal cord. He discovered only one case of disease in the muscle of the animal and he assumed this would have been from a nerve. The muscle is what we call meat and all muscle has some nervous tissue. In his view, the disease was not carried in the milk or blood of animals, nor the saliva, urine or faeces. The present scientific view is that if you can eliminate those tissues (mostly nerves) which can carry it, then what is already a very small risk will be minimised.

And what is the minimal risk? They don't know.

Derek Cooper asked research scientists if meat was now safe. They made guarded replies, and did not look directly at the questioner. 'If you want to know from a scientist if it's safe to eat meat,' Derek Cooper said later, 'you need only to look at their eyes!'

The shock that a large proportion of our cattle has been subject to a plague as fearful as those in the Old Testament sent us reeling, and for the time being we accept that the meat that now reaches the butchers' shops and supermarket shelves is subject to the most rigorous scrutiny that has ever been known. Many big supermarkets laid down new rules of their own for abattoirs. The head and nervous system is often processed separately from the carcass following the revelation of veterinary expert, Dr Helen Grant, who told a House of Commons Select Committee of practices she had witnessed in an abattoir where men with chain saws split the head in two, causing the brain to disintegrate into a fine spray which coated all the carcass meat around, spreading, she considered, the virus in the infected parts to the uninfected tissue.

After Germany refused to import British meat, the Government found £12 million in 1989 to research the disease but, to many, it seemed like slamming the stable door after the cattle had bolted. The money came after it had been announced that Bristol Meat Research Station was being closed down – on the grounds that it had no more important work to do.

It is not surprising that the tide is turning against intensive farming. The Conservative MP, Sir Richard Body, a farmer himself, says that Mad Cow Disease was a symptom of a wrong-headed agricultural policy, which concentrates food production in the hands of the few in order to produce sheer volume. 'But we cannot produce all the food we need, not even the quantity we actually produce, unless we farm very intensively. No other country tries to force out of its livestock so much in the way of eggs, meat, milk and other dairy products.'

The way we have been farming is a recipe for disaster: 'To keep tens of thousands of birds together like that is a major health risk and, according to the Central Public Health Laboratory, samples show that over 60 per cent are infected by Salmonella.

'Between 5 per cent and 10 per cent have also been found to suffer from some form of cancer. That cancer should afflict animals only a month and a half old seems evidence enough that the quality of this type of poultry meat has sunk to a low level.'

The whole system is balanced precariously, he says: 'Every vet in the business is agreed on one thing. The system would collapse if it were not for the antibiotics given to farm animals.'

Pigs are the worst example. It used to be said that pigs were 'walking cereals' because of the amount they ate; now they might be called 'stationary packets of antibiotics.' The majority of sows are kept in stalls throughout their lives, unable to move except to stand up or lie down; they leave the stalls only to be served by the boar or to farrow their litters. Such conditions have given rise to fourteen new pig diseases previously unknown. Only by pumping them with antibiotics are they kept going.

It will not be long, say some of the veterinary surgeons, before the system will break down. The bugs will beat the antibiotics. Meanwhile, a growing number of doctors are concerned at the way we use antibiotics in factory farms. Some human patients 'do not seem to respond to antibiotic treatment as readily as before.'

There is a political way out, Sir Richard Body suggests. A Government which separated the functions of the Ministry of Agriculture (representing farmers and representing the needs of the country as a whole) by creating a Ministry of Food and Health could start to make long-term plans on lines more relevant to everyone's needs, customer and farmer alike.

'Is it really fair to expect the Ministry of Agriculture to do the job making sure food is healthy? So long as it sees itself as the guardian and protector of the farmer, there is little chance of it also looking after the consumer.'

In his autobiography, the American Lenny Bruce, first and greatest of the alternative comedians, told of a job he had selling free-range eggs for a farmer at the roadside. He was so successful that he sold out. So he went into town, bought a load of battery eggs, smeared them with chicken muck and straw, and went on selling them.

The story ante-dates by twenty years the selling of free-range chickens and organic beef and pork. In appearances, many of these farm-gate, farm-fresh products have the ring of the real thing. But the 'Real Farm' image is often a cosmetic applied by the producer and his marketing and advertising team.

It is a subject about which farmers Richard Guy and Gillian Metherell feel strongly. Rebelling against the systems of intensive rearing, they founded in 1985 the Real Meat Company dedicated to 'Purity, Quality and Welfare'. They operate a business representing a group of farmers who agree to follow strict rules of production, monitored by an independent scientific adviser at Bristol University, responding to the increasing demand from people who want meat and poultry that tastes better – and that they are prepared to pay more for.

They spoke out to say publicly what many people have suspected: that not only is much meat and poultry dependent on an unhappy system of farming (weight-gain before quality, drugs and daily medication even when they are not required) but misleading claims are legitimised.

The consumer who reads a label on a meat product, say a packet of bacon, which says 5 per cent added water, would assume it to mean just that: that, for whatever reason (the producer would say to improve palatability), a small percentage of water has been added.

Labelling, permitted by the Ministry of Agriculture, is misleading. Five per cent water added actually means 15 per cent water added. The law allows the first 10 per cent of water, the brine, used in the curing process to be discounted! If the bacon is cheap, so it ought to be. Only 85 per cent of it is actually meat.

Another convenient law, which might have been conceived as a wild imagining from Edward Lear's nonsense books, is the law regulating the labelling of sausages. If you read a label claiming pork

sausage, you might innocently think that is a sausage made entirely
with pork. Not in Britain, it isn't – in Spain, Italy, France and
Germany it might be, but in Britain we do it differently. Because
they say the customer wants cheap sausages, because no-one cares
enough to make a song and dance about a packet of dreadful sausages,
we have this uniquely British standard. A pork sausage, first of all,
need only contain 65 per cent meat. That need not surprise us, that
over a third of the sausage may be rusk or filler and water, since they
didn't get the name banger for nothing (they used to explode in the
pan). But the pork doesn't have to be lean meat. The law allows half
of it to be fat. Well, that need not surprise us – what would a sausage
be without its sizzling fat, even if 50 per cent fat might be more than
we bargained for, especially if we thought we were getting a cheap
source of protein? (We might be unaware it was cheap protein only
because it was only half protein, the other half being cheap fat, which
the doctor was telling us to cut down.) But that's not all. Only 80
per cent of this pork sausage has to be pork, the rest can be other
meat. So, in extreme cases, if a company wanted to stay just within
the minimum requirements of the law, only 26 per cent – a quarter
of the sausage – need be lean pork. That's what the law, which is
protecting the consumer, allows. (How the manufacturer interprets
lean meat is something else: if the pork cannot be made into joints
or bacon or any passable cut, it will go into the sausages. But that's
another story.)

It is possible to be misled by claims for free-range chickens. Free-
range, to you and me, sounds as if fowls might range freely, as they
might have done in times gone by, scavenging in farmyards – a scene
you can still sometimes encounter in rural France. But free-range
birds often spend only one month of their short lives on the so-called
free-range farm; and the natural diet which is claimed for them
contains an antibiotic called coccidiostat which is certainly not
natural. Some of the 'free-ranging' birds are living in semi-intensive
percheries in fields, in houses on four or five floors containing as
many as 5,000 birds. The fowls don't have to scratch around, because
the feed enters automatically, and the eggs are collected by machine.
Only a very determined bird can get out, and most don't. The eggs
are a lovely appealing yellow – as if to assure you that they have been
feeding on leaves and vegetables rich in Carotene – Vitamin A – but
this is not so: artificial colouring has been added to the feeds. This
is not just allowed. It is done at the *insistence* of supermarkets which

say their customers want yellow yolks. They are insisting, in effect, that their customers want to be told this. Is it a harmless improvement – a little rouge, a little lipstick, a little cosmetic colour?

Now it turns out the descriptions are cosmetic too: farm fresh, farm gate, natural, free-range, traditional, have no firm definition matching the customer's expectations. Even the word organic – especially organic – has no legal definition and no meaning by itself.

It is only the best-informed consumers who can discover for themselves that there is a high organic standard – and that is the one promoted by the Soil Association, which was first to pioneer farming without chemicals. In the pursuit of quality, they have laid down requirements for cattle, pigs and poultry. Permanent housing of animals is not permitted, so this immediately disqualifies factory farming. Animals may not be tethered or confined for long periods. Herds or flocks must neither be too large nor too small – in such a way as to affect the animals' behaviour. (Animals kept singly suffer stress, as do those in mega-flocks.) All stock must have access to pasture in the grazing season. Animals must be fed for the most part organically grown foodstuffs, so there will be no chemical residues from fertilisers or insecticides in the feeds. The herds and flocks must not be given drugs or medication in their normal, healthy state, whether it is antibiotics or hormone growth stimulators. All food additives are prohibited, such as colouring for egg yolks.

The Real Meat Company follow these lines, adding some of their own: all feed, without exception, must be organic. They also stipulate the minimum age of slaughter to ensure the flavour that comes from maturity, and post-slaughter maturing, two factors which considerably add to the cost of the farmer, which of course results in more expensive meat and poultry.

The cost of meat and poultry is not as high in Britain as it is in other European countries, but this is hardly a blessing, as the quality in general is not as good (although at the premium end a Mayfair butcher like La Boucherie Lamartine or Harrods Food Hall will sell British meat which is the best in the world).

Cheap meat depends on the customer being unconcerned or ignorant about the quality and wholesomeness of the food, about what has been done to it, how it has been force-fed intensively and regulated by chemicals. Richard Guy, of the Real Meat Company, says: 'The British palate seems to tolerate almost anything, probably due to much practice. This is why Britain enjoys a position near the bottom of the league of world food quality, and why our food exports are so dismal.'

The intensification of livestock production over the last forty years brought down the price of beef, pork and chicken. As Guy observes: 'Manufacturers and producers could rely on the fact that a pack of bacon or a box of eggs that is ten pence cheaper than the next on the shelf will immediately be taken up by shoppers.'

It seemed to be a mark of efficiency to hold prices down, even reduce them. 'But efficiency in the area of food means, a chemical input into the food chain, degradation of animal welfare, and usually a lowering of taste and quality.' The crisis of confidence in animal husbandry has focused attention on the more far-reaching questions of what we want in the long-term. The scientists are galloping ahead. A Cambridge company called ABC (Animal Biotechnology Cambridge) is already promising services to farmers which will make present practices seem like the Stone Age. Philip Paxman, the veterinary surgeon who runs it, has been mass-producing cattle embryos from high quality beef stock to be implanted and grown in the wombs of low-grade surrogate cows (the embryos can be started in the wombs of rabbits or sheep before being transferred). The next step would be to sex the embryos, guaranteeing the farmer male or female offspring, as required. Cloning is the almost inevitable next stage, a process which has already made leaps and bounds in horticultural science. If an embryo can be split at an early stage, theoretically, each of the cells could re-form into a new embryo. The outcome would give us standardised meat every bit as consistent as the one-note supermarket tomato or Golden Delicious, and probably every bit as boring, as it would be bred for super-production, feed-to-weight conversion rather than taste and quality.

The question of the 1990s is not: Is meat safe to eat? It is: Is our meat healthy to eat?

Animals, bred for protein, the basis of our diet, give us by no means pure protein, but lots of fat. We all know how appetising it is to have a good roast joint with a marbling of fat, we love the crispy crackling on pork, we like crispy bacon; roast lamb drips its scented fat onto the potatoes in that lovely Norman dish, Le gigot qui pleure; and the golden skin of a well-roasted chicken is the effect of the fat-crisping it up.

But what we are not so conscious of is the level of fat in chunks of steak, buried in the tissues even when we cut the surplus off. In Britain, as I've already said, nearly half our calories (42 per cent) come from eating fat, and most of the fat is animal fat, what we call saturated fat, the fat that blocks the arteries and causes heart disease and heart attacks and, we now believe, breast cancer. The reason why our meat is fatty is that our animals are force-fed, reared intensively, without exercise, the only aim being to produce quantity and bulk quickly and cheaply.

In the 1990s, we must be looking for taste, quality, value, health and nutrition. The present methods of rearing animals do not satisfy any of these criteria – and gradually the public will reject them in favour of meat which does. For our health we should be looking at lean meat which comes from healthy, active animals, such as deer, hare, rabbit, pheasant, partridge, quail, pigeon, which belong to our not-so-distant past. We should be researching animals which use human's spare resources, not high-tech fertilisers, herbicides, insecticides, not large land masses to provide cereals for animals which are in turn trapped in pens and cages they cannot turn round in. We should also ask ourselves if the cost of eagerness to make meat the mainstay of our diet – instead of fish, fruit, vegetables and cereals – is not responsible for avoidable diseases.

GUIDE TO MEAT AND POULTRY

The gourmet view of meat and poultry is that animals and birds reared under the most natural conditions taste nicest, and that the cheapest is seldom the best value. This happily marries with the views of those concerned with health, nutrition, animal welfare and food safety.

BEEF. Safety continues to be an issue although most people accept that the Ministry of Agriculture has taken the correct steps to control the epidemic of Mad Cow Disease, bovine spongiform encephalopathy, known as BSE. But anxiety will linger on until scientists isolate the BSE agent. A remedy for the disease, if there is one, may be decades away.

The Meat and Livestock Commission, which represents the meat industry, paints a reassuring picture: animals in the advanced stage of the disease will not even get to the slaughterhouse. BSE is a notifiable disease and farmers get full compensation if they lose an animal in this way. In 1990 cattle were still being slaughtered at the rate of 1,000 a month. Tests showed that 16,000 of the first 20,000 slaughtered were positive for BSE, a figure alarmingly high in itself, but at least erring on the side of safety. At the slaughterhouse the brain, spleen and lymphatic glands which are known to carry the agent are removed. The head is removed before processing, and the spinal cord is removed with great care. The carcass, which might have been sprayed by the sawing action of electric saws, is wiped and washed in case any BSE agent has been spilled. If the remotest risk still remains, says the Commission spokesman, consumers should be reassured to learn that laboratory tests showed that it was one billion times more difficult to infect test animals by ingestion than by direct injection of infested material. 'The dose would be so small we don't think it would breach the immune system,' said a Commission spokesman. The small dose theory does not in fact impress all the scientific critics. 'The agent is carried in nerve tissues, and some nerve tissues in beef are one centimetre thick. So a small dose might be the size of a small grain of sugar. It might take forty years to show instead of ten years, which still isn't satisfactory if you're giving meat to your children.'

For those who fear that human error might still creep in, there is a rule of thumb. Buy beef from steers slaughtered at two years as it is extremely unlikely to carry the agent, which is predominantly found in animals aged four and five and in exceptionally few animals under the age of three. Young beef meat, however, represents only a proportion of the meat sold in Britain and it's not generally realised that quite a large amount is cow meat, that is to say, meat from cows removed from the dairy herd at the end of their milking service. The beef cows will be anything from five years to nine years old, well into the compass of BSE infection. Waitrose and Marks & Spencer sell only prime meat from young animals, and you can ask your butcher if meat is bull or cow (a higher price will usually indicate prime steak from young animals). If you're trying to avoid cow meat you need to realise that it will be used in processed meat products, canned meat, in many burgers and sausages, and probably in pies and stews in cafés and canteens, in schools and institutions, and anywhere which relies upon cheap meat to balance the budget.

Those who want further insurance against BSE can invest in beef from organic herds, from cattle which have grazed on insecticide-

free, artificial-fertiliser-free grassland approved by the Soil Association, and sold with their endorsing symbol. They are in the happy
position of being able to boast there hasn't been a single case of BSE
in organic herds, which they do not regard as a coincidence, but as
proof of the organisation's sound methods of husbandry. The Soil
Association can furnish a list of participating butchers and farmers
(send £2.50 to The Soil Association, 86 Colston Street, Bristol, BS1
5BB). There are other companies providing meat farmed to similar
standards, such as The Real Meat Company, East Hill Farm,
Heytesbury, Warminster, Wilts, BA12 OHR, and Greenway Organic
Farms, Freepost, Edinburgh, EH11 0AQ. Harrods sell organic beef,
at roughly 25 per cent more than the price of grass-fed Scottish beef,
and Safeway sell it in selected Home Counties stores.

The good news, the very good news, is that British beef is best.
Gourmets are unanimous in praising the quality, flavour and texture
of beef from Aberdeen Angus and Hereford herds. The bad news,
the very bad news, is that part of its rich, juicy succulence can be
attributed to its sweet marbled fat, which nutritionists now say
contributes to heart disease. The compromise is to enjoy it occasionally and, given its rare price, that shouldn't be difficult.

Supermarkets do respond to customer demands, and breeds which
develop less fat, but arguably less flavour, are being reared. Flavour
and texture also depend on how long the meat is hung. About twelve
days in a cold store is thought best, but hanging leads to evaporation
of moisture in the meat and loss of weight, so expect to pay more
for it. Meat which has been hung will be darker in colour, which
unfortunately puts off some customers who believe day-glo red
represents freshness and therefore goodness. Well-hung meat will
be sold with a label such as 'Traditionally Matured Beef'. Buy it and
taste the difference.

VEAL. Very young beef, often fed on milk, often produced in very
unhappy circumstances from animals tethered in a confined space
to discourage movement which would toughen up the muscles;
what's muscle to them is meat to us. For three centuries this has
been a basic meat for the classical chef, delicate to the point of
tastelessness, tender enough to satisfy the nursery palates of the
Kings of France.

Veal bones make the very best stock, or fond de cuisine, delicate
and gelatinous, but they actually cost half as much as some cuts of

meat, and are almost impossible to obtain since they are earmarked for restaurant chefs who buy them in large quantities.

LAMB. Lamb satisfies almost everyone on the grounds of taste, animal welfare, safety and nutrition, though its plentiful fat is saturated and the surplus needs to be cut off, or removed from soups, stocks, stews, when they have cooled. Although sheep infect each other with scrapie (a spongiform disease like BSE) it's not thought that it can be passed to humans since the animals are slaughtered years before they reach the infectious stage.

Chilled New Zealand lamb is good value, Welsh and English spring lamb is the tastiest in the world, mutton from Muslim butchers lends itself well to stews with vegetables (but the fat does not have a pleasant flavour and should be removed during the cooking). Look out for hoggets, year-old lamb, at the beginning of the year, for good flavour.

PORK. To taste the flavour of free-range pork against intensively reared pork is to enjoy a new taste experience. It reminds you that pork has been at the heart of the oldest cuisine in the world, China's, for a few thousand years.

The pig is the best of meats (when turned into charcuterie by the French or made into traditional hams by the British) and the most abused of meats (when, injected with water and polyphosphates, pork chops taste like soggy wallpaper, bacon spits in the frying pan, and the meat exudes a slimy effluent or fills the mouth with a mush of coloured, mechanically-recovered, jellied scraps).

Ask stores and supermarkets for pork products which do not have water added. They will cost a little more, but they are better value, as you are not paying for injected water.

Marks & Spencer has turned over half its pork production to free-range, and the taste is superior.

Pork seldom makes a bow on smart restaurant tables, but good pork is excellent value on every ground, and, as a favourite of the British for centuries, deserves to make a comeback in the home. Poor quality pork has no place at all.

VENISON. The old-fashioned, over-ripe haunch of venison bagged by tartaned guns in other days has been replaced by modern, farmed deer from Scotland, which is good lean meat lending itself to flavoursome steaks and stews. It is good value on every count.

HARE AND RABBIT. The one hard to find, the other under-appreciated. Both merit increased attention from the modern cook on grounds of taste, value, quality and good nutrition, but it means cultivating suppliers.

CHICKEN. In other centuries this colourfully plumed and exotic bird, which began life squawking in the rain forests of Burma, was a luxury so delightful that in the sixteenth century King Henry IV of France knew he could get to his people's hearts by promising them a chicken in every pot. But animal geneticists have got to it, and the twentieth century descendant is a wretched thing, victim to humiliations heaped on it by man. The modern bird has been bred to be a cheap and bland protein source of no interest on the grounds of taste and texture, of increasing anxiety on the grounds of health and of increasing distress to those concerned with animal welfare.

The average supermarket bird does not appeal to the serious cook; it is sloppy and wet because it has been injected with water and polyphosphates. But at least you can find birds which are labelled 'No Added Water'.

Corn-fed birds are yellow, because they are fed on bright yellow maize, but they are not usually reared under conditions any different from other birds. Quality varies, and the feed may help. But they shouldn't be confused with free-range birds which are also fed on maize.

Free-range birds promise better flavour and usually have it. The chickens have more room to move about which develops muscle and therefore texture. Their feed is usually more traditional than broiler birds', and they get cereal and green leaves, which are as good for growth in chickens as they are in humans. Moy Park in Ulster provides the largest number to the British market, some under supermarket own-labels.

The tastiest free-range supermarket birds are Label Rouge fermier chickens from the pine forests of Les Landes in south-west France. The variety is called Cou Nu (bare neck describes their unlovely appearance) and the birds have larger thighs and a meatier flavour. Tesco have the exclusive British supermarket rights to selling them.

The grandest of all chickens are the blue-legged Poulets de Bresse from the Burgundy in France. They live outdoors, and as chickens go they enjoy a gourmet diet. Like bottles of wine, the Bresse chicken has an appellation contrôlée, and each bird has its individual number if not name, which explains why they are about twice the price of any other free-range bird.

Organic chickens taste excellent, and also offer the customer a sense of moral good, as they will have met the Soil Association's exacting requirements.

DUCKS. An expensive alternative to chicken, because their size is deceptive; when you've taken very little meat off the bird, you find you are left with a large empty box which is the carcass. Most British frozen ducks are white, wet and anaemic and don't measure up to the large, tasty farm ducks which are the great heritage of the people of south-west France. Supermarkets offer pairs of breast of duck, the magret, which can be grilled like steak, pink or well-done. Duck liver makes the most delicious pâté.

WILD DUCK (mallard). The only game bird which shouldn't be hung, but eaten as fresh as possible. Gamey flavour and well worth seeking out. If you can, snap up other marsh birds from the marksman's gun such as teal and snipe.

GOOSE. Britain's Michaelmas as well as Christmas bird long before the economical turkey pushed it out. Top for taste, a roast for a feast, issuing delicious fat which should be collected and used, as a treat, for roasting potatoes. Pieces of roast goose (or duck) can be preserved in jars of fat to be used in rich winter dishes such as a cassoulet of beans. Saturated fat, so go steady.

TURKEY. White meat much approved by the health lobby, since it's good protein and low in fat; but its blandness doesn't offer much as a taste sensation. But smoked turkey is good in summer salads.

GUINEAFOWL and QUAIL. Two wild birds successfully farmed, available in the supermarkets, a healthy, attractive, tasty alternative to other meat.

WOODCOCK, GROUSE, PARTRIDGE, PHEASANT, PIGEON. In descending order of price and estimation. For the sheer gastronomic pleasure they give, they are all cheap, and excellent value, and repay every minute you spend consulting a good recipe book. And they give satisfaction on every ground.

4

FISH

We have become so used to receiving our fish in processed forms, filleted and wrapped in frozen packets, or in made-up cook-chill recipe dishes, we need to rediscover the thrill and wonder of real fish.

The sight of the catch being landed at a Mediterranean seaport is often one of the lasting memories of a holiday, and so is a visit to local fish markets. The variety of Continental fish and shellfish will have been so much larger than our own. Everything will have found a place in the cuisine: from large steaks of brown-fleshed tuna and firm meaty swordfish to creamy-white hake and grey and red mullet, which will feature on restaurant menus; from squirming octopus and squid, spiny lobster and rosy crab, to conger eel, bream, thorny rascasse, gurnard and bony rockfish, which will surrender their flavours into saffrony soups; right down to the dozens of tiny fish, sardines and anchovies, which will be deep-fried in piles or marinated in wine with garlic for tapas or hors d'oeuvres.

In Denmark, Norway and Sweden, fish will have pride of place at the breakfast smörgåsbord: everything from juicy chunks of poached wild salmon and slices of gravad lax to fillets of mackerel and herrings, pilchards, brisling and sild, preserved, soused and pickled in sweet and sour sauces, with wine, onions, shallots or dill.

On a sandy beach in Bahia in Brazil, the coconut palms nodding comfortably, a black woman in bright primary colours prepares spicy grilled fish on a tiny burner at a wooden shack of a café. The fish is fresh out of the water, and she scrapes off the scales, slashes it on both sides with a knife, rubs it with salt and fresh lime juice,

cooks it on both sides till it blackens, and serves it with a quickly
made sauce of lime juice with red chillies and green herbs. A group
of young people pick it clean with their fingers. There's almost no
way to enjoy fish more.

Yet, in spite of being an island, where no-one lives far from the
sea, we British fail to appreciate our riches.

In South Shields, Co. Durham, shipyard apprentices went on
strike 130 years ago to protest against being fed a daily diet of
salmon. In Dickens' time, the poor cursed their luck, that they could
only afford to eat oysters. Today consumption has dropped by 20
per cent since 1945, and the high street fishmonger is a rarer species
than the wild salmon.

We've always been cavalier towards our fish resources. The
treasures of our seashores and estuaries – Dublin Bay prawns, Kerry
lobsters, Isle of Man scallops, oysters from Galway, Helford and
Colchester – are better appreciated in Paris restaurants than in those
of our own capital. A mouthwatering cornucopia of fruits de mer is
almost unknown here, although our waters are brimming with shellfish and fresh fish.

Although some sixty species of fish are landed, most fishmongers
settle for cod, haddock, plaice, blaming the customer for being
unadventurous. Gone are the days of the cod wars, when we would
actually send Royal Navy gunboats to protect our vessels fishing in
Icelandic waters. In other centuries, we fought the Dutch to fish the
North Sea for herring.

In these days of shared fishing waters, we swap quotas with our
Common Market partners. The French take our coley, to sell it at
half the price of cod, the Germans take redfish (the ocean perch),
and the Scandinavians take up the slack of our herring (fish highly
prized for texture and flavour – by them but not by us). The
Germans, Danes, Dutch and Norwegians will trade us 100 tons of
our precious cod, haddock and plaice, for 1,000 tons of herring,
which they salt, pickle and souse. We have this priceless birthright,
and we squander it. Mackerel, we have no time for at all, selling the
bulk of it to the Russians, who anchor huge floating canneries,
known as Klondykes, off Liverpool. What the Russians don't take
we sell cheaply to Nigeria and Egypt.

A century ago, fish was a vital part of our food supply – and more
recipes for fish dishes than meat dishes appeared in cookery books.
But mackerel, herring, pilchards and sardines, sprats and brisling,

the so-called oily fish, have come to be considered the food of the poor, whether eaten fresh, salted, dried, smoked, canned in oil or with tomato. Fish and chips, the nation's most important convenience food, has a low social status. We do not give cockles, mussels and whelks the gourmet status of Italy, France, Holland and Belgium, but douse them in malt vinegar or non-brewed condiment, which makes them hard and indigestible.

You could argue that we don't deserve good fish. It seems we are not happy till we are nannied by the food industry and fish farmers. They'll present us with a modified product, farmed trout and farmed salmon. They'll clean it up, wrap it up and package it and advertise it, and then we'll take it, drained of all character and flavour.

Or we'll disregard fresh fish altogether and buy it only when it has been denatured and converted into something to disguise its origins: fish fingers, battered fish, fishcakes. At a convenience level, there are some acceptable products on the market, but inevitably companies compete to sell a cheaper product, and that may mean mixing mechanically recovered scraps with polyphosphates (jellying water), boosting it with monosodium glutamate, the flavour enhancer, bulking it up with breadcrumbs or rusk, frying it in saturated oil, and giving it a cosmetic golden finish with some colouring matter made from coal tar dye, such as tartrazine. Everything in it will have been passed by some Government committee declaring it safe, but common sense says the fish fillet straight from the sea must be even safer.

Fresh fish, cooked well, is a sheer delight. And fish contributes to good health, being a superb source of easily digestible protein. For those who may be at risk from heart disease, oily fish are particularly beneficial, as the fish oil thins the blood and reduces the likelihood of blood clotting, a major cause of heart attacks.

It may be no coincidence that heart attacks weren't known to Victorian doctors, when salmon, mackerel, herrings, pilchards, sardines, featured significantly in our diet. The Japanese, who not only consume a great deal of fish, but have traditionally eaten little meat throughout hundreds of years of their civilisation, have a particularly low rate of heart disease. But it increases when they change to a Western-style diet, as they have done in Hawaii, for example.

Fish has always been considered as good a source of vitamins as lean meat, and of iodine, phosphorous and calcium, with oily fish providing extra Vitamin A and D. But it was an extraordinary experiment in 1979 by the Oxford nutritionist Dr Hugh Sinclair, when he was nearly seventy, which established fish oil's blood-thinning properties, and therefore its value to patients at risk from heart attacks. Dr Sinclair had first encountered Eskimos on a trip to Canada in 1944, and was curious that they apparently had no record of heart disease. Yet they ate a diet which included seal blubber, and was higher in animal fat than any other in the world. In 1976, he was able to visit a remote colony in Greenland where they still consumed the traditional diet of seal meat and fish. They were free of heart disease and many other Western diseases (asthma, diabetes, psoriasis, and had low levels of dental decay, arthritis, diverticulitis) although those who had left the homeland to live in Canada had within a single generation become as vulnerable to these diseases as the rest of Western society. What he discovered was that the Eskimos' blood did not clot as ours does, and in 1979 he carried out an experiment on himself in Oxford, eating only seal meat, fish and shellfish for one hundred days. He found that the time it took him to stop bleeding after a cut (the bleeding time) increased from a normal four minutes to fifty minutes, then settled at fifteen minutes, an indication that his blood had become so thin that it would not quickly clot.

The significance lay in the composition of the fish oil, which contains two essential omega-3 fatty acids, EPA (Eicosapentanoic acid) and DHA (Docosahexahaenoic acid). They bring down the levels of triglycerides in the blood. This has been the basis of much research since, and Dr Reg Saynor (Director of the Cardiothoracic Laboratory at the Northern General Hospital, Sheffield) successfully used fish oil pills in a seven-year period of research study treating heart disease patients, the basis of a book he wrote with Dr Frank Ryan, *The Eskimo Diet*. The beneficial effects of the fish itself, or the oil pills, is now universally recognised around the world by nutritionists.

One of the most comprehensive studies of fish oil was made in Norway, and reported in the *New England Journal of Medicine* in 1990. In an experiment with 156 men and women who had a record of high blood pressure and hypertension, half were given six grammes of fish oil every day for ten weeks, and the other half were given six grammes of corn oil. There was no change in the blood pressure of those taking the corn oil, but 68 per cent of those taking the fish oil showed improvement. Among people who already ate fish two or three times a week, there was no substantial improvement, so it's not a case of unlimited improvement. Eating oily fish, or taking fish oil, can only raise you to a plateau, not take you beyond it.

A study in 1989 in Wales, among men who'd suffered one heart attack, established that regular consumption of oily fish or fish oil reduced the chance of a second attack by 29 per cent. This was achieved by eating no more than 150 grammes (five ounces) of mackerel, pilchard, herring, sardine, salmon or trout each twice a week, a total of 300 grammes (ten ounces) a week. A small price to pay for your health, even if you didn't think it was delicious. (Fish oil has now been developed with fruit flavours for children; it is ironical to think of the outcry that greeted the discovery just after the War that some ice cream was being made with deodorised fish oil instead of cream, lard or vegetable fat).

Another American report, from the National Heart, Blood and Lung Institute, analysing research over a nine-year period, sets a recommended dosage of an average daily intake of between a half and one gramme of Omega-3 fatty acids, which would be the equivalent of a teaspoon of cod liver oil. This is the equivalent of about half a pound of oily fish a week.

Atherosclerosis begins at an early age, and fats are laid down in the arteries in childhood; youngsters of twenty who died in Vietnam were found at their post-mortems to have had furred-up arteries, and had already laid the foundations for heart attacks later in life. To people at any risk from heart attack, this information is as relevant as the knowledge that statistically not smoking dramatically reduces the risk of lung cancer.

The intake of oily fish should be balanced by a corresponding reduction in the consumption of saturated fats, such as cream, butter, high fat cheese (stilton, cheddar, brie), lard, hardened white cooking fat, beef fat, lamb fat, chicken fat, and saturated oils such as coconut and palm oil.

The rediscovery of the benefit of oily fish may be only the tip of the iceberg. One of our leading experimental nutritionists, Professor Michael Crawford, for many years a close admirer of Professor Sinclair who made those important discoveries, believes seafood will very soon become recognised as an essential element of man's diet, which we forfeit at our peril. It is his view of evolution that natural selection is modified by nutrition and what food is available. Far from coming down from the trees which we shared with our ancestors the apes, Professor Crawford suggests that man has his origins at the point where water meets land. Those animal species which moved furthest away from the sea became degenerates, their bodies growing at a proportionately faster rate than their brains. It was to the estuaries that waters washed the highest concentrations of nutrients and mineral salts, and it was here that the fish and shellfish which consumed them provided the rich food which allowed man's brains to develop in proportion to his body. Only one other mammal in the world has a brain similar to ours, and that is the dolphin. Professor Crawford says there is no longer any need to look for a missing link: it was there, in the estuaries: a small mammal which was the mother of both man and dolphin.

Professor Crawford, who is Head of the Department of Nutritional Biochemistry at the Nuffield Institute of Comparative Medicine at the Institute of Zoology, London, analyses a series of world-wide studies which point to the health benefits of people with a high-fish diet, and suggests that research into its value has not even begun. 'It is certain that nutrition can affect brain development. The most important messages so far concern the relationship of fatty nutrients found in fish. The marine food chain is important for a brain and neural development breakthrough.

'Think of evolution. What we've seen is that the body can grow at a rate that outstrips the brain, so the brain shrinks in relation to the body. What needs to be addressed is the development of the human intelligence as a much more fundamental issue than the protection and development of a physical state. Humans are different from plants because they had to get food rather than photosynthesise. To get food you've got to have a brain and a nervous system. And the origin of brains and the nervous systems occurred first in the sea, so it's not really surprising to think we still owe an allegiance to that chain in the nutrient sense.

'What we are looking at is the human animal which has grown to a great size and now needs a significant input of nutrients. He also needs a great diversity of nutrients to meet all his requirements. We have Government tables on recommended requirements for our bodily needs but no requirements for brain development have been proscribed by science as yet. Fish, we know, is good for arteries, but what makes brains grow?

'Evidence shows that nutrition is clearly important to brain development. At the extreme end, when cretinism was discovered in the mountains of Europe at the beginning of this century, it was found to be due to the deficiency of the trace element iodine. Marine resources are the best source of trace elements such as iodine, and the brain degenerates without them. Minerals and trace elements wash out and fertilise the estuaries, where the food chain is beginning in earnest. Estuaries are the richest places. Nile delta was rich soil; at the estuary they had the world's finest sardines which fed off the nutrients washed down. The sardines were killed off when they built the Aswan dam.'

Professor Crawford says that all species denied access to seafood have suffered, and those that most utilise it have the best health and possibly, the best brain power. He instances the Japanese, who eat five times more fish than the British (they would need seven times their present land-mass to replace their seafoods with land-based foods).

Talking of the survival of the fittest, he suggests, with a hint of tongue in cheek, few are fitter than the Japanese. 'One could use the quantitative measurement of the financial markets, exchange rates, trade surpluses, drive and financial intelligence. If you consider the growing surpluses of Japan and the budget deficits of America over the last ten years by the end of the century Japan should be able to buy out America. The Japanese can be said to be the one remaining hunter-gatherer culture, but they specifically hunt and gather the sea. Is it possible that nutrition has played a role in shaping the success of nations?

'Man evolved at land and water interface. What it means is not only that seafood played an important part in our past history and that it will have to play an important part in our future history; but also that in the planning for the next century we have to take this on board.

'It is exceedingly difficult to build a society entirely on land-based agricultural systems. We have to develop the marine food chain in the estuaries and in deep-sea fisheries. We have to create a marine environment to stimulate a food chain which has been depleted by pollution. And we need to get into the business of harvesting rich marine sources. Instead, what we are doing at present is a hunting-

and-gathering business more appropriate 10,000 years ago, a random, hit-and-miss business we have no control over.

'Now we are killing the estuaries, and killing the resources, the starting point of the marine food chain. Another example of how research has been blinkered, focused in a narrow direction of land-based agriculture. And, within that narrow focus, we still haven't got it right: take Listeria, BSE and so on. Sewage, heavy metals, phosphate-rich detergents, industrial waste are killing off marine life, and will soon create pollution.

'Pollution is bound to affect the whole of the North Sea. Seals and dolphins and whales at the top of the food chain will get infections, as they are biologically weakened, and our whole marine supplies will be endangered, just at the moment that we are discovering their importance.'

The Friends of the Earth insist that pollution may soon dramatically reduce the fish in the North Sea because toxic heavy metals and agricultural chemicals are being emptied into it from the Elbe, the Rhine, the Meuse. Britain alone pumps a million tons of industrial waste into the North Sea, although there is an agreement to stop incinerating toxic waste at sea by 1994. The North Sea has become a lavatory for human sewage, an industrial tip for waste and a way of putting out of sight and out of mind all the chemical wastes which are too poisonous to leave around on land.

The best hope at the moment would seem to be fish farming. It is already well established, and farmed trout and salmon are already big business. The tradition of fish farming is a long one. In the Middle Ages, monks had their carp ponds in monasteries. Friday was designated a meatless day by the early Church, but Fast day soon became Feast day since carp is very much a delicacy in those cuisines where there is the patience and craft to prepare it well. In parts of Eastern Europe carp is actually Christmas Day fare. In the Far East, the Chinese have bred fish successfully in paddy fields, where they flood them to grow the rice. Professor Crawford reports that the North Vietnamese flooded bomb craters made by the American bombers and bred fish in them.

Britain's salmon farms are on a much vaster scale, occupying Scottish lochs, where the floating cages marked by red buoys offend the environmentalists, and incipient pollution from medicating the fish (and their occasional bouts of disease) offend the ecologists.

Farmed fish, like land-based cattle, pigs and chickens, have to be fed on expensive proteins processed by man, instead of taking them free from the wild. So the farmed fish is a designer fish for top tables – not a solution to providing cheap food.

Nevertheless the growth of the farmed fish business has been phenomenal. Within a decade it has grown from a £3 million to £100 million business – representing a fifth of all fish eaten in Britain. The value of the fish brought by trawlers from the oceans round our island represents a falling £400 million only. The seas have been over-fished by ourselves and our fishing partners, using nets with such fine mesh in our greed to get maximum catches that we take the baby fish which then never grow to be tomorrow's haul.

The challenge of restoring fish to the seas round Britain, so that we can harvest them as efficiently as the Japanese, should be tackled with urgency. We are able to use sophisticated modern chilling and freezing, to enjoy exotic seafood from Australia, New Zealand, Ecuador (which is where Marks & Spencer breed their monster tiger prawns), the Mediterranean, the Seychelles (which provides a dazzling rainbow range of colourful parrot fish to enhance the modern fishmonger's slab). So let us protect, develop and explore waters – and be a lot more adventurous with the resources which we do have.

GUIDE TO FISH

If you now consider that it may be important to increase your consumption of fish, here are a few ready tips.

Canned fish is an excellent source of its essential fatty acids, nutrients and trace minerals: mackerel and sardines are high, followed by tuna, salmon, anchovies. (See Table on page 58.)

The nation's biggest fishmongers are Marks & Spencer. They have done all the work for you, choosing, preparing, packaging, communicating final instructions on storage and cooking which you ignore at your peril.

But isn't it more fun to use your own judgement, and patronise the disappearing high street fishmonger? Choose a fishmonger that smells clean. Very fresh fish has no smell. If the fishmonger offers you the fish to smell, don't recoil. Lean forward and smell it. Ask him questions. He should know where the fish has come from, if it has been frozen or chilled. Even if you don't know much about fish, he'll respect your efforts. Even the innocent question, 'Is it fresh?' may have the unexpected effect of sending him scurrying to the refrigerated room at the back, and emerging with something better than he's showing on the slab.

Tell him what you want it for, or what you're going to do with it, and you will awake a glimmering interest. After all, you're reminding him that he's an expert, and that's quite flattering.

He will usually offer to gut the fish, behead, descale and fillet it to order. Ask for the heads, tails and bones of white fish to make stock (boiled for twenty five or thirty minutes with a little carrot, onion, celery, a bay leaf, peppercorns and a glass of dry white wine, they make a beautiful stock for fish soups, which can be strained and frozen for later use).

Freshness is everything. Fresh fish have a brilliant sheen, the gills are red. The eyes are clear, not opaque or sunken. The flesh is delightfully firm and springs back if you press with your thumb.

Having bought your fish fresh, eat it as soon as possible. Don't buy oily fish, such as herring or mackerel or shellfish, to eat tomorrow or the next day; they quickly develop an 'off' flavour. You can keep white fish overnight, but that's long enough. Unwrap it, put it on a plate and cover loosely with cling-film or foil, and put it on a lower shelf in your fridge. Smoked fish is already 'cooked' so it will keep two or three days without deteriorating.

An unusually enterprising fishmonger will sell up to sixty species. Marks & Spencer have thirty or forty, but some high street shops are sadly barren.

Here's a quick guide to the fish of the 1990s.

SALMON, SALMON TROUT (which is sea trout), rainbow trout (from Scandinavia) and rather dull-tasting farmed trout are the fashionable middle classes of the fish world, acceptable in any company, ideal for entertaining, city dinners, parties and picnics, special occasions and treats. They have firm flesh, a delicately rich flavour and are slightly dry and fat, so they need the help of sharp mayonnaises and sauces, and lemon wedges. Good for the heart, but not low in calories.

FRESH SWORDFISH, TUNA AND BONITO are the aristocrats of healthy fish, sold as meaty steaks, and grilled like them, delicious with lemon and a mustardy or horseradish sauce. Good for the heart, too, and of course, available canned in brine or vegetable oil.

MULLET: the larger grey mullet has the most delicate flesh, and is lovely steamed with herbs, or baked in foil. Red mullet is a delicacy in the hands of a good chef, a misery in the hands of the amateur. In this respect, like sea bass and sea bream, expensive delicacies, which can be completely ruined by overcooking.

MACKEREL, HERRING, PILCHARDS, SPRATS, WHITE-BAIT, in descending order of size, are our most unappreciated treasure, not only extremely healthy, nutritious, and good for the heart, but marvellous to taste. As we rediscover their merits, we may be able to return to preparing them and cooking them in an adventurous spirit: not only grilled or deep-fried, but smoked like kippers and bloaters; brined like roll-mops; simple deep-salted small herring out of the barrel, washed down with aquavit as they eat them in Hamburg; preserved in wine, a Norwegian delicacy; soused (cooked in a slow oven for half an hour in a covering of vinegar and water, with peppercorns, and left to get cold in the mixture); cured like gravad lax (fillets of mackerel, pin bones removed, covered with a mixture of sugar and spice, and left under a weighted board for twenty-four hours).

DOVER SOLE is the most highly prized white fish and is so arrogantly simple in its perfection that it wants nothing more than plain grilling. Other white fish (lemon sole, halibut, turbot, plaice) are well known for their delicacy, a light protein which some prefer to hearty red meats.

COD is the nation's most popular fish, probably the meatiest in character, and we eat so much we have to import 65 per cent of what we buy.

HADDOCK is the most popular white fish in Scotland, but they've mastered its blandness by smoking it, and incidentally, creating one of the world's most succulent foods, Arbroath Smokies, young haddock smoked whole.

MONKFISH, which used to be poor man's lobster because of its firm, chewy white meat, is now anything but a poor man's dish, winning fashion in spite of its awesomely horrific looks. It is a daring fishmonger who shocks his customers by exhibiting the whole creature. It's a marvellous fish for the experimental cook to try inventive skills on, with pretty saffron sauces.

SKATE, with its firm texture, and hake and whiting have their fans. We deep-fry our skate to sell in chip shops, but the French raise the fish to gourmet status by grilling it and serving with capers and nutty burnt butter. And the hake in Spain is by no means plain when it's called Merluza and served with Romesco sauce made from powdered, dried pimentos and pine nuts.

REDFISH (ocean perch), coalfish (coley or saithe) and dogfish (huss or rock salmon) are splendid for the chip shop, but they aren't popular on the slab. The Germans and French have no such reservations and eagerly grab British European Market quotas when we don't take them up. Companies like Marks & Spencer have ways of making us eat them and soon we'll be eating a lot more than we think in their excellent fish pies and fish cakes.

SQUID is an attractive price, reacts well to chilling, and is much bought by minority groups in Britain. It needs a cook prepared to look up Chinese and Mediterranean cookbooks. Squid is delicate, needs shortest cooking time. Unlike the octopus which is tough and needs pounding with a wooden mallet, and long stewing.

LOBSTER may be the most sought-after shellfish, but it is high in cholesterol, with few essential fatty acids. Marks & Spencer sell half a lobster at a daringly attainable price, but it is Australian, and has less flavour than our cold water lobsters. The best are probably those from the chilly waters of the North Sea off Harwich, weighing about a pound each, and harvested from the wrecks which wartime German E-boats left strewn at the bottom of the harbour in the early 1940s.

CRABS are a British glory, usually presented as a crab salad or sandwich and which deserve universal acclaim for their contribution to crab soup, one of the tastiest soups it's possible to make. Crabs need to be extremely spanking fresh. The trick of buying one is to weigh one crab against another of the same size, and choose the heavier one.

SCALLOPS, OYSTERS, CLAMS, MUSSELS, COCKLES, WINKLES AND WHELKS, razor clams, fill our estuaries and line our coasts, but until we regard them as delicacies worth paying a decent price for, the best will continue to go abroad. Consider the vongole of Italian cooking, and what they do with their cockles in a meat sauce for spaghetti. And then compare it with the cockles sold on the sea front at Southend, steamed as hard as rubber, soused in non-brewed condiment to scorch your tongue and throat. No wonder we don't consider them a delicacy. But mussels are finding their way back, though they have a long way to go before they enjoy the status they hold in Germany and Belgium.

DUBLIN BAY PRAWNS, also known as Norwegian lobster and scampi, are hard to find in their native state, but often sold ready battered. Warning: the scampi you order in the high street restaurant are probably made from a mixture of pulped, mixed and mashed extruded shellfish tails and other fish with polyphosphates. The same may be said for crab sticks, a coloured mess of mechanically recovered fish scraps, of nil cooking value.

This is a league table for fish with a high proportion of beneficial Omega-3 fatty acids listed in grams per 100 grams (by kind of permission of Dr Reg Saynor).

	grams per 100g		grams per 100g
Mackerel	2.2	Trout, oysters	0.6
Herrings, pilchards, sardines	1.7	Skipjack and other tuna, shark, hake, mussels	0.5
Bluefin tuna	1.6	Shrimps, crab	0.4
Salmon and anchovies	1.4	Cod, squid, clams	0.3
Mullet	1.1	Plaice, lobster, scallops, eel	0.2
Halibut	0.9	Haddock	0.1

5

NOVEL PROTEINS

If the world's food resources were ever severely threatened, it ought to be comforting to know that food scientists and food technologists will find an answer. But the fact is that, when they do find answers in the laboratory, people are not necessarily ready for them. The psychological attitudes to eating are so firmly rooted that people are not always ready to change, even when faced with starvation. The celebrated food scientist, Dr Magnus Pyke, has given examples of milk powder being sent to Central American communities where it is not a regular item of diet – and social workers arriving in the villages to find the houses freshly white-washed, but the people still undernourished. A powdered fish protein supplement sent to Africa failed to satisfy taste expectations and was hopefully dispersed on the land as a fertiliser.

For most of our lifetime scientists have been concentrating on developing protein on the assumption that it provides the building blocks to human growth, whereas carbohydrates simply fuel the body, while oils and fats are already in excess of human requirements and there is no shortage of them.

Protein is plentiful in affluent countries, and is found in meat, poultry, fish, eggs and milk. Some foods are incomplete proteins such as beans, which do not have the essential amino-acid Lysine, and cereals, which lack the sulphur-containing amino acids. But combinations of the two, such as beans and rice in South America and the Caribbean, or baked beans on toast in Britain, successfully complete the nutritional equation.

A good protein can be obtained by fermentation of beans or rice, and this has been understood for thousands of years in the Far East. Although they couldn't have known they were making protein, they must have understood they were achieving nutritional value. Rice and beans were fermented to make miso (which means 'meat of the earth'). It can be preserved as a brown paste (it's prized for its maturity) or solidified into hard lumps so that it can be grated into nourishing soups, a daily source of protein in Japan; and so is tempeh, another fermented bean product. The Japanese eat an average of four ounces of miso and tempeh every day. Soya beans are also fermented by the Japanese to make soy sauce, and the characteristic black beans and black bean paste of Chinese cooking.

The most modern novel protein, Quorn, the new wonder protein food created by new technology, is produced by the same technique of fermentation, but doesn't have the advantage of having been tested on humans for many centuries.

Many possibilities for meeting protein shortage are available. Without international funds those with the most commercial possibilities are inevitably the ones which have been most prominent. A company which could invest sufficient time and scientific skills and resources into developing a protein food for the world's protein-starved would be doing the world, and themselves, a very good turn.

And the companies in a position best to exploit these opportunities have been those with waste by-products of other activities. Particular interest has been shown by oil and gas companies, atomic energy agencies, and the big millers. They can grow bacteria, fungi or algae – nourishing them on their plentiful waste products. Some of the food successes of our time have developed in this way. Meat extracts made by hydrolisation are an example. Meat which can no longer be offered for consumption as whole meat or processed meat or even pet food can be turned out into great pits and flooded with hydrochloric acid, so that its action causes the carcasses to dissolve in water (that is what it means to hydrolise) thus retaining the nutrients. Yeast waste from breweries is treated in a similar way, then salted and coloured, to give us those attractive yeast extracts so rich in B vitamins.

It follows that the people with the most waste have the strongest motives to try to exploit these possibilities.

The novel protein which got off the mark first was TVP – Textured Vegetable Protein, made from the by-product of the soya bean oil

industry. Next to corn oil, made from maize, the soya bean is the
most important oil crop in the United States, and it's a high quality
oil, low in saturates. But only 20 per cent of the bean is oil. Forty
per cent of it is protein, and after pressing it was only good for
animal feed. It was this waste product that the Americans developed
in St Louis, heart of the Georgia bean-belt, and launched in the
States in the 1960s and 1970s as a meat analogue, appearing with
meat in school meals, as extenders in meat products. Its success
owed much to skilful promotion and advertising – as the product
itself is not particularly tasty. The bitter taste of the soya bean has
always been against it (like margarine, which is remembered for
its disgusting taste in the War fifty years ago, soya flour was
another nutritionally useful, appalling-tasting product that had to
be suffered.)

Soya beans are one of those 'natural' foods which in reality are
quite harmful to humans until they have been processed. They have
toxic agents which induce gout (goitrogens) and they have enzyme-
inhibitors, haemagglutinins, which impede the digestion of the
protein, but it is removed by moist heat, as is the hexane-rich
petroleum solvent which has been used to extract the oil from the
bean, following drying, dehulling and flaking. The resulting mixture
is by now 50 per cent protein, and two-thirds of its volume of
water is added to make a paste which is extruded from nozzles
into atmospheric pressure. When the pressure is released, internal
cavities are created, and their size and character can be controlled
to produce a required texture. The extruded pieces are cut up and
dried. When water or liquid is added they quadruple in volume, and
assume much the same texture as meat, and can be flavoured as such
or blended with meat in stews or pies.

Other oil-producing seeds leave residues of protein which offer
opportunities for exploitation. Examples are peanuts, sunflowers,
rape, sesame, coconuts, cottonseed; these offer opportunities for
developing proteins, although the groundnut is regarded with
caution because it is prone to contamination from mycotoxins, particularly the mould aflatoxin, which causes liver cancer.

The British rayon-spinning company, Courtaulds, harnessed their
technology to treat a processed field bean, and produce a superbly
textured meat analogue which they call KESP. The harvested bean
is stripped of its tough outer coat before being ground to extract
the protein which is then pasteurised. The protein is precipitated,

washed, and prepared in spray-dried form. Then it can be mixed with water and forced through the holes of a spinnaret to produce thousands of tiny threads which are stretched in a bath of salt and acid. It's then ready to be formed into suitable shapes, flavoured and coloured, and combined with egg white. It can be heated to produce a firm, stable texture, very much like the substance of good meat or chicken.

Professor Bill Pirie, when he was head of the Government's experimental research station at Rothamstead, Harpenden, in Hertfordshire, showed how protein in green leaves and grasses can be intercepted and separated from their indigestible fibre (no barrier, of course, to cows, sheep and horses which get their protein in this way). For human consumption, the protein can be extracted by a 'dairy' process, the same process by which curds are separated from milk for cheese or white bean curd is separated from soya bean 'milk' (which is a dilution of soya flour in water). Bill Pirie demonstrated a simple Heath-Robinson press driven by a low-powered motor. In Rothamstead he used a broad-leafed plant, lucerne, which is usually considered juicy rabbit feed. He visualised his process having significant value in wet tropical countries where the ripening of seed crops is unsure. Preferably the leaves would be the by-product of some other process (cane sugar, jute, cotton) or they might be weeds growing at the margins of lakes which could be easily harvested mechanically.

On the same principle of by-passing the animals that consume these basic foods, scientists have already experimented to effect with algae, plankton, bacteria, yeast, moulds and fungi.

Yeasts have a prolific rate of growth, and over a few square metres of the surface of a substrate, say waste sulphite pulp liquor from a paper mill, half a ton of yeast can generate fifty tons of protein. Petroleum by-products also serve as a feed for yeasts, and the process was successfully being employed to provide protein supplements for animals, instead of fish meal, when it became too expensive. Bacteria that feed on waxy paraffins in the petrol-refining process are a huge source of protein, which needs only the addition of phosphates and nitrates. The nitrate can be provided from a by-product of methane, another waste product of the oil industry. Algae may be used as protein sources and were considered a food by the Aztecs of Mexico. Most seaweed is not suitable because it is multicellular and a poor source of protein. But unicellular varieties such as Spirulina Maxima and Chlorella grow in lakes in South-East Asia and Africa. Tribes living beside Lake Chad eat the bitter tasting bluey-green plants, which are slightly indigestible but over 60 per cent protein. The plants photosynthesise carbohydrate from sunlight; they would need extra feeding with nitrates and phosphates to be produced on a commercial scale.

And, last but not least, fungi. An example of what can be done by scientists given the resources and motivation is illustrated by the appearance four or five years ago of Quorn, a protein developed to be used rather as TVP has been, that is combined with meat, or replacing meat, in pies and made-up recipe dishes sold in supermarkets. But unlike TVP, which is a modification of a regular foodstuff, Quorn is an entirely new food.

Its inventor, Dr Gerald Solomon of the Lord Rank Research Centre at High Wycombe, suggests it's the first new food since the French scientist Hippolyte Mége-Mouriès invented margarine by processing beef tallow and skimmed milk 120 years ago. Quorn is made by growing and fermenting *fusarium graminearum*, a tiny member of the mushroom family, no larger than ten microns by twenty microns.

It was Lord Rank, head of the great milling company, who set up the project. 'Lord Rank was a keen Methodist,' said Dr Solomon. 'And he wanted to employ talent and money to help the world situations. Not food for animals but food for people. An American had published a paper on fungi as food for people, instead of yeast or bacteria, and I was asked to look at it.

'If we could find suitable bacteria, we had the material at Rank Hovis to grow them on. We have a place at Ashford in Kent where they separate gluten and starch from wheat. The gluten is used in baking but the starch has less uses. We could use that as food for the bacteria.'

First, they had to track down a food source. 'In 1967 we started a three-year screening programme, and examined 32,000 soil samples from all over the world,' said Dr Solomon. 'Soil is the great reservoir of bacteria and most of our antibiotics come from soil-searching. Soil is the permanent resting place of bacteria.

'So, anyone who went on holiday had to bring back soil samples in sterile glass phials.'

Without realising it, they found the fungus they would eventually use on the very first day – and, if they had known this, they would have saved themselves three years' further searching. It was April Fools Day – 1 April, 1968, and it was labelled A 3/5. 'A' represented year one; the figure '3' meant it was the third sample (out of a subsequent 30,000) and the figure '5' represented the number of bacteria and isolates found in it. This tiny *fusarium graminearum* was found not on the other side of the world but just a few miles from their High Wycombe laboratories, in the pretty Thameside village of Marlow.

The bacteria were tested in the labs. A shortlist which would respond to the vast enterprise ahead was drawn up. Dr Solomon remembers it as a dramatic and exciting challenge. 'This was the 1960s when a world food shortage was forecast. We knew others were planning to make novel proteins. Our philosophy was to do better research, to get a better product that people would want to eat, that would achieve an acceptance. We guessed it would be a hard long slog. If we could make it excellent quality, people would find it attractive.

'Nobody had done anything like this before. There wasn't the technology. Fungi cannot be grown as surface culture, which is how penicillin is grown, but shaken in flasks. It wasn't economic in batches so we invented a technique called loop fermentation, growing the fungi in a liquid feed derived from glucose (from wheat starch), with added ammonia (for nitrogen) and some minerals.

'Some fungi kill you, so toxicity was an important issue. You can pump drugs 1,000 times their strength into an animal and if it survives then you can assume humans will survive the tiniest amounts. But you can't make an animal eat that quantity of feed.

'However we fed 1,000 tons of fungi to animals in a year which is a lot. The tests were OK. Then we had to test for carcinogenicity. With rats it takes four to four-and-a-half years; it takes two-and-a-half years to grow them in vitrio, then you have to examine ninety-two tissues, and take 20,000 histological samples. We didn't take short cuts; we had to jump every hoop. It took eight years.'

Eventually, they submitted a twenty-eight volume report to the Ministry of Agriculture, Fisheries and Food, with detailed reports of tests on rabbits, rats, pigs and humans.

'In blind tests only two humans ever reacted badly,' said Dr Solomon. 'In one our managing director collapsed after the meal, with overheating and respiratory problems. Why did he collapse? It turned out later that he had been tiling the bathroom and had inhaled vapour adhesive. The other one had a straight allergy.'

Meanwhile they were watching the competition. Both ICI (the chemicals giant) and BP (the petrol company), had been investing in research into novel proteins – but Dr Solomon knew they would drop out. 'Fermentation is expensive so it's important to develop an expensive product, not a dirt-cheap one, that's to say, protein for animals.

'Then along came soy TVP. We thought it would be a flash-in-the-pan, because it was more expensive than meat. Soy had to be woven. Fungi is filamental by nature, so it has the texture from the start. It looks good, it has structure, it has filaments exactly the same size.'

Quorn makes an attractive appeal to the modern housewife. It brings down the blood cholesterol. It is high in protein, low in fat, and a source of dietary fibre. Not to mention an absence of chemical additives, colourings and preservatives. It is not associated with intensive farming at a time when there is a growing anxiety about meat.

And Quorn provides the answer to those who call for us to use resources more economically. Whereas cattle take twenty-six weeks to double their mass, and chickens three weeks, fungi take six hours. Fungi are many more times as efficient at converting starch to protein; 1,000g of starch produces 13g of beef or lamb, 49g of poultry, but 136g of fungi.

Dr Solomon is very relaxed about Quorn's future. 'Getting acceptance is not the technologists' problem. That's for the applied psychologist. My secretary is a food snob, and won't buy any supermarket made-up dish. She wants to cook with the raw materials. But we're looking at the woman on the Clapham omnibus with three kids screaming at home. Frankly, I would expect acceptance to take fifty to seventy years. The transistor was developed in 1947, but took forty years to come good.'

And as for the intended purpose which Lord Rank saw for it, feeding the world's needy, he was doubtful. 'The technology is too expensive. It's not a poor man's food.'

If it turns out that man doesn't need all this protein after all, he might need some of its components, and there is yet another way in which protein can be conjured up – by synthesising, separately, each of the twenty-two amino acids which make up protein. Our nutritional requirements can be broken down to constituent parts in modern science, and it is a matter of pure chemistry to replace these parts artificially, with manufactured synthetic ones. Many vitamins are produced in this way already for use in the food industry. Fat, too, can be made synthetically, and in Germany, during the course of two World Wars, the process was developed on an industrial scale. The source was paraffin from the petro-chemical industry.

The processes are too costly at the moment – but the seeds of a future development which might have their uses in another age have been sown. The most likely next step is to utilise those essential amino acids (there are eight of the twenty-two which the body cannot make, and the synthetic versions of two of these, Lysine and Methionine, already have plentiful uses in foodstuffs).

Dr Magnus Pyke, in his book, *Synthetic Food*, gave an account of twenty-four men who volunteered to go on a diet containing only chemical nutrients, over a period of four-and-a-half months. They survived in full health. The mixture, served as a syrup, was particularly uninteresting, and it was considered advisable to keep them locked in their quarters in case they reacted against its monotony. The exercise had been prepared in the course of evolving a diet which might be suitable for a spaceshot – so its unrealistic cost was absorbed by the project. This syrup was indeed an elixir of life: it contained protein in the form of eighteen amino acids, including the eight essential amino acids, twelve water soluble vitamins, thirteen mineral salts, carbohydrate in the form of glucose (a pound in weight), and some fat and fat-soluble vitamins. Palatability wasn't a requirement, but it would be if it was ever decided that synthesising food was economically viable.

Dr Pyke points out that it will inevitably happen that synthesising some products will be cheaper than natural products which depend on agriculture or animal husbandry. The discovery in the nineteenth century of a way to synthesise indigo and other vegetable dyes resulted in the ruin of the indigo farmers of Bengal. However the manufacture of synthetic fibres did not totally displace traditional natural materials such as cotton and wool.

Of course, the world may decide that the protein emergency has passed, and what is required is a balanced diet, in which protein plays a small part and can be found in judicious combinations in legumes (seed-bearing plants and particularly the bean family) and grains. The National Academy of Sciences in Washington, USA, took the view that the world should be looking to increase its supply of leguminous crops. They not only have the advantage of providing protein, but most of them have the ability to supply themselves with nitrogenous fertiliser through bacteria which live in nodules in their roots. They convert nitrogen in the air into soluble compounds the plant can feed off, converting them to proteins, vitamins and nitrogen-containing compounds. This is of tremendous advantage in poor countries which are invited to enjoy the Green Revolution and then can't afford the expensive inputs of nitrates which derive from the petro-chemical industry and are required by this kind of agriculture.

The legume family embraces 18,000 species of seed-bearing trees, shrubs and plants, which have many more uses than their edibility. They provide the world with the common bean (*phaseolus vulgaris*) which is the staple of Latin America; the lentil family in India; the pigeon pea of Africa and the Caribbean; and the soya bean of the Far East. Some are rich in oil, such as soya beans and peanuts, but most edible legumes contain 24 per cent protein, sometimes 60 per cent.

Beans are important in Europe too, and were the staple food of the poor before the potato was introduced. Ironically, the Green Revolution which introduced cereals – such as maize and rice – did so at the expense of beans, reducing the production in ratio to grain, and therefore reducing protein in countries where it was most needed. So a programme of increasing bean production is a far more attractive prospect than trying to boost the production of animal protein.

The legume family is second only to the grass family in its importance, but has never been exploited in the same way – with the notable exceptions of soya beans and peanuts. Legumes grow quickly and represent an efficient way of easily supplementing protein needs.

There are enough edible varieties in the world to suit most people's needs, but there is still a good case for searching for new uses for existing varieties, or taming entirely new types. Some of the legumes which could be developed for wider use include 'fruits' such as the Mediterranean Carob bean, which is a sweet chocolate substitute and makes a high protein flour, root crops such as yams and other leguminous tubers, and some prolific tropical plants like the Lablab with its high protein seeds (used at present as animal feed).

The African Marama bean has more protein than a peanut and twice as much oil as a soya bean, and a delicious flavour; it actually survives in the dry Kalahari desert. The vigorous Jackbean is a hardy, productive crop, but it needs the help of the scientists to breed out some of the toxins (as they have nearly achieved with the Tarwi, a kind of lupin which grows in the high Andes on the equator, breeding out the alkaloids present in the seed). The Jackbean is as rich in oil and protein as the soya bean.

Not all the legumes are suitable sources of edible protein. Many are poisonous, most notably the seeds of laburnum, one of the many lovely trees in this family, along with wistaria, and many beautiful flowering trees in the tropics – the raintree, cock's comb coral tree, orchid trees, golden shower. Legume seeds are as small as sweet peas and as large as tennis balls, and some beans grow to a yard in length. Sometimes it's the timber which is sought after – the beautiful rosewood which makes such elegant furniture, and lends itself to fine carving. The pods of the senna are famous as laxatives, and other legumes yield gums like Guar and gum arabic. The root of another legume gives us licorice.

Colonists staked their claims to parts of the world which produced valuable dyes obtained from leguminous trees and shrubs. When Portuguese explorers found in South America a tree which yielded a wine-red dye called Bresil, they named the country after it. British Honduras was founded on the basis of a purplish-red dye they extracted from logwood, a leguminous tree, and it was another shrub producing the brilliant blue dye indigo which was a major reason for the British, Dutch and Portuguese to colonise India.

Legumes aren't complete protein foods, and not well balanced like the proteins in meat, fish and milk, but they mostly include the amino acid Lysine which is lacking from most cereals and edible plants, and although they lack Methionine this can be provided by cereals in the diet.

As plant foods, the legumes are associated with the problem of toxicity, which can be eliminated by fermentation (soy sauce and tempeh and miso in the Far East) and many of the alkaloids, flavonoids, and non protein amino acids can be neutralised by soaking in water or by thorough cooking. Sprouting the seeds, the Chinese bean sprouts of stir-fry cooking, is another way of producing from them pure, edible, untoxic material.

The biggest objection to the bean family is possibly social. Eaten in more than small quantities they have the anti-social effect, shared with members of the cabbage family (onions, turnips, swedes), of making gas in the gut, a problem well-known to vegetarians. Dr Alan Long, research adviser to the Vegetarian Society: 'The problem with beans is trying to remove the fartinaceous substances. These are due to complex sugars, oligosaccharides, which can't be digested by enzymes in the gut. Bacteria get to work on them and ferment the sugars, and carbonaceous gas is the result.'

The Non-meat Protein Guide

Meat, fowl, and fish are conventionally the prime sources of protein, along with dairy products such as eggs, cheese and milk. But protein is also available in sufficiency in cereals, nuts and vegetables, especially pulses.

The accepted human requirement in the UK is fifty-five grams of protein a day, which many think unnecessarily high, and Oxfam suggest that forty-five grams a day is sufficient. In the UK it is extremely difficult to go short on protein; deficiency usually occurs in those countries where they eat rice three times a day – but even then it's usually possible to add lentils to the diet, the dhal of India, or the processed bean products of China and Japan (the soya bean curd known as tofu, and fermented rice and beans as in tempeh and miso).

THE POTATO. One of the lowliest protein sources, containing only 2 per cent protein. Yet, until the Irish famine of the 1860s, a person eating four and a half pounds of potatoes a day, and nothing else, as some did, was getting his full protein requirement of forty-five grams. A smaller quantity, with some added milk stirred into it would also suffice.

CEREALS. Wholemeal wheat and other grains, such as barley, rye and millet, contain around 10 per cent protein on average, oatmeal slightly more. Buckwheat (known as kasha in Eastern Europe) is a good source.

NUTS. From almonds (around 20 per cent protein) to peanuts (over 28 per cent) nuts are a good protein source, similar to cottage cheese.

PEAS AND BEANS. They are 5 to 6 per cent protein. Broad beans are 7 per cent. But because vegetables are mostly water, flour from peas, chick peas and beans is a much more concentrated source.

TVP (textured vegetable protein). This is processed soya bean flour, which has been re-formed to make meat analogues. It is used commercially as a cheap meat substitute. Either as mince or in chunks, it is combined with real meat to make low-price pies, burgers, stews and mince, both in supermarkets and in institutional catering. It is also offered as a meat substitute in health food shops under various brand names. In the UK it is mostly sold by British Arkady, the subsidiary of an American company. The British-invented product, KESP, was discontinued when the process became uneconomic.

QUORN. The newest novel protein, made from a minuscule member of the mushroom family, as high as chicken in protein, and attractively marketed in supermarkets with Indian and Chinese spicing, or occasionally available unflavoured for the home cook to experiment with.

THE SOYA BEAN FAMILY. The world's most useful bean, providing a good low cholesterol oil, as well as good protein:

Soya Milk. The Chinese and Japanese mix the flour with water to make high protein soya 'milk'. This is the only acceptable milk to the Chinese, who are mostly allergic to dairy milk.

Tofu. An almost tasteless white curd made from soy milk used to add protein to soups and in vegetarian dishes. Smoked tofu has a certain character.

Tempeh. This is fermented tofu, and has more substantial texture and flavour.

Fermented soya beans. Black salted beans sold loose, or in tins, used as a seasoning, especially with seafood dishes, such as crab, squid, eels.

Yellow bean sauce. Fermented beans sold in tins, either whole or in a paste, and used like black beans to flavour sauces.

Soy sauce. Not just a condiment, but a source of concentrated protein. Roasted soya beans are injected with a mould, and after a few days exposed to a yeast-like bacteria to ferment. The best take two years to mature, the cheapest are made of hydrolised vegetable protein and salt. Japanese varieties (such as Kikkoman) are considered better than most Chinese soy sauces. Japanese soy sauce is usally known by the name Shoyu, and contains wheat as well as beans. Tamari, when authentic, is a soy sauce made entirely from fermented wheat.

Miso. Beans fermented with rice or barley to make a concentrated protein, the basis of Japanese nutrition for centuries. It is taken three times a day in soup, blended with dashi, a nourishing fish stock made of dried bonito flakes and dried seaweed. The three most common kinds of miso are Shinsu (yellow miso), used in soups and sauces; Shiro (white miso) which is sweeter, and used in sauces, pickles, and as a savoury spread on food to be grilled; and Aka (red miso), dark, salty and savoury, which keeps indefinitely at room temperature.

6

NUTRITION

Among the brightly coloured paintings which decorate the notice-boards along the corridor of a West London school is one by Julia (aged eight). It shows a glass of cola, and beside it seven spoonfuls of sugar. In spidery, clear capitals, she has written the caption: EVERY TIN OF COLA CONTAINS SEVEN SPOONFULS OF SUGAR TO ROT YOUR TEETH.'

The cola companies are on television week in and week out adver-tising the glamour, excitement, reassuring significance of their prod-ucts. They spend hundreds of thousands of pounds. But Julia is advertising right back, there in junior school.

In Julia's class, Alexander (also eight) defines his preferences: 'I like crisps but I know they aren't good for me.' Others volunteer that junk food is bad for you, and that you should eat lots of fruit instead of sweets. The parents are a social mix, but the message is there.

Is their awareness due to the result of some hugely funded Depart-ment of Health initiative, some massive Government advertising campaign? No, on the contrary. It is the human response to every parent's and teacher's concern for the well-being of children.

Denied a lead from the authorities, parents and teachers have made it their business to establish the truth about nutrition, and to attempt to implement its lessons. How have they been able to estab-lish these guidelines?

The credit for putting nutrition on the national agenda must go to Professor Philip James, now head of the Rowett Research Institute in Aberdeen. Throughout the 1960s and 1970s thousands of nutritionists around the world had been amassing mountains of data which pointed to a desperate need to act quickly. But reports were confusing: the evidence of one scientist appeared to conflict with another. It was an education minister, Sir Keith Joseph, who said impatiently there should be a committee to sort it out, and the man who emerged as the voice of the committee was a persuasive Welshman, Professor James.

A character rare in the world of science, he conbines an intellect equal to any of his academic colleagues with the manoeuvrability and pragmatism of any Front Bench politician. Like some great politicians (such as Harold Macmillan with his catch-phrases, 'Winds of Change' and 'You've never had it so good') he has the unusual ability to extract essential data from millions of words in thousands of reports, and encapsulate the relevance of the main points in one pithy comment. It was he who coined the instruction: 'Eat less fat, sugar and salt; more fibre.'

In those eight words he effected a reversal of our understanding of the previous fifty years of work in nutrition.

It is rare for a scientist to have a sense of newspaper headlines, and Professor James is only too conscious that other scientists are suspicious of colleagues who get quoted in the press or appear on television. But it was through these media that he found himself launching his controversial discoveries.

His first experience had been writing and narrating a BBC Horizon film, *Fat in the Fire*, based on his work on obesity at the Dunn Nutritional Centre at Cambridge. There had been criticism of an uncomfortable episode which showed how patients' fat was measured by inserting needles into the flesh. 'People objected violently to this scene,' he says. 'But the bloke they were putting the needles into was me.'

The BBC liked his direct, informative style and came back for more. They suggested a six-part series on health, to be called *Feeling Great*, with the comedian, Roy Castle, as compère. Professor James initially backed off. 'My instinct was that a proper doctor doing research would not do that. But I was persuaded by Professor Jerry Morris of the London School of Hygiene who said that to refuse would reflect a lack of public responsibility, so I agreed.'

He thought it would be a good idea to make the point that, far from not eating potatoes when on a diet, that was exactly what slimmers ought to eat. 'Potatoes are carbohydrate, and that's good.

They provide bulk, they give you a full feeling.' It was fat that slimmers should cut out, the fat you fry potato chips in, or sautée them in, or roast them with, or the butter you melt on to them, and the grated cheese you sprinkle them with, or the cream you mash them up with, and the fat that makes up 70 per cent of the calories of a potato crisp.

At this time the notion was so revolutionary that even the members of the BBC film unit were disbelieving. It was like telling them the earth was round, when they could see for themselves that it was flat. 'The director of the film resigned because he said I didn't know what I was talking about,' says Professor James. '*His* grandmother told him that potatoes were fattening, so why was I saying that they were not? It was an outrage.'

It was the first time anyone had considered nutrition might be a lively subject for TV. 'I wanted an unconventional approach. I suggested that we should pay for fifty council house families to record their food intake for a week, and they'd get £5 a time if they did it.

'The film unit couldn't believe what a big problem we had in Britain until we discovered that out of the fifty families, the diets of forty-nine of them were absolutely appalling. We showed the most loquacious families, with the cameraman sitting right above the cooker, and discussed their diet over Sunday lunch, and we told them how to change what they ate. That was cinema verité.

'The series caused a riot, but it was extraordinarily successful in the sense that the BBC Education Unit had never had such a response in its history. I was accused of having set nutrition back thirty years by that programme because it was non-scientific, and by "fancy talking" to the public like that. It summarises the dilemma for nutritionists: how do you make science out of this whole area when it's of such immediate concern to the public? How do you maintain your integrity? And how do you persuade your scientific colleagues that it's appropriate, and at the same time talk to the public?'

The Health Education Council (as it was then) invited him to help think about health education. They were struggling. 'They were telling children how to brush their teeth. That was *nutrition* education! I asked about obesity and diabetes, heart disease, cancer. Where were we on that?'

His obvious feeling for communication prompted the people who had set up ACNE (Advisory Committee on Nutritional Education) to invite him to advise them. ACNE also invited Professor Derek Miller, of Queen Elizabeth College, London, noted for his bow-tied, telegenic performance on chat shows, and his zeal to inform. (In fact it was Miller the BBC had first approached for the *Feeling Fit* series, but the peripatetic professor was always wandering off to India, Nepal, New Guinea).

ACNE was formed in the mid-1970s after Sir Keith Joseph addressed the British Nutrition Foundation's annual lecture and said it was inappropriate for everybody to be giving different messages. The Health Education Council, the British Nutrition Foundation, the Royal College of Physicians, not to mention World Health Organisation reports, were apparently offering conflicting advice. Sir Keith Joseph wanted to address the educationalists, home economists in the teaching schools, health visitors' associations, dieticians and representatives of industry with a single, straightforward message. 'In his market-based way he wanted to bill the people who might be involved in producing the food as well as the educationalists. He wasn't going to start a costly campaign from Central Government, because there already were organs for integrating and developing the health message.'

Let Professor James tell the story in his own words from the point where he joins the committee with Professor Derek Miller. 'This was much to the fury of the Department of Health because by then the DHSS wanted to minimise the significance of the committee, as it was coming out with totally sweeping and unbelievably new policies, which, looking back, now seem to be totally banal and ordinary.

'In fact there already existed a Government Committee which covered this area, the Committee on Medical Aspects of Food, COMA, which is chaired by the Chief Medical Officer of Health, is responsible for developing policy, so resentment about the function of ACNE could soon develop. The COMA report itself in 1974 had already made various points. Then there was actually an extraordinarily good Coronary Heart Disease report from the Royal College of Physicians, in 1976, but typically the College thought all they had to do was produce a report and everything would follow. It was the fact that nothing happened following that report that led to a few members of that committee setting up the Coronary Prevention Group. Dr Christopher Robbins was their first director.

'The Royal College of Physicians, provided the right group of people were picked, could say whatever they liked, as long as their council would accept it. There were no pressures on the Royal College in this domain. The people they actually had to convince were the GPs, the cardiologists, the epidemiologists and internists in medicine. The attitude of the average GP was: 'I don't know anything about this; it's a completely different game; I can't do anything to help; I'm busy.

'The fact was that most people thought the report was irrelevant which was not true but the report remained in a vacuum. The College had no mechanisms for following through because then you were into the doctors' conservatism. Cardiologists were totally against it.

'I offered a little paper that essentially said we should be dealing with obesity, heart disease and so on. They said: "Good Heavens, yes!" I thought we should have a think-tank because it was such an amazingly different story – we hadn't thought about these things before. So I was given £500 by the committee to organise a weekend conference, in the Dunn Clinical Nutritional Centre in Cambridge. I invited Derek Miller and a number of people who were close to me because I had to hunt for people in the nutritional world who would be able to think in the same way as I did.

'Essentially I presented the World Health Organisation guidelines and the Royal College of Physicians' report, and said that we now had to generate a set of guidelines based on all this, which would be meaningful and could be integrated.

'From that weekend we produced a first draft which was pretty pathetic. The main committee however thought this draft reflected the most dramatic and devastating change in thinking. They questioned this paragraph and that, but they asked me to extend the draft. So we extended it. The British Nutrition Foundation (BNF) and the Department of Health representatives confused by us saying: "What do you mean by extending it?" But I told them we would remain entirely consistent with every Government report that had been produced.'

Now Professor James realised he'd run into a brick wall. He concluded that the sugar industry, because sugar was implicated in the review, was bringing pressure to bear in both the Government and the BNF. The word got back to him that MPs at Westminster were predicting that the report would not emerge.

'By this stage I was advised by all my colleagues that I should drop this report because my whole future was at stake.' They said he was putting at risk the work of the Dunn Nutritional Centre, which was becoming world-famous for its chemical research.

The argument moved to the actual title of the committee and, therefore, its sphere of authority.

The DHSS was the policy-maker and was annoyed when ACNE rechristened itself NACNE (National Advisory Committee as opposed to Joint Advisory Committee) to signify that it was now a truly coherent, national body. So ACNE in becoming NACNE symbolised its message that it was not concerned with minority sections of the community who might need special care, but with a huge public health issue.

'Eventually the Department of Health told us we could not proceed with the NACNE report because it had established the COMA Committee. And I said to the person concerned: "You absolute devil!" at which he burst out laughing. He said: "Well, what do you expect?"'

The editor of the *Lancet*, Ian Munroe, eventually decided to publish the report intact, but while he was preparing it, Geoffrey Cannon blew the whole story in the *Sunday Times*, alleging that there had been an attempt to suppress a report which was in the national interest.

Questions were asked in the House of Commons. The Prime Minister, Margaret Thatcher, didn't go along with her civil servants, 'she said in effect she had no objection to the public being informed and being given advice on how best to eat for their health. Her instinct was absolutely right, of course. Suddenly, within twenty-four hours, I was being told "How did you ever get the idea we were against publication?"'

Professor James feared that he had upset too many people and that his career would be at an end. 'When it actually emerged I thought I would normally be reprimanded or even sacked but fortunately I'd moved to the Rowett Research Institute in Scotland and was protected because they have a great sense of supporting their own.'

So the message got out. No doubt the publicity and the questions in the House confirmed its importance. And what was the message they sought to suppress?

'Essentially that the problems of nutrition in Britain were not the problems of the elderly or other vulnerable groups. We were not looking at those sections of society that needed special care, but at the total population. We were talking about huge public health issues, not just minor fiddles. That was pretty shocking. Then to say that the British diet was wrong was the most outrageous critism that you could make of what the medical establishment had been doing for the last forty years!'

'Despite the Government response, dieticians were now gung-ho, feeling in part involved because members of the committee had forewarned them. They moved rapidly, particularly on the community side, and so within two years practically every health district in Britain had a new diet and health policy. Community physicians were outraged by the lack of information and the dieticians, irate at not having been involved earlier, were taking on the NACNE report as the basic document from which they developed their policies.

'It was the most extraordinary grass roots development. The publicity and the media played a vital part in that. The House of Lords reacted and was suddenly up in arms over health education. I had Church of England committees writing to me – did we want any help, because this seemed so important. The sense of social responsibility was staggering. The Women's Institute were all agog. There was a sea change in consumer opinion.

'The COMA heart disease material came out in 1984. That report was brilliantly contrived by the Chairman, Sir Philip Randall from Oxford, who wrote it himself under pressure from the NACNE report and he came out with something very close to NACNE and that was a vindication that we were not completely crazy. The COMA report is of enormous significance; it's an official Government policy with its implications being accepted by both the Ministries of both Agriculture and Health before it was published – that's never happened before.'

The drama of the public stage is a long way from Philip James's own family background – he likes it when Americans call him a 'poor old long lost Welsh shepherd's son'.

He was brought up in a small village in North Wales. His mother was English and taught English in the village girls' school. His father, who was Welsh, and headmaster of the boys' school, was a charismatic man, a Methodist, a conscientious objector who was put into solitary confinement in Wormwood Scrubs in the First World War. Music was his passion and he ran the local brass band.

Philip was six when his father died, and was sent to a Quaker

boarding school in Yorkshire, where he won all the school prizes.
He went on to read Medicine at University College, London, but
after qualifying soon became disenchanted with the Establishment.
'I discovered that the British medical profession was hierarchical,
pompous, aggressive and competitive.'

He volunteered for a job in Jamaica, working in a clinic which was
studying malnutrition in children. 'I had studied paediatrics, but I
knew nothing of nutrition. I didn't even know that Kwashiorkor
was a disease of the undernourished.' He was shocked at what he
saw in Jamaica. Children at death's door, their skin flaking off. His
job was to run a metabolic unit for the study of acute medical
problems in malnutrition, and at once he had to learn how to do
research.

'We went on Emergency services. We'd travel in a Landrover
with a nurse and got up into the mountains, ending up in a single
hut which was made out of corrugated iron and cardboard boxes.
We'd find a child dying from diarrhoea. The hut would have nothing
in it except newspapers plastering the mud walls. We might find two
bananas and an old tin of milk with a dirty bottle and so on. They
were living in a patch, perhaps twice the size of a small room. The
locals were very poor indeed and couldn't buy any food. They could
live off a tin of condensed milk for a week if they diluted it.

'When I got to Jamaica I didn't know why children got diarrhoea,
which was a big killer in the tropics. So I developed a whole series
of techniques for looking at that problem. I think I may have
managed to drop the mortality rate in the ward by up to a quarter.

'The children's guts were so shot to pieces that you couldn't give
them standard milk diets or sugar enriched diets, and their capacity
to digest was so impaired that you had to give them small volumes
extremely frequently, because their small intestines couldn't cope.
I worked out why, if you gave them a full meal, it would shunt down
the intestine, dragging fluid out of the body.

'We thought at that stage that it was because malnutrition affected
the gut, which turns over new cells so fast that it needs an excellent
supply of nutrients of the right sort. That may not be true. Subsequently I did a study where we seemed to show that the bugs in
the intestines could grow and damage the intestines – so there is an
interaction between nutrition and infection.'

He returned to London. By now he was curious to know more
about the way food affects the health of patients, and whether food

caused disease, or whether food could be used to treat disease. His work immediately showed a startling similarity to research in Jamaica; patients in British hospital wards were adult images of the undernourished children.

There was serious malnutrition in British hospitals.

The subject of nutrition, which had enjoyed huge importance in the 1920s and 1930s when all the discoveries about Vitamins were being made was far from advancing. By the early 1970s it had been pushed to the sidelines, except in the tropics.

So when the Medical Research Council told James they wanted some research done on obesity he was faintly annoyed. He didn't know anything about the subject, and when he inquired about it he found that nobody else did either. He wrote a review to that effect.

This immediately aroused interest. He asked the question – What makes people excessively fat? The view accepted at this time was that most people could change their body weight with a bit of self-discipline, but there seemed to be exceptions. One theory was that some people were born differently with a fixed number of fat cells. Another was that infant overfeeding led to excess fat cells and adult obesity. Neither theory was right.

But this was the unlikely line of inquiry which was to lead to the discoveries which established nutrition as a central issue in the study of health. To make a start, he formed an ad hoc team at the Dunn Nutritional Centre in Cambridge, grabbing what facilities he could. First of all, he moved into an instrument-cleaning room in the back of an old clinic. Nurses would come in and out to boil dirty instruments. Then he moved to a Portakabin at the Animal Research Institute, Babraham, near Cambridge. It could have made a perfect location for filming *Dad's Army*, but somehow it worked, and they occupied a pig chamber, adapting for human use the calorimeters which had been designed for measuring fat on pigs. Lack of funding failed to stem their enthusiasm, and they annexed an old radio-therapy unit, with thick walls for cobalt therapy, and that became a laboratory.

All the scientific research which would eventually fuel the NACNE report was originated here. But what also became clear in Cambridge was that it's one thing to make scientific progress, it's quite another to put it into practice. Cambridge provided his first taste of politics, the need to jockey for funds, battle for a place to work, even the struggle to find patients to work on. But he relished the difficulties.

He hit the Cambridge 'Mafia', as he calls them, a group of academics who have the idea that work is a competition rather like croquet, where you progress by knocking a rival's ball off the lawn. The Mafia very soon resented that James was held up as an example of how to get things done in spite of lack of funds. 'I discovered that if you make a lot of waves, and you are quite successful, you threaten people. I got locked in battle with a major character who was responsible for medical research in a competing institution.'

When Professor James finally communicated his important health message to the country at large, he realised that his openness actually counted against him in the small, but fierce, world of academic funding, and that there were people looking for excuses to get him out. He didn't mind, and he was planning to battle it out, but quite suddenly he was offered the directorship of the Rowett Research Institute in Aberdeen, where the greatly admired Sir Kenneth Blaxter was retiring.

James hesitated, but a visit to Aberdeen soon convinced him that it would be a rewarding career change. 'I was astonished by the enthusiasm and welcome the key decision-makers gave me. I wondered what the plot was. In Cambridge everyone is plotting.'

The Rowett is the largest animal nutrition research institute in Europe, and he was stunned to realise that funds for which he had fought so energetically for human nutritional research were freely available for animal research.

Typically, Professor James has already reversed conventional thinking on some aspects of animal nutrition. Out of his concern for the high level of animal fat in human diet, one of the first questions he asked at the Rowett was: 'Why can't we rear animals with less fat?' The immediate reaction was: 'Oh, you and your heart disease!' And then the astonishing answer: 'It's not difficult.'

'Within weeks they had produced some calculations showing that farmers had been desperately fattening their animals for decades because they thought that was the right thing to do. Then they were confused by the butchers, saying fatty meat was wonderful to taste, although it's not true – taste and tenderness are not related to fat content – contrary to what everybody says.'

Initially the Meat and Livestock Commission was outraged. When he put his arguments they 'collapsed, said they have terrible problems and couldn't do it because the producers give them the money. We then agreed that they would go in on a major new development on lean meat. I then went gung-ho on the radio again, saying we had a mediaeval system of marketing and carcass analysis and that it was time the whole of animal husbandry changed. Now the Agricultural Research Council at MAFF conduct a policy to produce lean animals. How incredible!'

Under Professor James, the Rowett continues to enjoy great international prestige for its animal research work, but the study of human nutrition is expanding. Professor James has established that nutrition is vital to our understanding of health.

What does the future hold? The logical question is, if nutrition is the key to good health, can we deploy our knowledge of it to manage ill health? He think this is very likely. But having a sensible theory is one thing, and proving it scientifically is another; and overcoming resistance to those who object to what you have proved is yet another.

But it's a challenge he does not fear. Within the space of twenty years, nutrition, which was supposed to concern none but the sick and children in run-down tropical zones is now a science recognised as absolutely central to our lives. Much of the credit must go to the ducking and diving, the wit and intelligence, of one man, and his ability to bring the force of many great intellects in science to the service of mankind, conquering the opposition which resists change on the grounds that it may discredit its own position.

Professor James has more insight into diet than any of us. Does he match his own lifestyle to what he thinks is right for others?

'Everybody is terrified of coming to eat with us. [His wife Jean is a good cook.] They think we must be freaks, but we're not. My cholesterol level is equivalent to that of an African living in a rural society.' (Scottish males have the highest levels of cholesterol anywhere in the world – so by local levels the professor is freakish!)

But his experiences in the last twenty-five years have completely changed his diet. 'As a student I ate Mars bars and drank creamy milk. Nowadays my diet is near that of the Italians'. I eat meat (I'm not against eating meat) and fish, and we do eat cheese – to enjoy good nutrition you don't have to be a weirdo and eat nothing but beans. But the main elements of our diet are: cereals, including pasta and rice, potatoes, vegetables (we often have three vegetables at a meal). We have fruit twice a day. We start the morning with home-made muesli with oats, wheatflakes, raisins, no sugar. (It's cheaper to make your muesli, and you can make it to choice.)'

The Jameses cook with olive oil, or small amounts of butter, and grill rather than fry. He keeps his fat intake to a minimum.

Salt, he has reduced to a lower level than most people, without cutting it out. 'We eat low-salt bacon and that sort of thing.'

Sugar, he has almost cut to zero. 'We adapted steadily, and now we hate sweet things. Except fruit.'

Exercise? 'I work a hundred hours a week – that's my exercise. I have the weight problem in the family and readily put on weight. I don't take as much exercise as I should but feel better when I do.'

Travelling: 'The hardest thing is to get the food you want in hotels. When I go to dinners, too, I try to find the right foods but it's very difficult. I'm desperate to get home after a trip abroad. I went to Hungary and actually saw posters where they were advertising fat as healthy!'

7

HEALTH

The secret of living a healthy life is no secret. Nutritionists established a healthy blueprint for us as long ago as the 1970s, but the message wasn't communicated clearly and Britain has continued to have a record of premature heart disease and cancer as bad as any in the world.

The message is: 'Eat more vegetables and fruit and cereal, less fat, sugar and salt, and lead an active life.' It seems obvious now, but this simple instruction was more or less buried for fifteen or twenty years, and it took the efforts of an assiduous investigative reporter to play the midwife and bring the news into the world.

When Governments failed to act, when they went as far as shelving a significant report prepared by the country's top nutritional scientists as described in the previous chapter, journalist Geoffrey Cannon stepped forward.

Today, Cannon is the leading campaigner for health, yet ten years ago, he now realises, he was completely ignorant of what a healthy lifestyle meant. Like everyone else, he yo-yoed from business lunches to semi-starvation diets. Cannon believed the diet message was simply: 'Eat less.' He was wrong. It never occurred to him that the key to slimming and to long-term health is rarely the quantity of food but its quality. This, in 1979, is what he set out to discover for himself.

What seems most extraordinary, is that, given the knowledge available to the scientists, he could go to no public source of information that was energetically disseminating the news of sensible diet. He found the opposite.

It was as the result of this quest that Cannon went on to write (and co-write) a series of books which completely altered our thinking about health and diet, especially *The Food Scandal* and *The Politics of Food*. The basis of Cannon's work was the nutritional report, produced under the supervision of Professor Philip James's National Advisory Council for Nutrition Education, known as the NACNE Report (see Chapter Six).

In the early 1980s when Britain had just about the worst record in the world for premature deaths from heart attacks, common cancers, and other Western diseases, the official line was that non-infectious illness was 'just one of those things' – bad luck. Smoking was accepted as unhealthy, but any idea that food had anything to do with health was ridiculed. But in other Western countries scientists and governments had accepted that heart attacks, in particular, were largely preventable by eating a diet with less saturated fat. Why wasn't the message getting across in Britain?

The necessary information existed, but was scattered, like pieces of a jig-saw puzzle. 'I was trying to assemble them without knowing how big the picture was, or how many pictures they would make.'

Cannon's career, up to this point, had not touched upon food. He'd been a founder of *New Society*, editor of the *Radio Times* for ten years, and entertainment and leisure editor of the *Sunday Times*. It was here that he became involved in the national awakening to jogging and with Hetty Einzig wrote a searching book called *Dieting Makes You Fat*. It was research on this book which put him in touch with scientists who care about public health.

'During early 1983 I kept on meeting health professionals who hinted that I might be on the track of a Big Story,' said Cannon. 'One scientist actually said to me, "This is the biggest scandal since Victorian days, when public officials refused to act on the fact that cholera and typhoid were caused by open drains."'

Eventually, in the best traditions of the leak to Fleet Street, a draft (officially secret) of the NACNE report arrived in the post. Its arrival was timed to the very day of an annual conference organised by the food industry, funded by the British Nutrition Foundation, on the subject of dietary guidelines. This was Cannon's first experience of the BNF and the Foundation's first experience of him. Half-way through the afternoon, he stood up and asked if there was any document containing dietary guidelines he could recommend to his readers. 'Should I perhaps publish details of one document that, curiously, nobody has mentioned, the report compiled by the National Advisory Committee on Nutrition Education?' he asked. Pandemonium. 'Because the NACNE document was meant to be a big secret. The BNF bosses were appalled to realise I knew about it. At that stage they didn't know I actually had a draft copy of it with me. As soon as I'd uttered the magic acronym "NACNE", two groups of people made a bee-line for me. One lot from the BFN told me there was nothing in the document, there was no need to worry myself about it, and also that there was no need to worry my readers about the Great British diet. The other group told me that NACNE and its suppression revealed a gigantic scandal, and the reason why British food and therefore British health was just about the worst in the developed world. Well, there was no doubt which was the more interesting story!'

So he determined to tell the story in the *Sunday Times*. At first when he approached the paper's chief news editor there was no reaction. The subject of nutrition was completely misunderstood; he couldn't at first explain the significance of his news. In exasperation, Cannon asked: 'You think that nutrition is about meals-on-wheels and Asian school children with rickets, don't you?'

'Well, isn't it?' said the news editor.

Cannon persevered: 'Suppose I were to tell you that an expert report originally commissioned by the Government has come up with the conclusion that the food that we typically eat in Britain is a main single cause of the diseases we now mostly suffer and die from, and this report has been blocked by the Government because of its implications for the food manufacturing industry?'

The *Sunday Times* in those days had a long tradition of investigative journalism, pioneered by editor Harold Evans and executives such as Ron Hall, Magnus Linklater, Bruce Page and Don Berry. It was Berry, features editor in 1983, who worked with Cannon on the NACNE story, turning 13,000 words of detailed documentation into publishable length, and it ran as: *Censored: a Diet for Life and Death* on the front page. There was a dramatic and immediate response from readers, and the news editor urged Cannon to prepare follow-up stories. William Laing, a health economist who'd been deputy director of the Office of Health Economics, helped him prepare a feature: *Biting a Billion off the NHS Bill*.

'What I did was to get views from a dozen professors on how the cost to the taxpayer of hospitals, doctors, dentists, drugs, and so forth would be reduced if the nation chose to adopt a healthy diet. Or rather, if the Government accepted responsibility for cleaning up the food supply.' Bill Laing constructed an economic forecast of these savings. In the case of heart disease, the general view was that a healthy diet could prevent something between 30 per cent and 70 per cent of the cost of the treatment. Tooth decay, which was expensive, and effectively caused by sugar, was easy to calculate. 'Bill estimated that the total savings every year for a range of diseases would be in the region of a thousand million pounds, at a time when the National Health Service budget was £15 billion a year.'

It was another '*Sunday Times* exclusive', a provocative follow-up to the initial scoop. To Cannon's amazement, the story was rejected by Frank Giles, an ex-Foreign Office man who had succeeded Harold Evans as editor. 'I walked into Frank Giles's office, told him my first story had attracted more readers' letters than the rest of the paper put together, and asked him to explain,' said Cannon. 'I remember him saying, "I'm not the editor of the *Nutrition Gazette*." I thought this was an idiotic thing to say. Then he asked me to leave his office. I got the story in, though, a couple of weeks later, after Don Berry came back from a holiday he'd taken just after my first NACNE story was published.'

It was at this time Cannon met the nutritionist Caroline Walker, who'd been secretary to the working party which prepared the NACNE report. 'Once the story was published she effectively gave me a crash course in nutrition and public health; and also introduced me to scores of leading scientists and other health professionals, many of whom knew, as she did, that Government was determined to keep the truth about British food a secret from the British public.'

With her, he wrote *The Food Scandal*, which was published in the summer of 1984. It tells the full story of the NACNE report and interprets its findings for the average family.

Fats. Choose oils and margarines that are high in polyunsaturates.

Meat. Choose very lean cuts of beef, lamb, pork, bacon. Eat more poultry, game.

Fish. Eat more fish and shellfish of all kinds. Fat fish like herring and mackerel are high in polyunsaturates.

Dairy. Buy skimmed or semi-skimmed fresh milk.

Carbohydrates. Eat lots more good quality wholemeal bread; potatoes, pasta, rice. Eat more potatoes, whole, with their skins, but go easy on the butter.

Fruit and vegetables. Have fresh fruit instead of puddings or sweet snacks.

Breakfast. Choose wholegrain breakfast cereals without added sugar or salt.

Snacks. Fresh and dried fruit and nuts, and sandwiches, are better than 'convenience' biscuits, cakes and confectionery.

The Food Scandal challenged the unholy trinity of British processed food: saturated fat, commercial sugar, added salt. It was rude about specific branded products.

At much the same time, Cannon wrote three major features for *The Times*, to accompany *The Food Scandal*. The first – *Food, Treacherous Food* – summarised the scientific evidence showing that typical British food is an important cause of many diseases, including major killers such as heart attacks, strokes and common cancers. The second, *The Cover-Up That Kills*, made the point that: 'Few now doubt the fatal connection between eating Western food and suffering from Western diseases. Yet this important message is not reaching the public.' A third feature, *So You Think You Eat Healthily?*, showed how everybody can switch from unhealthy to healthy food. The features caused an uproar. *The Times* had to employ extra staff to handle the hundreds of letters that were sent; and over thirty readers' letters were actually published, mostly expressing strong views on what Cannon had to say.

'The views published in *The Times* and *The Food Scandal* were not my personal views, nor those of Caroline,' says Cannon. 'We were revealing that all over the world *scientists* agreed that Western food was a massive public health problem – except in Britain.'

In 1990, Cannon proved this point with a book-length report published by the Consumers' Association called *Food and Health: the Experts Agree*, which analysed the contents of seventy-five expert scientific reports published between 1965 and 1990, almost all of which have the same message – essentially the NACNE message.

'In the mid-1980s the pressure on me, and on Caroline, was pretty intense,' Cannon says. What kept him going, he says, was his partnership with Caroline, whom he married in 1987, a year before she died at the age of thirty-eight. 'She knew we were right,' he said.

'And we gained support from many eminent people in science and medicine who urged us on.'

Geoffrey Cannon's entry point into health and fitness, in the late 1970s, 'was fear of the Big F – my fortieth birthday,' says Cannon. 'I started jogging and writing a monthly column for *Running* magazine. I learned to ski by means of a wonderful Californian method called the Inner Game. And by getting interested in exercise physiology, I realised that all the dieting books, gathering dust on my shelves, systematically underrated the value of the right kind of exercise.'

Keeping fit is not an obvious course for one dedicated to the pursuit of the intellect, but he hit the physiology books, decided that the conventional, low-calorie, no-exercise wisdom was wrong, and wrote a feature for the *Sunday Times* in January 1982 called *Dieting Makes You Fat*. He gained much of his scientific research material on a visit in 1981 to the heart disease prevention unit at Stanford University in California. The book that developed out of the article (by Hetty Einzig and Geoffrey Cannon) was a worldwide bestseller.

'The human body is a machine that improves with use,' says Cannon, quoting one of his heroes, Swedish physiologist, Professor Per-Olof Astrand. 'The way to be well is to eat high quality food and to be physically active, every day.'

Cannon makes a distinction between exercise and activity. 'Exercise involves taking your trousers or skirt off: for activity short of exercise, you can keep them on. Vigorous exercise, which puts the heart and circulation system into gear, like running or swimming for more than twenty minutes at a time, is great. But you can also get fit and healthy, and lose excess fat, by everyday activity. For example, I avoid lifts, and use stairs rather than escalators at underground stations when I can.' He has just moved upstairs from the ground floor, to the second and third floor of his house, enjoying the exercise afforded by the extra forty-nine steps.

In *Dieting Makes You Fat* Cannon explains that exercise of the right type keeps the body going at higher revs all the time, not just when you are exercising; and the habitual low calorie dieting trains the body to work at lower revs. 'That's why middle-aged people, usually women, who have lived their adult lives on or between diets, are so flabby, and get fat on small amounts of food,' he says. 'There's no mystique about it. Everybody who goes from fat to fit by means of regular exercise and good food feels warmer all the time – central heating turned down, windows open more often, fewer bedclothes and sweaters.'

The lexicographer Jonathan Green chose *Dieting Makes You Fat* as one of the *Sayings of the 1980s*, much to Cannon's satisfaction. 'After the book, all the main slimming clubs changed their regimes: they all got interested in nutrition and exercise,' he says.

The jogging boom, though, was thoroughly jogged when Jim Fixx, the American jogging guru, keeled over and died of a heart attack at the age of fifty-two while running. He evidently couldn't fix it for himself. Cannon had a ready answer. 'Jim Fixx is an example of what I call the "Finnish lumberjack syndrome". Not long ago the worst rates of premature death from heart attacks in Europe were in northern Finland. A lot of the men, who were dying very young, were very physically active lumberjacks, for example. So obviously exercise by itself didn't protect them. The Finnish diet at that time was very heavy in saturated fats from dairy produce. Active people eat more; so they put more saturated fats through their bloodstream, clogging their arteries faster.' This is probably what happened to Fixx, who believed that running was the answer to everything, and boasted in his books about his love of steaks and hamburgers. 'The more exercise you take,' says Cannon, 'the more important it is to cut out hard fats.'

Since 1983, Cannon has been in correspondence with a large number of scientists to discuss, debate and check the messages in his books and journalism, and in the unpaid work he now does for many consumer and professional groups. His files of professional correspondence fill two cabinets. Under ABC, for starters, his contacts include: Dr James (oat-bran) Anderson; Sir Francis Avery Jones (the gastro-enterologist); Dr Keith Ball (co-founder of the Coronary Prevention Group); Sir Douglas Black (former President of the Royal College of Physicians and of the British Medical Association); Professor Norman Blacklock (sugar and kidney stones); Dr Denis Burkitt (fibre); Dr David Buss (chief nutritionist at the Ministry of Agriculture); Professor John Catford (head of 'Heartbeat Wales'); Dr Kenneth Cooper (aerobics); Professor Michael Crawford (essential fats); Dr John Cummings (fibre and the gut); Dr David Cuthbertson (former Director of the Rowett Research Institute).

Cannon also edits a series of booklets produced by the McCarrison Society, *The Founders of Modern Nutrition*. The three so far published are on Surgeon-Captain T.L. Cleave ('who showed why sugar is such a great evil in the Western diet'); Dr Hugh Trowell ('who coined the phrase 'Western Disease'); and Dr Hugh Sinclair ('who almost alone in the world, realised the vital importance of essential fats'). Cannon devised the series, obtained grants to underwrite the cost, designed as well as edited the booklets, wrote introductions to each of them, and circulated them to leading nutritionists all over the world. 'People wonder why I do this kind of work,' Cannon says. 'A director of Sainsbury was overheard saying recently: "Exactly how does Geoffrey Cannon earn a living, anyway?"

'Well, I believe Cleave, Trowell, Sinclair and a few others are great nutritional scientists, that their work is important, and that they should be commemorated. Nobody else is doing it, so I encourage fellow-scientists to write the booklets.

'The public mood about food and health has changed now,' says Cannon. 'Colin Tudge, then on the *New Scientist*, and Oliver Gillie, then of the *Sunday Times*, were pointing out the connection between Western food and Western disease, back in the 1970s. And in the 1980s the London Food Commission, with Tim Lang and his colleagues, have made a great difference for the better.' In Cannon's opinion, the great change came with BBC TV's *Food and Health Campaign*, a monumental sequence of series of programmes, over fifty in all, broadcast on BBC1 and BBC2 in 1985 and 1986. He and Caroline Walker advised the BBC and helped to devise four of the *Campaign* series. Simultaneously, he and Caroline advised and helped devise two *World in Action* programmes for Granada Television, and a two-part series for Thames Television. What with this, and Derek Cooper's Radio 4 *Food Programme*, and BBC2's *Food and Drink Programme*, which started to take an interest in nutrition later in the 1980s, healthy food was finally on the national agenda.

'There were two phases in the 1980s,' says Cannon. 'First, the great food scandals between 1983 and 1986. Second, the food safety horror stories, the great bug scandals between 1988 and 1990. National newspapers and networked television programmes were falling over themselves, with scores, hundreds, of features and programmes, all of which could have been called "What Are They Doing to Our Food?"' In the 1990s he sees a very different scene. 'The food retailers have got the message. Leading food caterers have got the message. And so have the farmers: for example, Sir Simon

Gourlay, when President of the National Farmers Union, calling for a national Food Health and Safety Executive, independent of Government.

'In the 1980s, Government and the food manufacturers were frantic. Civil servants and public relations people working for the food processors spent fortunes trying to discredit people like Caroline and me, Tim Lang and Derek Cooper, and scientists like Professor Richard Lacey. We were subject to an orchestrated hate campaign. The story they put out was that we were only interested in self-publicity and to enrich ourselves; that we were scaremongers, rabble-rousers, food activists, food Leninists, food terrorists; that we had a hidden agenda, to tear down the fabric of society. The general idea is to marginalise you; to hold you up as an object of hatred, ridicule or contempt. There was no attempt to address the issue, to debate the science of what we were saying.'

'Those days are gone,' says Cannon, and he now considers that it's the Government and the manufacturers of sweet, fat foods, which are 'marginalised'. Change is happening now, because most of the food industry recognises market opportunities in healthy food. 'The more people value food, the more money they are prepared to spend on food. What we in Britain have been suffering from, for forty years and more, is a cheapened food policy. We've been brought up to believe that food is good because it's cheap. In fact, cheapened food is unhealthy and, eventually, unsafe – as we all now know.

'As long as we think cheap food is a virtue, we will continue to play into the hands of the food manufacturers,' says Cannon. 'In Britain the manufacturers who make highly processed products out of hard, saturated fats, commercial sugars, white flour, and cocktails of chemical additives, are very big business indeed. They are not about to change their ways or retool their production lines. British food manufacturers spend hundreds of millions of pounds every year, pumping out propaganda promoting their gut-busting, artery-clogging, tooth-rotting products.'

He believes the time has come for a dramatic initiative. 'Successive governments have had a pathological inability to admit there is anything wrong with the British food supply. As everybody knows now, after the great bug scandals of 1988 and 1990, ministers and civil servants constantly made outrageous use of the Official Secrets Act, in attempts to mislead the public and defend their indefensible policies. And, finally, almost all scientists can't or won't speak out and confirm that British food was a massive public health problem, because to do so would risk their careers.

'That's where I come in. There is still a lot to campaign for, and I shall continue to fight for public health. The difference between 1983 and now is that the healthy food message is an idea whose time has now come.'

CANNON'S CANONS OF DIET

Geoffrey Cannon turned fifty in 1990 and his lean physique reflects a philosophy of health and fitness. He jogs regularly, and still tackles the occasional twenty-six-mile marathon. The London marathon may be sponsored by a famous sweets company, but sugar and sweets are not on his agenda in his training diet. 'In my teens, I had the feeling that sugar was toxic, and I didn't take drinks with sugar. I didn't kick the confectionery habit till much later on.'

When he knew more about health and diet in the 1980s, he decided to cut out salt (which is associated with high blood pressure). 'After a three-month break without it, which was hard, I went into my favourite local Greek restaurant, ordered some soup and found it tasted like saline solution. The manager gave me some implausible culinary explanation, and then admitted it was restaurant practice to make food taste as salty as possible, because they made most of their profits from sales of wine. So that's why pubs put saucers of free salted peanuts, salted crisps and salted everything on the counter!'

As a convert to fibre and its protective role against heart disease and cancer, he eats a lot of cereal, grain, vegetables and fruit. Breakfast is usually muesli, to the recipe of its inventor, Dr Max Bircher-Benner; lots of fresh fruit, such as bananas, apples and mango, cut up in a big bowl, and a little wholegrain cereal, a few nuts and seeds, and some biodynamic live yogurt. 'The muesli you buy in the shops, all grain and dried fruit with nuts, is OK provided it has no added sugar: but the main item should be fresh fruit.'

As an occasional treat he eats croissants – plain, certainly not with butter or jam. He buys wholegrain bread, breads with seeds and nuts (he's lucky to live close to one of London's best bakers, Pierre

Pechon in Bayswater), and good baguettes. 'I'm not against white bread if it's good quality.'

Cutting down on fat was not difficult – the animal fats which are saturated, and therefore lead to heart disease. He uses oil freely, especially on big salads with garlic and lemon juice dressings.' The test of a unhealthy meal is washing-up next day – washing-up dishes covered with the congealed grease of saturated fat is very unpleasant. A test of a good healthy meal is: 'Does it taste good cold?' Ratatouille is a perfect example. Made with extra virgin olive oil, it tastes almost better the next day.

'If you want to eat meat, eat the flesh of an animal which was physically fit in its life. By which I don't mean ask the butcher if the cow ran the 100 yards in ten seconds, but free-ranging animals, living natural lives, like deer (if you're rich) or rabbit (if you're poor).'

He regards fish as important to the diet, and recommends eating it at least twice a week. The oil in fatty fish, like mackerel, herrings and sardines is good for the brain and nervous system. 'The oil in fish is liquid, because, as Caroline Walker used to say, a mackerel wouldn't get very far, swimming with a tail full of lard.

'I always eat fresh food, not processed. My motto is: 'Good food goes bad.' By that I mean it hasn't had the life processed out of it. But be sure to eat it before it goes bad! I avoid white food and coloured food. White food is sugar, salt and white fat (like the fat on meat). By coloured, I mean artificially coloured, and probably artificially flavoured, chemicalised food. I stick to food which is the colour nature intended.'

8

SUGAR

The people most vulnerable to over-dosing on sugar are mostly those least able to do anything about it – young children, the old, invalids.

Not many people are still ignorant of the dangers of eating too much sugar, although the sugar manufacturers have fought a splendid defensive battle to guard their lucrative market. As Mandy-Rice Davies once said so precisely: 'They would, wouldn't they.'

Those who remember the days when the tobacco companies insisted that the link between cigarettes and cancer hadn't been proved will recognise a similarity in the arguments used today: it isn't proved that sugar causes tooth decay, it isn't proved there are links with diabetes, heart disease, gallstones.

When one of the sugar industry's supporting scientists made the claim that sugar was not the unique cause of obesity, the nutritionist, Dr John Garrow, pointed out that 'we can all think of teetotallers who have road accidents, non-smokers who have lung cancer, and trees that fall over on a calm day when a lorry runs into them. Nevertheless I think that we could all agree that alcohol, smoking and high winds could reasonably be classified as contributing to road accidents, lung cancer and fallen trees respectively .... I think it is fair to say, on the evidence, that the consumption of sugars contributes to obesity.' And obesity contributes to heart disease, and so on.

Sugar is the sweetest thing in our lives. It is seductive and beckoning, comforting and reassuring, a reward promised to us from our first rays of consciousness. The milk in a mother's breast contains a form of sugar, lactose.

Of the £500 million spent every year to advertise food products on television and in the press, a large part is devoted to glorifying sweetness. Every emotional string is pulled. Young pubescent girls swim in slow motion with an inviting bar teasing their parted lips; suitors do daring deeds to bring to the lovely maiden in the castle a box of chocolates. Sweet carbonated drinks emphasise wholeness, freshness, healthy activity, belonging, friendship. A chocolate bar helps you rest, work and play, and the same company sponsors marathons. You need energy to run twenty-six miles. Chocolate bars are packed with energy. Ice creams are advertised to imply elegance, sophistication, style, keeping ahead of the Joneses. Sweetness fills every longing.

The long aisles in supermarkets, banked on both sides as far as the eye can see with colourful packages as dynamic as fireworks, reflect the excitement in the world of sweets. It can't do any harm, the odd packet of chocolates. Would you deny a child sweets?

Sugar is one of the most delightful discoveries man has ever made. It is present in ripe fruit and berries, though you'll have to eat six pounds of apples to extract five ounces, which is the amount of sugar the average Briton eats each day. Starches in grain, onions, potatoes and certain foods turn into sugars when they are heated. The sweetness of fried onion is what gives succulence to cooking worldwide, and especially in India where it's the basis of most curries. Sugar, exposed to the action of yeast bacteria, ferments into alcohol, which has much the same effect on us nutritionally as the rest of the sugar family – sucrose, dextrose, glucose, lactose.

Before sugar was discovered, honey was our sweetness, and apart from its impurities and trace minerals it's exactly the same nutritionally as our granulated or caster sugar.

Sugar cane, a fast-growing member of the grass family, which speedily grows to the height of bamboo, was the source of the first sugar. Children around the equator chew the sticks in the street, and drinks made from cane sugar are sold at stalls. It tastes nothing like sugar as we know it – it's like demerara sugar, or even rum. This is the assertive, rather pleasant flavour of the original before it is refined. In its original state its application – to the confectionery industry, the drinks industry, the food manufacturing industry – would have been severely limited. When sugar is described as natural it's a reversal of the meaning of the word: it is, along with salt, an extremely highly processed concentrated unnatural food.

Although salt occurs naturally in foods, man managed to separate
it from sea water (where it is 3 per cent of the volume) and, later,
by washing it out of underground deposits, and served it in great
quantities to make food more savoury and appetising.

Neither salt nor sugar in the form we use them are natural – that
is to say, as they appear in Nature. The work of food technologists
of this century has been to extract more and more essences from
their natural state, and return them to our food supply in another
form – where we can no longer control the intake in the natural way.

Sugar, delicious sugar, was probably developed in India. There
is a record of sugar cane juice being pressed as early as 500 BC. It
was known in Egypt as early as 375 BC and Alexander the Great
would have used it. In China, too, where they have eaten more types
of food than we would dream imaginable, records show they had
been eating it in 100 BC. The Persians developed the techniques of
extracting sugar in the sixth century AD, and invading Arabs then
took it round their North African empire, and as far as Southern
Spain. It was during the Crusades in the twelfth century that it came
to the knowledge of the English. Not only did the Crusaders bring
home sugar, but they mixed it with mint, another Middle Eastern
speciality, and vinegar, and hey presto – we had invented mint sauce.

Venice, the centre of the spice trade, became the European centre
for sugar, and by the fourteenth century regular supplies were
arriving along with other spices of the day – pepper, ginger, liquorice,
cumin. Sugar was used largely in cooking and making sweet
puddings. Much of it came as marzipan, mixed with almond paste
and egg. Apothecaries coated their powders with sugar – 'sweetening
the pill'.

The Portuguese introduced sugar cane to Madeira, and by 1456
shipments of sugar were on the way to Britain in larger quantities.
It prompted Christopher Columbus, who discovered America in
1492, to give a colonial impetus to the sugar trade which was to make
it universal. On his second voyage, he carried sugar cane plants to
Dominica and Haiti (then Hispaniola) and the example of the
Spanish (in the Caribbean) and the Portuguese (in Brazil) was soon
followed by the French, Dutch and English, who brought slaves
from Africa to work sugar plantations, thus forming the basis of a
slave trade which later extended to cotton picking in America's deep
south.

Sugar was initially extremely expensive. Edward I had a £6,000-a-year bill for sugar. Queen Elizabeth I was exceptionally fond of it, but as toothbrushes were not, unfortunately, invented until the twentieth century, her teeth were noticeably rotten and black. In her reign, consumption of sugar was something like four pounds a head a year. Due to trade with the West Indies, it rose to twelve pounds a head in the seventeenth century, and became permanently twinned with coffee and tea, the fashionable new drinks. Consumption is now one hundred pounds a head in industrialised countries like the USA and UK.

In France they invented lemonade. Limonadiers mixed lemon juice, sugar and water and patrolled public places with the drink slung in metal containers from their backs. Eventually they formed themselves into a compagnie des limonadiers, setting up shops to compete with coffee houses and tea shops. Thus was established the pattern for sweetened drinks which would eventually be carbonated and flavoured to produce modern cola and other sweet drinks.

The history of sugar is in fact a history of slavery, the unacceptable face of our benign empire. For 400 years West Africans were seized and transported in chains to work the cane fields, hacking and stacking the twenty-foot high, tough stalks, thicker than broom handles. Of twenty million slaves, seized in this way who survived the journey to America, it is estimated two-thirds worked the cane sugar fields. As years passed the provision of slaves became a matter of pride for corrupted African tribal chiefs, and indeed a matter of trade. Slaves were consigned to life sentences, and there was no breeding. It was cheaper to buy than to breed, they argued.

Great Britain abolished slavery in 1807 and it would be pleasant to think that this was a triumph for humane instincts and high moral fervour; but Dr Magnus Pyke punctures this view and believes abolition was only achieved because mechanical technology for sugar processing had reached the stage where heavy labour resources were no longer necessary.

The end of slavery coincided exactly with the biggest increase in the world production of refined sugar. But by this time a Prussian chemist, Andreas Marggraf, had discovered that sugar crystals could be isolated in white beet – and it was to this Europeans turned when slavery was abolished.

In Britain the sugar trade had created unimaginable wealth, financing the growth of the great shipping ports, Liverpool and

Bristol, largely providing the money which would create the Industrial Revolution. And sugar would become so cheap it would be a major source of carbohydrate for working people for the next centuries – sugar in tea, sugar in jams, and one day, sugar in everything.

Originally sugar was made into sugarloafs, the shape which gives its name to Sugarloaf Mountain, towering above Rio de Janeiro. The sugar cane stalks were chopped and crushed in a mill, and the juice was cleared of impurities with lime, egg white or animal blood, then cooked in pans till most of the water was boiled off. The solids were poured into conical clay containers several feet long to drain, 'claying' – and covered with more wet clay which would drain through, removing much of its sticky, brown colour due to what we call molasses, the powerful flavour we know in treacle. Indeed, this is also the flavour of old-fashioned rum, which was rationed out to all Naval personnel daily.

Modern sugar is produced by centrifugal spinning. Mills which can exert a pressure of 200 to 500 tons crush the cane which has been cut into chips. This produces raw juice. Lime is added to neutralise organic acids, and the heat is raised to boiling point. A sediment falls, and the resulting liquid is concentrated to a syrup in an evaporator, and eventually cooled into crystals, which are cleaned up in the centrifuges and then mixed with porous charcoal made from animal bones.

But a large part of British sugar today is beet sugar. Rising like a castle in the once proud mediaeval abbey town of Bury St Edmunds in Suffolk are five towering silos which stand out for miles around, and a complex of machinery which resemble an oil refining plant. Farmers throughout Norfolk and Suffolk have a ready price for growing beet, and plant geneticists have developed beet of enormous size and great yield, and a sugar content of 18 per cent which is 4 per cent more than sugar cane. The process is similar, with the beet chopped small and the juice subjected to a series of boilings; and the same centrifugal procedures. The result is even, consistent, clean, and concentrated. The sugar in our packets is 99.8 per cent pure sucrose.

It's pure. It's white. And Dr John Yudkin would say it's deadly. His book, *Pure, White and Deadly*, dropped like a bombshell on a comparatively ignorant public in 1972.

Many nutritionists had been voicing reservations about sugar in the context of other dietary recommendations. For a long time the nutritional manuals had summed it up along these lines: 'It is a cheap and easily digested form of energy, and therefore a useful food. But it also lacks every nutrient except carbohydrate and so in its attractiveness there is a danger that it can displace more nutritious foods from the diet.' Professor Yudkin pointed out there was more to it than this.

Professor Yudkin is a biochemist who became Professor of Physiology at Queen Elizabeth College, London, in 1945, and then moved to the new Professorship of Nutrition. In this capacity he introduced the first degree course in nutrition in Europe.

'The interesting thing is that I got on extremely well with the food industry, except for the sugar industry directly – and even they used to ask my opinion. I take an opposite view from my colleagues who say you mustn't have anything to do with the food industry because of the rogues they are. I take the view that you cannot on the one hand complain that they don't take any notice of nutritional values because they don't ask anybody; and on the other hand get huffy when they do ask a nutritionist and the nutritionist then advises them.

'I'm very happy to be an adviser to Nestlé for example. I was invited to their new premises in Croydon. They took me to lunch in their dining room which was on the twelfth floor and one of the directors, a good friend of mine, took me to the window and said jokingly: "It wouldn't be very difficult to push you out ..."'

His book highlighted the intake of sugar in the diet, two pounds a week on average, and then drew conclusions about the effect of this excess.

'Supposing you went to your doctor in the 1690s and said you were eating four ounces of sugar a week he would tell you that you were eating too much. Yet we were eating a twenty-fifth of the amount of sugar we eat now. We eat on *average* two pounds a week, including the people who eat four to five pounds a week. It's almost unbelievable but it's true.'

So there are some children taking aboard as much as 1,000 calories a day from sugar, possibly half their daily calorie requirements, to the exclusion of other, more nutritional foods. It isn't only the eating of sweets, but sugar in soft drinks, in ice-creams, desserts, jams, biscuits, cakes, in canned foods, especially baked beans, in bottles of sauce, in pickles, where sugar has a preservative effect as well as adding desirability of flavour.

Professor Yudkin produced evidence on dental rot, or caries as they call the holes which the sugar acid etches in the tooth's enamel coating, and he raised the spectre of other long-term illnesses, not only arising from putting on weight, and the pressure that it puts on the heart, but sugar as a direct contributor to heart and other diseases.

It wasn't so much that Professor Yudkin was unravelling the laboratory work of thousands of scientific experiments; it was his direct and provocative challenge to the sugar industry which in the end had the effect of isolating him academically – but not before he'd handed on the torch to others.

For a long time he nursed a feeling of anger that the sugar industry should have been able to have him discredited and cold-shouldered at conferences. 'I'm not paranoic, but there are so many instances. I have been asked why I'm not on the British Nutrition Foundation Science committees. Under two different chairmen the BNF failed to invite me to join, and I was later to find out that otherwise sponsorship might have been withdrawn.'

He was in for a rubbishing, he realised, but his opponents went too far when they wrote about his book, seven years after publication, in the quarterly *Bulletin* of the World Sugar Research Organisation (WSRO), a newsletter which disseminates 'Good News' about sugar, and takes to task sugar's critics.

Under the headline *For Your Dustbin*, a reviewer dismissed his book, *Pure, White and Deadly*, in a single sentence. 'Readers of science fiction will no doubt be distressed to learn that according to the publishers the above work is out of print and no longer obtainable.'

Most book critics would have got away with that, one might have thought, on the grounds that it was tongue-in-cheek. But the professor saw red and sued them: four years later the *Bulletin* settled and published an apology. It was a matter of honour, he had cleared his name.

Besides his carefully-argued theme, Professor Yudkin took to task the communicators who were putting over the picture of good, healthy, nourishing, vitalising sugar, and he singled out the use of the word 'energy'. 'Sugar gives you "energy".'

Professor Yudkin quoted from a pamphlet put out by the sugar industry: 'Sugar works for you with each bite you eat, for your body is an energy factory with sugar as its fuel.'

'All food contains energy,' says Professor Yudkin. 'But the physiologist and the nutritionist who talk about sugar and energy mean something different. When you say that Johnny is full of energy you picture him rushing around, leaping up and down the stairs, climbing a tree or tearing along on his bicycle. So when you hear that sugar gives you energy you imagine that this is what you need to leap up and tear around like Johnny.'

In the language of chemistry and nutrition, energy means that sugar, like every other food, after it has been digested and absorbed, can be utilised to release the 'energy' you need for all the functions of the body – breathing, making the heart beat, the function of digestion, the involuntary metabolic changes in a living body, as well as the resources to walk and run. Fuel it is, but putting some more in the tank doesn't improve the performance of your car or make you more 'energetic'.

What fuel the body doesn't use for energy, it stores. As fat.

'I sometimes wonder whether the insistence that sugar contains energy arises from the fact that it contains nothing else,' says Professor Yudkin. 'All other foods contain energy together with at least some nutrients in the way of protein or minerals or vitamins or a mixture of these. Sugar contains energy, and that is all.'

'I have a very sweet tooth and I spent all my pocket money as a child on eating sweets. I went to the cinema once a week and bought half a pound of sweets to take in with me. Even in my early marriage, fifty years or so ago, I expected my wife to have some cooked dessert or at least some buns or cake for tea.

'My views changed more and more as we did research after the War, when I was beginning to think about instituting a nutrition degree. I began to say to myself that sugar is not really the sort of food that comes into our diet without the tremendous intervention of human activity, cultivation of the sugar cane and beet and its extractions. I got more and more intrigued with the distance of sugar and the sugar products from what might be considered the proper diet of man. So, my actions were never prompted by any feelings that I didn't like sugar and therefore shouldn't eat it. They were a conscious move away from the consumption of large quantities of sugar.

'I still chew the odd sweet. When my wife makes stewed fruit, say

once or twice a week when one of my sons may come and have
supper with us, it is sweetened with an artificial sweetener, one of
the nice-tasting ones. But otherwise we do without. So our meals
end with fresh fruit at least once, perhaps twice a day.'

Sugar became a national issue when the NACNE report was published in 1983 (National Advisory Committee on Nutrition Education under the chairmanship of Dr Philip James). The report
suggested an all-round change in diet. The battle moved to new
grounds.

Campaigning figures such as Caroline Walker took up the fight.
Miss Walker was committee secretary to Dr James on the NACNE
report. He was an academic; she was a great communicator. Above
all, she felt the social importance of his findings. The less well
off, the less well informed, the disadvantaged, would continue in
ignorance to depend on diets which could ultimately destroy their
health.

After analysing a Department of Health statistical report on teen-
agers' eating habits, she wrote:

'Children now eat more cakes and biscuits than fruit or vegetables
(excluding potatoes), more chips and crisps than plain potatoes,
more sweets than wholemeal and brown bread, more sugar than fish.

'Taking into account all the sugar in soft drinks, cakes and biscuits,
ice-cream flavoured yogurts, and all the other processed foods these
children eat, their total consumption of sugars must come to at least
one-fifth of their energy (calorie) intake.

'This is a nutritional disaster, because processed sugars supply no
nourishment, only calories. Saturated fats too, from cakes, biscuits,
chocolates, fatty meats and margarine, and from high-fat dairy foods,
are present in large quantities in this food.

'The total amount of whole fresh foods, lean meats, fresh fish,
vegetables, brown and wholemeal bread, needs to be increased a
good deal to bring this teenage diet in line with the medical recommendations of the Royal College of Physicians, the Department
of Health, and the World Health Organisation.'

Her target was the Department of Health and what she saw as its
responsibility to children. How much were they prepared to spend
on putting across a healthy message in the face of the vast sums
spent by the processed food industry on advertising? And she made
the pointed observation: 'As a general rule, the more heavily a food

is advertised, the worse it is likely to be for your health.'

Caroline Walker died in 1988, but her husband, journalist Geoffrey Cannon, (see Chapter 7) continued to campaign. In his book, *The Politics of Food*, he investigates the politics of the sugar lobbyists. It may not have been intended as such, but it makes a merry tale, and you have to smile at the desperate defence of the sugar industry by, it turns out, a huge squadron of Conservative MPs.

For the journalist, no tale is better than Saatchi and Saatchi's role in sugar, which Geoffrey Cannon uncovered.

The Health Education Council retained Saatchi and Saatchi, the globally great advertising agency, to put over their health story. Saatchi and Saatchi had done a brilliant job warning men of their role in accidental pregnancy, showing memorable pictures of 'pregnant men'.

The Health Education Council invited them to put over the main findings of the NACNE report. They produced a superb set of four full-page advertisements on eating less salt. The headline was: *What shook 100 million Americans into eating less salt.* On fats: *Why thin people should be as worried about fatty foods as fat people.* On fibre: *If you're overweight try eating bread and potatoes.* On sugar: *How many lumps does your body really need?* Strong stuff, and Saatchi and Saatchi signed off with the message: 'We believe you have a right to receive totally unbiased advice about your diet. The only thing we are interested in selling you is better health.' That's integrity for you, rare enough, you might think, in the advertising industry. Three of the advertisements were approved by the Department of Health and subsequently appeared in the press, and indeed, in 1984, won a silver design award for an outstanding public service campaign.

The one that didn't appear was the sugar advertisement. The DHSS turned it down.

Saatchi and Saatchi's expertise didn't go unnoticed. British Sugar retained the company to launch their £2 million sales push in 1984, the biggest ever campaign by a sugar company. That's advertising. One day you push one point of view, the next day the opposite.

Cannon puts on record a series of running battles which make fascinating reading, including the importation of American experts to tell the sugar story. Take the visit in 1986 of Dr Elizabeth Whelan, who had 'made it her life's work to debunk food faddists', and who said there was no proof that sugar adversely affected behaviour, caused cravings or obesity, or was associated with diabetes or heart disease. She even made headlines in the *Guardian* with 'Food faddists are bad for your health'.

The most recent report from COMA (Committee on Medical Aspects of Food Policy) was published by the Department of Health in December 1989, and this is Gospel: Limit sugar consumption for the good of your health.

The biggest risk is to children, adolescents and the elderly. Don't put sugar in bottle feeds for babies and young children, and don't give them sugared drinks. At home, reduce the amount of sugary snacks, such as biscuits and muesli bars, between meals.

The COMA report doesn't come out and say, 'Cut your sugar intake by half', but the British Medical Association and the Royal College of Physicians and the World Health Organisation all do.

It seems unlikely that Britain's consumption of sugar will drop by any serious degree. Sugary foods and drinks are desirable, and not manifestly as deadly as tobacco is.

The sugar industry produces bags of statistics and retains nutritionists to defend the industry. When they go on the attack, as they do in this newspaper advertisement, part of a £12 million television and press campaign, they are formidable indeed. On television commercials there was the image of the humming bird supping nectar. With the permission of the British Sugar Bureau, I reprint it in full.

SUGAR:
The more you know about it, the sweeter it tastes.

The Lucifer Humming Bird is one of Nature's athletic wonders. If you're lucky enough to glimpse one in its native South America it will be just a flash of iridescent plumage, nothing more.

On wings beating up to eighty times a second, it can fly upside down and even backwards; callisthenics beside which Olympic champions look puny.

Wherever does this bird get such fantastic energy? From eating the nearest thing to the sun's rays themselves. Sugar.

Sugars are the simplest of all foods. Pure and easily digestible, they are a fundamental natural energy source. So basic, in fact, that they aren't just confined to sweet foods. Have you ever wondered why crunching a raw carrot is so delicious? Or why a succulent grass stem is so pleasant to nibble on a summer's walk? It's because all plants contain sugars. They make them from sunshine, air and water.

Why don't all plants taste sweet? Simply because these sugars are also built into more complex foods. Starches like potatoes, rice and corn. And fibre: the stalks, leaves, husks and other parts of the plant's structure.

Scientists call all these sugar-foods carbohydrates, because of the carbon, hydrogen and oxygen they contain. When animals eat carbohydrates, they rapidly break them down to simple sugars again. (Try thoroughly chewing a piece of ordinary bread. After a while, you'll find it begins to taste sweet.)

Obviously some foods contain more simple sugars than others. Nectar, honey, milk and many fruits and berries are all rich in sugars. A glass of fresh orange juice contains about as much sugar as a glass of cola (that's another story).

But two plants contain more sugars than all of these. Sugar cane, a juicy, thick-stemmed tropical grass. And sugar beet, a white root vegetable which grows in cool, temperate climates like our own. These are the plants from which household sugar is traditionally extracted. It's a simple process. The juice of the pulped plants is mixed with water, filtered, cleaned and boiled down to a thick syrup, from which pure white sugar can be crystallised. Left behind is a dark treacly substance called molasses, which gives brown sugars their names.

There's hardly any nutritional difference between brown and white sugars. And neither contain any colouring, flavouring or preservatives.

When the merchant caravans from the Orient brought these exotic crystals to Europe in the eleventh century they became a rare delicacy. A few ounces cost a year's pay, so they had to be stored in lockable caddies. They were used to flavour meat and fish and mask the dreadful tastes commonplace before refrigeration.

Only when Columbus took sugar cane to the fertile soils of the New World did prices fall and sugar become widely available. Since then its amazing properties have gradually come to light.

Sugar is a natural preservative. It enhances flavour and provides bulk and texture. Sugar feeds the yeast which makes bread rise and ferments to make alcoholic drinks. It can set like plaster and also change into candy, creme, toffee, caramel, syrup, fondant or floss. It can brown, glaze and fix flavour. It prevents foods from going stale (just leave a lump in the biscuit tin).

But that's not all. Sugar can be turned into an explosive. Dissolved in water, an ounce or two will lower the freezing point by several degrees. A teaspoonful after a vindaloo will extinguish the furnace in your mouth. You know the bottles and plate glass windows that stuntman use for their tricks? Guess what they're made of.

Sugar hardens asphalt. And slows the setting of ready-mixed concrete. In vase-water, a spoonful gives cut flowers a longer lease of life. A pinch of sugar on the tongue is a traditional remedy for hiccups. Lifeboats and aircraft carry sugar in their survival kits. Astronauts, athletes and mountaineers use sugar tablets as emergency energy supplies.

'Eat thou honey, because it is good,' says the Book of Proverbs. 'Honesty coupled to beauty is to have honey a sauce to sugar,' wrote Shakespeare in *As You Like It*. Sugar has been praised by Chaucer and immortalised in the nursery rhyme. (What are little girls made of?)

For over 2,000 years sugar and sweetness have been bywords for goodness and love. Until recently. Because today it's a very different story. Sugar now stands accused of causing fillings, flab and worse. Is it to blame?

Sugar is undoubtedly a factor in tooth decay. But it isn't sugar which damages your teeth. It's acid, released by bacteria in the mouth. These bacteria live on sugars and starches left on the teeth after eating. So it follows, keep your teeth clean and the bacteria will starve. Brush your teeth with a recognised fluoride toothpaste at least twice a day. Avoid eating too frequently between meals. And visit your dentist regularly. Then sugar shouldn't harm your teeth. What about your waistline?

So many people now believe sugar is fattening, it's become widely accepted as the truth. 'Sugar tastes so good,' runs a perverse logic, 'that it must be bad for you.' Yet how many calories are there in a four gram sugar lump? The same as protein and half as many as in fat. (You probably add more calories to your coffee or tea with milk than with sugar.)

Every day an average person needs 1,500 calories. Just to breathe, keep warm and make your heart beat. Half these calories, nutritionists say, should come from carbohydrates – sugars and starches. So keep things in proportion. Even a weight-watcher can enjoy sugar in moderation.

As to other charges, scientific studies the world over confirm that sugar is not a direct cause of disease. Indeed, judiciously sprinkled, sugar can lead you into much healthier eating habits. Think how it transforms a sharp grapefruit or even breakfast bran.

Don't miss out on a treat from Nature on account of empty rumour. As one person said, avoiding sugar won't make you live any longer. It'll just seem that way.

No Q.C. in the land could have pleaded the case of sugar more persuasively. The advertising agency surely deserved its fee. How the food faddists are put in their place. In another series of advertisements, in magazines, sugar pleaded its case against artificial sweeteners, emphasising the natural source of sugar, the beet, Beta

Vulgaris, and the cane, Saccharum officinarum. They ask: 'The question is, do you prefer your sweetener made from sodium saccharide, aspartic acid, aceto-acetic acid, and phenylalanine? Or sunshine, air and water?'

Sweet talking.

A Government not so closely tied to the food industry might possibly insist that clearer warnings of the effects of excess are spelt out, especially to schoolchildren. Those who improve their diets will be the better educated and better informed, and probably a social divide will differentiate sugar refusers from sugar users. It will be smart to suck your sweetness out of fruit and sweet vegetables such as carrots. It won't be fashionable to use granulated sugar at all.

But it's doubtful if the sugar industry will be too worried. World markets are opening up which make you gasp at the scale. Consider the amount of sugar the soft drinks industry are going to need once Russia falls (as it is beginning to) to Coca-Colonisations: Every can of cola contains the equivalent of eight level teaspoons of sugar. India – with 700 million people. China – with over 1,200 million. The world beckons.

Sweet pickings.

ARTIFICIAL SWEETENERS

Public concern about dieting has led to a boom in diet drinks. Cyclamate led the field in the 1960s, but now it is banned and only four artificial sweeteners are allowed in Britain: saccharin, aspartame (NutraSweet and Canderell), thaumatin (Talin) and acesulphame K.

SACCHARIN The earliest artificial sweetener was saccharin, a derivative of coal tar, discovered as long ago as 1879, by a German student called Constantin Fahlberg at John Hopkins University in the USA. It was first marketed in 1900 for the use of diabetics, but didn't come into its own until the 1914–18 war when sugar was scarce.

It is 300 times sweeter than sugar, but it has a bitter aftertaste. It is most successfully used in combination with other artificial sweeteners or sugar itself, but is widely used in diet drinks.

Some doubts about its safety in large quantities persist, due to experiments which produced tumours in the bladders of mice. The World Health Organisation and the European Community lay down a recommended maximum dose of 2.5 milligrammes per day, but a review of British consumers revealed that the dose is often exceeded, and many children under five had high intakes for their weight, more than double the recommended maximum. Dr Erik Millstone of Sussex University puts this down to their high consumption of soft drinks.

In the United States products containing saccharin must carry a warning. For example, a chewing gum produced expressly to avoid tooth decay will also say: 'This product contains saccharin which has been determined to cause cancer in laboratory animals.'

CYCLAMATE A sweetener discovered by accident in Illinois in 1937 by a student chemist called Michael Sveda, while making a nitrogen-substituted sulphamic acid. Unlike saccharin it has no other taste than sweetness, and by the 1960s had been adopted as a popular artificial sweetener in place of sugar in diet products.

When research into substances which combined cyclamates and saccharin suggested it induced bladder cancer in laboratory animals it was withdrawn. But scientists argue that cyclamates were not the guilty party, and they are not banned in Europe. In 1992 EC law will permit their use throughout the community, so they can return to Britain.

ASPARTAME The trade name in the UK is NutraSweet and Canderell. It was another accidental laboratory discovery, this one by an American chemist named James Schlatter. It is a combination of two amino acids, aspartic acid and phenylalanine, and produces a sweetness 160 times stronger than sugar. It is now the leading sweetener in diet drinks.

Phenylalanine cannot be digested by people with a genetic deficiency known as PKU (phenylketonuria), which is said to affect one person in 15,000. In America and France products must be labelled 'contains phenylalanine' so that parents of PKU children can avoid it. There is a voluntary code in this country, but it is not usually observed. Dr Erik Millstone records that many people in America are complaining that the ill-effects of phenylalanine may be underestimated, and some 10,000 people who have written in complaining that the sweetener has caused headaches, dizziness, blurred vision and seizures have not been satisfactorily answered.

THAUMATIN The trade name is Talin, and it has been developed in Japan. It is an extract made from a jelly which surrounds the seeds of an African fruit called katemfe, first discovered in 1855 by a British surgeon, W.F. Danielli. It is 3,000 times sweeter than sugar. It is also a flavour enhancer which has been used in combination with monosodium glutamate in Japan. Its use has been legalised in Britain since 1983.

ACESULPHAME K Similar to cyclamate, acesulphame potassium is derived from sulphamic acid. It is 130 times sweeter than sugar. Developed by the German company Hoechst, and legal in Britain since 1983.

Research continues into many other artificial sweeteners. Although too expensive to market, the most interesting is a 'left-handed' sugar, developed in the United States as Lev-O-Cal. It is a chemical mirror of sugar. It has the same properties as sugar but, because the human body's enzymes do not recognise it as such, they do not attempt to digest it, so it passes through the body without releasing any calories. It doesn't even attract bacteria which cause decay on the teeth.

9

ALCOHOL

A wondrous mixture of cultures gives Britain an exotic range of alcoholic drinks: the Celts mastered distilling to give us Irish and Scotch whisky; in the West Country they turned their hands to converting apples to cider; traditional British ale made from barley lent itself to the continental practice of hopping to give us modern bitter and stout; the Romans planted vines, and the English wine industry has been revived in the last thirty years. As importers of wine, we have no equals.

The range of wines sold in Britain runs to many hundreds of thousands of labels, not only from France, but from Italy (the world's largest producer of wine); from Spain, cheaply; from East Europe, very cheaply; Bulgaria, Yugoslavia, Hungary. Unlike major wine-producing countries, we import from California, Australia, New Zealand, South Africa, from Chile, Argentina, the Lebanon, North Africa. In wine we have the most cosmopolitan and catholic tastes of any people in the world. Even the French respect our claret experts for judgements on their vintages. The British supermarket wine buyers have set new standards for wines, and in the last twenty years they have worked a high street revolution.

Readers of comic works like *The Diary of a Nobody* by the Grossmiths will recall the social snobbery attached to the purchase of wine from a grocer's. Now Sainsbury, the grocers, sell more wine than any wine merchant. And some of the best wine comes from a store which used to be famous for the strength of its knicker elastic, Marks & Spencer.

And in our time we have seen a social change: wine writing has been wrenched from the hands of club bores musing over a case of claret from a St James's address or a Bristol shipper, and passed onto an energetic band of young professionals, a generation with the application to assess weekly the staggering output of several dozen supermarkets and high street wine companies.

They have to reflect society's changing attitudes to drink, the surprising decline of the national drink, beer, and its replacement by so-called lager (a pale carbon copy of the long-stored, slowly fermented drink of the same name brewed in Germany for centuries).

Beer was hurried into unpopularity when it was hi-jacked by the five largest brewing companies in the 1960s. They used their monopolistic control of tied houses (pubs owned by them, run by hired managers) to market a beer which wouldn't go stale – what came to be known as keg beer. It was filtered, pasteurised, and carbonated to do away with the living yeast that made traditional draught beer so difficult to keep and so unpredictable in character and flavour. Filtering made it bright and clear, pasteurisation killed the bacteria and stopped fermentation, and carbon dioxide conditioned it, the sparkle giving an impression of freshness. Unfortunately, the metallic taste of carbonic acid makes the taste of this bland product even more unacceptable, and the only claim that can be made for it is that if your taste buds are completely out of action due to tobacco tar or curry vindaloo, it makes you drunk.

Richard Boston, in a weekly column in the *Guardian* in the 1970s, criticised this terrible beer and within weeks he had released a snowball of discontent which rapidly gathered momentum. It was the basis of the Campaign for Real Ale (CAMRA) which started a swing back to traditional cask-conditioned ales, and every beer buff can rattle off their ABC of good beer: A is for Adnams, B is for Brakspear's and Boddington's and Bateman's and so on.

But sadly, perhaps like poetry and jazz, real ale is becoming a cult drink for a growing minority, represented by its own writers such as Michael Jackson who discovers unusual beers like Benny Green digs out dusty, long-forgotten records. Jackson, one of the leading figures in CAMRA, became *The Beer Hunter* of television, bringing back the message from Europe that they'd been there a long time before, and the message from America that they haven't arrived yet. Among 350 brews he sampled was a beer 'hopped' with chillies, another seasoned with basil, another with ginseng. He seems to be signalling the end of beer as we have known it.

And of course, commercial lager made by all the bigger companies may herald the end of beer. But so it was that hopped beer, introduced by the Flemish in the sixteenth century, was the end of ale as the Elizabethans knew it. And ale introduced from the Middle East was probably the end of mead, as early North European tribes knew it.

The drinking of lager and wine divides the classes. The well-to-do and upwardly mobile drink wine, and the downwardly mobile, indeed not even mobile at all, but absolutely legless, drink lager, that triumph of modern commercial and marketing skills. Lagers are to traditional beers what sugar is to fresh sweet fruit. They provide the essential alcohol in the least offensive way, and in their blandness are designed to appeal to the most immature palate. What these innocent drinks do contain, however, is alcohol a-plenty. And in communities of young people where getting drunk is an act of bravado, a sign of machismo, they surely contribute to many of the disturbances which erupt every weekend in every major town in Britain. It prompts the thought that, if alcohol is to be drunk to excess, why can't it be in the form which confers a spirit of warmth, friendship and companionship, as indeed many drinks do?

Of all the chemical crutches we use in our society, legally and illegally – stimulants (caffeine in coffee, in tea, in cola drinks), tranquillisers and pain-killers (aspirin, paracetamol), mind-numbers (heroin, cocaine), consciousness-alterers (cannabis) and mind-dislocating hallucinogens (LSD) – the one which has been with us longest is alcohol.

Alcohol is the naturally occurring by-product of the activity of wild yeasts which are present in the air in billions, and which also coat grain and fruit (the bloom on peaches and plums is the yeast). Windfalls in the orchard left in the long grass, apples, plums, pears, ferment and may give you a little burst of alcohol when you squeeze them, which is very pleasant, if other bacteria haven't already joined in the chase and turned the juices to vinegar.

The satirical American writer Kurt Vonnegut once commented to the effect that the booze which we love and respect so much is no more than the excrement of copulating organisms. Yeasts are indeed inactive until they are fed sugars, whereupon they immediately start feasting and reproducing at a tremendous rate, excreting alcohol and breathing out carbon dioxide.

This chemical phenomenon is harnessed in the activity of breadmaking, the yeast culture feeding on the starches in flour. Wheat flour, which contains gluten, traps the gas bubbles, and expands accordingly to give us those desirable, well-risen loaves. The Aerated Bread Company earlier this century produced loaves by a straight injection of the carbon dioxide gas. Soda bread is made by fusing sodium bicarbonate and tartaric acid to release gas.

And the alcohol? It emerges in miserably small quantities. But at the old-fashioned bakers, when doughs were started with a loose batter (equal parts of flour and water, instead of normal breadmaking dough which is two parts flour to one of water), the liquid in the bubbling troughs soon took on an alcoholic character. The small amounts of one day's liquid dough which were held back to start the next day's baking, were known as barm, and the young bakers, who supped the juice and got fairly crazy as a result, became known as barmy.

Mead may be the oldest form of alcohol. It's estimated that man fermented honey solutions some 10,000 years ago. Naturally-occurring alcohol in grapes gave us the idea for wine. The barm from making doughs for bread (the Egyptians were first to do it on a commercial scale) gave us the first ales. But everywhere in the world, at who knows what time in history, people were extracting alcohol from the process of fermentation. Milk contains a sugar, lactose, which allows the tribesmen of the central Asian plains to make a milk alcohol (koumiss and kefir).

The wives of the Quechua Indians of Peru chew maize, and the enzymes in the spittle activate the fermentation process. It produces a mild milky brew, called chicha, like a bowl of milky porridge rinsed and strained, with absolutely no property worthy of mention except that it makes Quechua Indians tipsy (but not those brought up on the West's hard-drinking traditions). The Chinese convert rice to 'wine', although it's closer to an ale in its chemistry. Country people everywhere make 'wine' of carrots, parsnips, elderberries, black-berries, and it can be potent underneath its cloying, sickly sweetness.

Distillation was truly one small step for mankind: the means by which quite horrible alcoholic concoctions are stripped to their essence, leaving the muck behind: the brandy of Cognac and Armag-nac is made from the most inferior grapes in France; potatoes as well as grain are the fermented source material for great North European vodkas and aquavits. Cactus juice is the base of Mexican fire water, tequila. Rough cider converts to Calvados. Wheat, and more specially, malted barley, contribute to Scotch whisky, perhaps the world's most prestigious distillate.

Raw spirit can be extracted easily from beers, ciders or home-made wines by heating in a kettle or still, letting the vapours run through tubes of rubber or metal and cooled under running water. Alcohol is driven off at a lower temperature than water (173°F, 78°C, compared with water's 212°F, 100°C) so the vapour that first passes through the pipe is neat alcohol, which re-forms as liquid when it condenses on cooling.

It is illegal to make 'moonshine' which gets its name from secret stills worked at night on the moors, on heaths and Irish bogs, where the smoke of the fires wouldn't come to the notice of the Excisemen. But beware, poteen and its sisters often contain toxic impurities and may be sold at strengths far in excess of usual levels of spirit. There are numerous cases of death and illness following consumption of home-made spirits.

The chemical obverse of distillation is freezing. Spirit freezes at a lower temperature than water, so a container of cider placed in the freezer will first turn the water in it to ice, leaving the spirit unfrozen, and easily drained off. On American farms, barrels of cider left out in the winter yield the spirit they call Applejack.

These crude and unpleasant spirits can be aged, or else flavoured with essences of fruit, like Russian and Polish flavoured vodka. The sugar cane spirit, rum, is mixed with fresh tropical fruit juices such as Brazilian white rum batidas or Caribbean limes; or they can be subjected to craftsmanship and artistry, put into oak casks, subtly coloured and flavoured, and aged for three, four, five or ten or twelve years to assume a mystical, highly bankable identity like old brandies or the malt whiskies of Western Scotland.

Pure spirit is around 100 degrees alcohol, which is pretty toxic. It is usually diluted with water and sold at around seventy degrees alcohol, which is often described by a confusing and ancient measurement called proof. Proof was a simple way for Customs and Excise inspectors to distinguish low duty, low alcohol wines from high duty higher alcohol wines. A piece of rope dipped in a high alcohol wine can be lit with a match, just as you pour brandy on the Christmas pudding and it burns with a pretty blue flame. Another 'proof' was to wet gunpowder with alcohol and judge its strength by the way it spluttered or exploded into fire. (Retaining this measurement from the eighteenth century is a crazy and irrelevant custom like twentieth-century judges presiding in seventeenth-century wigs, a mumbo-jumbo which the cognoscenti can disentangle, but which mystifies all others.) So, pure spirit, if it was ever sold, would be around 200 degrees proof.

The alcohol content of wines, beers, lagers, ciders, spirits has always been mystifying, but this is one area where, in defence of the young, the innocent and the ignorant, educators have fought for clear labelling.

The wine world has actually changed more in twenty years than in several centuries. The New World, especially California and Australia, launched their vineyards using every modern skill available, the best viticulturists, the best oenologists, the most advanced scientific knowledge, and applied it to what has been traditionally a peasant fruit-farmer's craft.

Their successes were noted in France, which had until then had two classes of wine. The better class is fine burgundies and clarets (in 1855 the French classified four Bordeaux chateaux as premiers crus, Latour, Margeaux, Mouton-Rothschild, Lafite-Rothschild, adding a fifth, Haut-Brion, later, to create an aristocracy of wine). The other class of wine is plonk. To meet rising export demand, France grubbed up poor quality vineyards, replanting better varieties of vine, and pulled ahead of Italy and Spain, who in turn saw their own share of the market falling, with the result that many of the appalling wines of Italy and Spain have now been consigned to the past. With this general improvement, and the watchful and eager buyers from Britain and other countries, cheating and fraud seem to have been largley banished, and tend to take the form of fanciful exaggeration rather than dishonesty.

The most popular red wines on the British market, and like none at all drunk in France, are rounded, sweetish and bland, but these blends are honest and by no means the kind of trickery which has gone on for centuries.

The Mediterranean port of Sète in the South of France was famous for its chemists who would blend the huge, dull yields of L'Hérault, the biggest wine production area of France, mixing its inferior grape juice with tanker-loads of more generous wines shipped in from Spain, Italy and North Africa. It is only twenty-five years since Nicholas Tomalin, the investigative British journalist, made news with the revelation that an Ipswich bottling plant was putting fanciful chateau labels on vin ordinaire. His article, *The*

Art of Cooking Bogus Burgundy, opened a Pandora's Box of similar tales. Like the party of journalists in Portugal who saw a local red wine being put into bottles labelled Product of France and who protested to the manager. 'That's all right,' he said. 'The wine's going to Canada.' People who aren't knowledgeable about wine buy it on a snobbish basis: what they were doing in Ipswich was re-bottling the ordinary wine of France that is sold in plastic bottles, good enough for them but not for drinkers who drink wine for its snob value.

In 1974 there was the first of a number of wine scandals in Bordeaux where they bottled wines from Provence, where yields are higher due to the longer hours of sunshine, and passed it off as Bordeaux. They also doctored wines which had been designated as unfit for consumption, chemically treating them to alter colour, taste and smell. The negociant was unapologetic when convicted, and retorted: 'I am guilty, but so are thousands of others. In thirty years in the trade I have seen fraud practised everywhere among owners, dealers and professional associations. Baptising, as we call it in the trade, is a common practice.' He means that the chemist can work little miracles which would mean avoiding the loss of perhaps an entire vintage – due to spoilage caused by weather, by bacteria, by disease, by going rotten.

The Italians managed to make news when a no-grape wine was exposed in the 1970s. One of the ingredients used by Gianfranco Ferrari in this celebrated case was sludge from the bottom of a banana boat. In court it was explained that he made 1,000 gallons of un-wine every eight hours, despatching it as Barbera, Chianti and Valpolicella (you may even have tasted some in London Italian restaurants in your day.)

The Austrians were caught out adding to their white wines an ingredient which is found in anti-freeze. The good name of Austria was sullied and trade came to a virtual standstill. The news rippled to Japan, where they confused the name, and stopped buying excellent wines from Australia. So clean had the name of Austria been that Hirondelle, the first successful blended commercial wine in Britain chose it as the country of origin for their blend of Iron Curtain wines, Hungarian, Yugoslavian and Bulgarian. They did not see this as misleading. As long as the wines passed through Austria, and stood on Austrian railway sidings for twenty-four hours, Austrian law allowed them to call it Product of Austria. When this was pointed out in the British press, the practice was discontinued.

Chemical trickery is hard to spot. Chapitalisation – adding sugar to raise the alcohol level – is illegal in France (though not in Germany where the grapes don't ripen so fully in the more northern climate). The French Government offered a £20,000 reward to chemists who could discover a foolproof way of detecting it.

The Germans use carbon-dating apparatus to detect frauds. On one occasion they were examining a bottle of port from a consignment which claimed to be of 1963 vintage. Port is made from a high-alcohol wine, but its alcohol level is raised even higher, to about 26 degrees, by the addition of spirit. By law, this spirit must be grape brandy. To their astonishment, the carbon-dating apparatus revealed that the spirit which had been used was much older. They had discovered a scam. It wasn't grape brandy at all, but imported potato spirit from Russia which happened to be older.

No one has improved upon Shakespeare's summary of the effects of alcohol: 'It provokes nose-painting, sleep, and urine. It provokes lechery. It provokes and unprovokes. It provokes the desire, but takes away the performance.'

It takes two to six hours for alcohol to be taken up by the blood stream. Drinks with fizzy content, champagne, sparkling drinks, gin with tonic, whisky with soda, seem to have the quickest results. Alcohol is more quickly absorbed on an empty stomach, and its effects are slowed down when taken with food, especially fatty, oily foods which slow down absorption in the stomach wall, hence the old saw that you should drink a pint of milk before going out on a boozy session. Men metabolise alcohol more slowly than women, and large people more effectively than small people. On one merry occasion when the breath test was brought in, a group of famous drinkers was assembled to wine and dine to the utter limits: the loud stout males lasted the course to the bitter end, the cigars and brandy; the tiny female editor of a wine encyclopaedia was shattered and deeply ashamed to find herself over the limit before she had reached the main course. She didn't realise it was no reflection on her ability to 'carry her drink'.

Alcohol provokes urine, and in its turn dehydration – prompting another wise saw, drink a glass of water before going to bed.

Alcohol is a narcotic and its reputation as a stimulant is wrong. It depresses the central nervous system, which depresses the higher functions of the brain, and so removes inhibitions. Larger quantities affect concentration, interfere with memory and muscle co-ordination (you start to see double, then you fall over). Flushing is an early sign of alcohol's effect, as the blood vessels dilate, and an increased supply of blood rushes to the skin.

As the alcohol pours in, the body's metabolism is trying to get it out, which it does by means of detoxification. The liver contains an Alcohol Digesting Enzyme (ADH) which removes alcohol at the rate of about seven grams an hour: so the eight-pint-a-day drinker never gets the alcohol out of his system, the sure path to serious health problems.

A hangover, the unpleasant after-effects of an alcohol binge, represents withdrawal symptoms. The body which adjusted to a high alcoholic intake the night before is now screaming because it's not being given any more. Only the brilliant Germans could have applied such punishing logic as the Underberg hangover cure, which is a shot of alcohol mixed with herbs so poisonous that the idea of having a drop more than necessary is unthinkable. The alcohol stabilises the body, but a breakfast glass of champagne, in contrast, would surely start you on a road to the next, worse hangover.

Although there is no such thing as a hangover cure, the best breakfast to have is coffee, orange juice and a slice of toast (or plate of cereal). The caffeine in coffee has the effect of contracting blood vessels which have been expanded by the alcohol (and contribute to your headache). The vitamin C in the orange juice starts to restore the body's acid-to-alkali balance (alcohol stimulates the gastric juices, causes acidity which can affect ulcers; the body balances itself by producing excessive alkalinity, adding to the body's general stress). Meanwhile, the overworked liver can't metabolise glucose at sufficient speed, and the result is depressed blood sugar levels. The carbohydrate in the bread or cereal will help restore them.

Pure alcohol, like sugar, provides empty calories, but beers and wines have added nutritional benefits. Beer is a highly calorific carbohydrate, and a pint of stout used to be given to old folk in hospital to restore them in convalescence. A pint of Guinness contains 400 calories, a generous contribution to daily needs (an average person's daily needs are around 2,500 for a desk-bound male, 1,700 for a female, but up to 6,000 and 7,000 for people doing hefty physical work in iron foundries and the like). One pint of lager contains from 150 to 250 calories, depending on alcohol volume.

Spirits have an average of 60 calories per pub measure, and the soda or tonic adds another 40 calories, unless it has artificial sweetener. White wine is the slimmer's choice, with 60 calories for a pub glass, but more like 90 calories for the size you pour for yourself.

The Bible urges you take a little wine for your stomach's sake. The alcohol industry is fond of quoting a study which suggests a little alcohol is better for the heart than absolutely none at all. But this evidence has been energetically refuted by Professor Gerry Shaper of London & Royal Free Hospital in papers in 1989 and 1990. A French doctor (well, he would be French), Dr E.A. Maury, wrote *Wine – The Best Medicine* in 1974, claiming wine improved most conditions, and nutritionists agree that wine, especially, contains beneficial vitamins and trace elements, which are of course present in grapes – the vine having abnormally deep roots which suck up trace minerals from great depths. A study in Berkeley, the University of California, shows that wine taken with food aids the absorption of minerals such as zinc, (which is now believed to have an increasingly important role in our well-being), calcium (which we need to renew for our bones), phosphorus and magnesium. Another study, in South Africa, indicates that drinking white wine aids the absorption of iron, which helps tone up the blood. Research chemists who can find good things to say about alcohol will never be short of sponsorship funds.

Although alcohol is such a dear friend, it is, unfortunately, also a treacherous enemy. It contributes to around 40,000 deaths in Britain every year, the next largest cause of premature death after heart disease and smoking. It is one thing to guard your own life by drinking moderately, but you may not always be safe from others who over-indulge. Over a thousand people a year die in road accidents due to drunken driving, and 20,000 more are injured.

While smoking has halved in the last twenty years (two-thirds of Britons were smokers, and now only one-third smoke) the consumption of alcohol has doubled over the last thirty years.

The Government allows £1 million per year to combat alcohol abuse, half of it as advertising on television. But beer, lager, whisky, gin and vodka companies spend £100 million on advertising and sponsorship.

The Government recognises heroin as a dangerous drug and acts accordingly: it has spent £400 million combating heroin abuse, and in a year spend £17 million on advertising alone. It doesn't consider alcohol abuse dangerous to this degree, although it kills 100 times as many people, and, in addition, contributes to a great degree of misery to whole families.

We look back in history in wonder upon the social evils of gin palaces depicted so graphically by William Hogarth, but other unhappy social conditions afflict our own society, and they are not being addressed.

This is a view held passionately by Dr David Player, one of the most forceful social health reformers of our day, former Director-General of the Health Education Council. He now addresses alcohol abuse as Secretary of the Public Health Alliance, a grouping of eighty organisations with members such as Friends of the Earth, health authorities, local authorities, churches and diocese, community health councils for England and Wales, trade unions, Shelter, the Royal College of Nurses, the Royal College of General Practitioners.

Dr Player was head of the HEC from 1982 to 1987 when the Government closed it down and replaced it with the Health Education Authority which is directly responsible to the Department of Health, depriving the body of its independence. The HEC had been created as a QUANGO – a quasi-autonomous non-government organisation – and often, to the embarrassment of the Government, took an unmistakably political line. In 1987 they published *The Health Divide*, commissioning Margaret Whitehead to bring up to date *The Black Report* of 1980, a study by a working group chaired by Sir Douglas Black, which put forward some thirty-seven recommendations for action. The Whitehead report showed that health inequalities between rich and poor had increased. For all causes of death, except skin cancer and breast cancer, the rates were higher in social classes IV and V than in social classes I and II: overall health, they accepted, had been improving, but the gap between the haves and the have-nots had widened.

Dr Player's preface to this report was deliberately provocative: 'Such inequity is inexcusable in a democratic society which prides itself on being humane. To eliminate it, or even reduce it substantially, would be a major contribution to the health of the people in this country.'

His stand brought him into immediate conflict with Junior Health Minister Edwina Currie. She said: 'Yes, there is a health divide in this country. There is a divide between those who know what they should be doing with their own health, and do it; and those who know, and don't do it.'

Now that's a classic example of victim-blaming, claims Dr Player. 'This is one of the things that annoys me about this Government, and the do-gooders. They blame the public for the high crime rate, the victims. And they blame the victims for their health.'

When Dr Player took over at the HEC, he made alcohol and tobacco his two prime targets. But he also insisted that society must tackle the causes of addiction rather than the symptoms. This put him in a long line of reforming public health officers – the medical health officers who tackled the environmental problems of the 1840s, the roots of so much of the illness and disease of the day: reducing infectious diseases that sprang from bad housing, appalling sanitation, and dirty water supplies.

David Player is a Glaswegian, the first from his school to go into medicine. It was when working as a GP that the truth dawned on him that much of the illness and disease he was treating could be attributed to social conditions. 'I felt that as a GP I was putting the elastoplast onto situations. I remember being a GP in West Cumberland, a coal mining and iron mining area with very poor housing. They were mainly Irish labourers, imported during the last century. I remember getting called out one day to see this old miner, not even old miner, he was only fifty. Most of the miners there had silicosis and bronchial diseases. It was common to keep them on antibiotics, give them two cylinders of oxygen so that they could get up to go to the toilet. I put him on the usual antibiotics, gave him more oxygen, and said I'd come and see him the next day. Then, looking around his bedroom, I saw they had pans all over the floor to collect the drips from the leaking ceiling, and I realised that it wasn't medicine he needed. He was needing decent housing, as he had been needing decent working conditions.

'So I thought – I'm wasting my time. Five years study at university and I'm putting on elastoplast. I went back to university to study public health medicine. As I understand it, I am getting them out, downstream. I want to see, who the hell is pushing them in, upstream? As I went further up the river, I found commercial and industrial interests. The alcohol industry, the tobacco industry, the pharmaceutical and the food industry, are the people who are really causing the ill-health. And we, the doctors, are really down the other end of the stream.'

He became Medical Officer of Health for Dumfries, then Director of the Scottish Health Education Group. In 1982, joining the HEC, he found himself in a position to lead public opinion.

'We started to take on the anti-health forces, the health antagonists, what I call, The Enemies of the People (Ibsen's play is very relevant to that). Number One has to be the Tobacco Industry. In the US, latest figures suggest that 32,000 *non-smokers* died from cancer-related diseases – from 'passive' smoking. (In the UK, we reckon about 3,000.) Add the 32,000 to the 390,000 smokers who die in a year in America, you get a total of 422,000 Americans dying every year from smoking, which is more than the 405,000 Americans killed during the whole of World War Two. The report went on to say that in only three years smoking kills more than all who died in all battles in all United States wars, including the Revolutionary War. I worked out the same figures for Britain and found we lost more people in a year than we did fighting the Japanese and the Germans in the last war. I don't want to be too dramatic about it. But we are involved in a battle for health, as serious as the battles in the war. In America, tobacco companies are ruthless in pushing their products into Thailand and other poor countries of South-East Asia.

'Now, nicotine is a stronger drug of addiction than heroin. Alcohol is also a drug of addiction. If you lived in the conditions that some people in this country live in, the lowest 10 per cent, smoking and alcohol are the least of your problems. They are drugs of solace. Consider the Colombian and Peruvian peasants. They chew coca leaves to get through the day.

'It was the Surgeon-General of the United States who called nicotine a much stronger drug of addiction than heroin. When the Vietnam soldiers came back they found it easier to get them off heroin than smoking. This is what annoys me about the pushers of cigarettes, the companies. They've got to recruit 100,000 young people to smoking every year, because 100,000 people are dying every year because of smoking. It's too many. The figures are too large to be meaningful!'

There are no brakes on the tobacco companies. 'They are spending hundreds of millions of pounds every year on advertising and sponsorship to get people hooked. We find that if people stay off cigarettes until they are twenty it's unlikely they'll start, so they've got to get them young. They've got to make it glamorous, and macho and exciting.'

Alcohol presents exactly the same problem. 'We can draw a scientific line measuring the per capita consumption of alcohol and the amount of harm done in the country. We're not against alcohol, but against alcohol abuse. Our aim is to reduce per capita consumption and this is where we come into conflict with the alcohol industry, whose primary objective is to increase consumption, because that means profits.

'I've had many discussions with the alcohol industry and we've tried to cosy up to each other because they like to be good guys. They all go to church on a Sunday morning with their families, and they don't see themselves as bad people, and they are not bad people. But after all discussions with them we break up in the end because our aims are not compatible. This goes in cycles. I've gone through several of them. The big bodies are the Scots Whisky Association and the Brewers' Society, representing spirits and beers. The other one is the Licensed Victuallers' Association, but they are worried about alcoholics because they are not good for business. We produced low alcohol drinks with publicans and they were promoted very well. We work better with the publicans than the producers.'

Alcohol, he believes, is a drug of addiction. 'Anybody, if they drink long enough at a certain level can become addicted. When you talk about alcoholics, it's just the end result, poor chaps sleeping out rough in London. But there are many gradations, the alcoholics at home, the secret ones.'

He says that about thirty MPs are in direct reward from consultancies to the alcohol industry. 'So when it comes to debates in Parliament these guys get into filibusters. Then we're really up against it. In the States, they have paid lobbyists who've got to be shown as such. In this country we've got MPs. The alcohol industry has a lot of political power. It is one of the biggest contributors to the funds of the Conservative Party. At the 1987 election many of the big poster sites which had alcohol and cigarette ads were given over to the Conservative Party not for payment, but a contribution in kind. So instead of saying "Buy Beer", it said "Vote Conservative at the next Election". They have an extremely powerful influence.'

He would like to see a ban on alcohol advertising except at point of sale. 'There should be no alcohol advertising on television. I object to the advertising per se, and also I object to the way they aim it, at young people, particularly, and downmarket.'

Football fans are an obvious target. 'At the Heysel Stadium riots in Belgium, I was convinced that alcohol was at the root of the trouble. Most of the fans were tanked up on lager. We talked about lager louts, but this was denied, and it was suggested that it was the National Front. I think that's a load of baloney. But the alcohol industry would try to find a scapegoat.'

The National Front story wasn't believed. 'After that the Prime Minister took it seriously. In Scotland there's been no drinking at football matches for years and the amount of trouble has gone down just like that. So that's been started in England. And how does the alcohol industry get round that? At the moment there are at least sixteen football teams in the first four divisions which have the names of beer or lager on their chests. So you get these punters coming in, dying for a drink and you've got twenty-two guys running around saying "Drink me, drink me." It's like a scene from *Alice in Wonderland*. You've got the situation where every top-selling lager sponsors a football team. You talk about lager louts, but this is going on subliminally.'

The message goes out to under-age fans. 'I remember that Norwich City was sponsored by Fosters Lager, and I remember a picture of a boy holding up a Fosters Cup and the caption said "This competition is for boys and girls from twelve to eighteen". The boy was perhaps thirteen, and wearing the Canaries strip, saying *Fosters Lager*. They are exploiting the heroes of these young kids.'

Looking to the future, what can be done? Dr Player hopes the Public Health Alliance will disseminate the vital information that those in charge of administrating health most need. A political answer is the solution that is most called for. He wonders if people know, or even care, how desperate the situation is for the unemployed, the very poor, the people at the bottom of the social scale. 'I'm not against drink. I love a beer. But in Scotland one million people drink 80 per cent of the beer and whisky and that's too much.'

Sir Donald Acheson, the Chief Medical Officer, has pointed out that for the first time this century, there is a declining life expectancy because of drink, and that's the age group fifteen to twenty-four. 'The reason is the abuse of alcohol, particularly on the roads. It's a serious issue.'

Dr Player's short-term answer is to aim at the doctors. 'Doctors can help.' He laughs: 'One definition of an alcoholic is someone who drinks more than the doctor. (Actually there are other professions who do drink a great deal more than doctors. Above them in the national league table are publicans and barmen, hoteliers, club owners, restauranteurs, chefs and cooks, shipworkers and fishermen, and authors, writers and journalists.)

'But the GP is at the front end of the problem. The doctor finds that a lot of the symptoms he's presented with are related to alcohol abuse. In some of the large hospitals in this country, 25 per cent of the acute admissions are due to alcohol-related diseases.'

The Scottish Health Education Group has created a kit for doctors called DRAMS, short for Drinking Reasonably and Moderately with Self-Control, which is issued free, and they arrange courses in which they teach a brief form of counselling which doctors can utilise in an average seven-minute consultation session.

The GP can give the booklet to patients and get them to keep it for weeks or months so they can monitor themselves, and it's effect-ive. It's based on a similar kit to help people give up smoking, and it's the most effective way there is. 'I think it's the best thing in the world when a GP says: "I'm your doctor. I think you should give up smoking. I think you should cut down your drinking".'

SAFE LIMITS

Most people who enjoy drink find their own levels by trial and error. The occasional hangover is a jarring reminder that you have pushed your body off limits.

But social occasions, pressure of work, sometimes family or per-sonal problems, can often push up consumption, forcing the body to adjust and exacting a cost which will certainly damage your health, not to mention the obvious social side-effects. Excess alcohol consumption leads to cirrhosis of the liver, high blood pressure, strokes. Certain types of cancer are more common among heavy drinkers. So are stomach upsets, poor concentration and difficulty in sleeping.

This guide, prepared for the Health Education Authority and Alcohol Concern by Dr Peter Anderson and Dr Paul Wallace, suggests the happy mean for safe, happy, healthy, social drinking, a target of less than twenty-one units of alcohol per week.

Ten reasons to cut down drinking

1 Less risk of having an accident, developing high blood pressure and liver disease.
2 Improved concentration and a clear head.
3 Fewer hangovers, headaches and stomach upsets.
4 Sounder sleep and less tiredness generally.
5 New sense of being in control and feeling fitter.
6 Time and energy for activities other than drinking.
7 Fewer arguments and rows with friends or family.
8 More pleasure out of your sex life.
9 More money. Work out how much you've spent on alcohol during the last week. Over a year, you could save fifty times as much.
10 If you are pregnant, your baby will stand a better chance of being born healthy. During pregnancy you should cut down as much as possible – it's best to stop drinking alcohol altogether until after the baby is born.

Finding out how much you drink

The pub measures below all contain roughly the same amount (one unit) of alcohol. Score one for each one you drink. Drinks poured at home are usually more generous and should be scored double. Also, score three times as much for extra-strength beers.

A drinking diary (described at the end) will help you tot up how much alcohol you are drinking regularly. Fill it in every day for a week, noting down all your drinks. Then add up your total score and compare it with our target below.

You also need to record where you do your drinking and with whom. It's these factors that make up your individual drinking pattern.

Your drinking target

Using pub measures as a guide you can assess your consumption by adding up the units.

½ pint beer or lager	1 unit	1 small glass sherry	1 unit
1 single whisky	1 unit	1 measure vermouth	1 unit
1 glass wine	1 unit	½ pint extra strength lager/beer	3 units

Low Risk Drinking

Men with score of 0 to 21 units per week.
Women with score of 0 to 14 units of drink per week.

When spaced throughout the week, this level of drinking is not likely to harm your health. But, for some people, even this amount may be too much and you should aim for at least two or three alcohol-free days a week. There are some situations where it is unwise to drink any alcohol at all, such as during work, when driving, before playing sports or during pregnancy.

Medium Risk Drinking

Men with score of 22 to 35 units of drink per week.
Women with score of 15 to 21 units of drink per week.

Danger to health and safety increases. 'Binge' drinking is especially risky, making accidents, fights, arguments and sickness more likely. Continuing at this level could lead to trouble. Try to cut down.

High Risk Drinking

Men with score of above 36 units of drink per week.
Women with score of above 22 units of drink per week.

If you drink this much you're running the risk of liver damage, accidents and alcohol dependency. This level of drinking could lead to social difficulties such as drink and driving offences, problems with your family, or loss of job.

Planning to cut down

1 Choose a date in the next few days to cut down on drinking. Try to pick a day when you'll be under least stress.
2 Decide what weekly limit you're going to aim for.
3 Plan to do things other than drinking: going to a film, playing sports or exercising, starting an evening class or doing some DIY at home. It's up to you: the important point is to find activities you enjoy which don't involve alcohol.
4 Use your drinking diary to find which times of day, where and with whom you drink more than usual. You need to be prepared for these 'risk' situations and to plan your life differently at these times and to avoid the urge to drink.
5 Try to get someone else to cut down on drinking with you. You could be a great help to each other.
6 Tell people you are cutting down and tell them when. They could be helpful instead of pressuring you to 'have another little drink'.
7 Stock up on plenty of non-alcoholic drinks – there are alcohol-free beers and wines available in many supermarkets, pubs and health shops now. These are a good alternative to the usual fruit juices and bottled waters and, when you're with other people, it's less obvious that you're not drinking alcohol.
8 Keep thinking about the positive reasons for drinking less, and the benefits. If you make up your mind, you will easily succeed.

Make a Drinking Diary

List the days of the week, and make five columns to fill in each day.

> When (am/pm)
> Where (pub/office/home)
> What (spirits/beer/wine/cider)
> Who with (group/friends/alone)
> Units (total of drinks per day)

At the bottom of the page make a total for the week.

10

ADDITIVES

The holiday ice cream, made in Barcelona, was delicious. Obviously it was free of additives. But no. The wrapper revealed it to be packed with them, preservatives, emulsifiers, flavours and colours. How come it tasted so good?

We've come to associate additives with awful taste and colour and we angrily respond by complaining they are probably dangerous, too. But lots of natural foods are toxic to an extreme degree (the green bits of potatoes are packed with solanine which is highly toxic) and we cheerfully submit to high doses of sodium in spite of what we know it does to our blood pressure (sodium chloride as salt, and monosodium glutamate, especially in Chinese foods).

If only all Britain's additive-rich ice creams tasted as good as those in Barcelona instead of turning over in your stomach and leaving your taste buds indelibly branded for hours afterwards. Our average commercial ice cream, eaten in parks, at seaside resorts and cinemas, is a profound insult to the national palate, with the assumption that the public doesn't know any better. Any Spaniard, Italian, Frenchman, German, anyone in the world, seems to appreciate flavour better than our food scientists.

Ask a food scientist, and he'll shrug. He'll say it's what the market research people have arrived at. Ask a market researcher, and he'll say it's what the public want, at the low price they've been led to expect. So it goes round in a circle. If additives satisfied us, there surely wouldn't be so much public resentment against them. But they don't, and they fan the flames of general mistrust towards the greedy elements in the food industry.

People who care about the taste of food have come to think of additives as second rate, but they could be mistaken. The eight notes on the tonal scale don't necessarily limit us to playing *Three Blind Mice* on a recorder; in the hands of Bach, Beethoven and Brahms the same notes lift the mind and the spirit. Unfortunately, many of the people who play with food flavourings don't know their A flat from their E sharp.

But the flavour artists have had their successes and there is no greater success story than margarine. At a cost of hundreds of thousands of pounds the Unilever scientists identified twenty-two of the most essential flavour components, out of several hundred, that give butter its unique taste. These they were able to manufacture synthetically and incorporate into margarine, enabling the product to be marketed as a realistic and cheap substitute for butter. The advertising campaign for Stork margarine was launched on television and proved that the man-and-woman-in-the-street couldn't tell Stork from butter (when it was spread thinly on bread and you had to give an instant decision). In fact, if you go to the Tilbury factory in Essex where Unilever's margarines are made, extruded like so much toothpaste in a computerised operation, and dip your finger in a tub, you'll be struck by the instantly clean and clearly distinguishable butter flavours. But the flavours disperse quickly on the tongue and you are left chewing something far less pleasant – although this will depend on the base of the fat used for the margarine – animal fat, saturated or unsaturated oils.

When the Frenchman, Hippolyte Mège-Mouriés, invented it a century ago, distilling a drop of white beef suet the size and colour of a pearl (to give it its name, from margaras, Greek for a pearl), it was conceived as a cheap substitute for butter. The British had it forced upon them in the 1939–45 War. Reinforced with vitamins, but it was so unpleasant to the taste that the expression bread-and-marge came to symbolise a new low in our sinking gastronomic identity, along with snoek, a horrible-tasting, oily fish caught in South African waters. The food scientists who turned round the taste of margarine were alchemists indeed, and their rewards came when butter was identified as a luxury which should be limited for sake of our hearts, and margarines made from unsaturated oils like sunflower became premium foodstuffs in their own right. But its appeal to the palate is aided by the quality of the raw product, the oil, in the first place.

The criticism, on taste grounds, against additives, is that they can be used to mislead, some would say defraud, by being used to disguise poor quality materials.

Flavours may well become the issue of the 1990s, but additives play very many other roles, many of them in the best interests of the consumer – such as preservatives, because they inhibit spoilage, therefore checking toxic substances which lead to food poisoning. On the other hand, these same additives are in the best interests of the food industry, extending shelf-life and therefore profit.

The additives used for colouring provoke the fiercest debate, and many are implicated in research, which suggests they are responsible for allergies and hyperactivity in children, as well as cancers in laboratory animals. I list these at the end of the chapter.

The referees in the debate are Government Ministries, the Department of Health and the Ministry of Agriculture and Food, advised by the scientists who sit on a panel called the Food Advisory Committee. They evaluate evidence offered by scientists around the world, but the cost of initiating thorough research into all the additives in use, and combinations of them, is prohibitive, especially where we need to know not if a dose of E-1000 will immediately make you glow like a traffic light, but if it will give your children cancer in twenty, thirty or forty years time as part of the build-up of any number of additives.

Some tests for cancers take five years, while generations of mice and rats are bred specifically so that they can be fed overdoses. It can cost several hundred thousand pounds to put one single chemical through its paces, and there are some 1,800 additives in general use in the US and UK, the chief users. Some additives will be found safe used on their own, but it's understood that two or more additives can act synergistically to promote tumours in laboratory animals, so the mathematics of testing all the combinations of additives, in twos and threes and fours, clearly show it's not feasible.

Because we live in a climate of anxiety about our foods in general, it's only natural the finger of suspicion should fall on additives, and this happened dramatically on 1 January, 1986, when our membership to the Common Market required our food manufacturers to identify additives with E-Numbers, E standing for Europe. So alarmed were the British public that publishers had a field day. Maurice Hanssen's *E for Additives* became an instant bestseller, but unlike *Nineteen Eighty Four* or *Lady Chatterley's Lover*, which also sold a million copies, it is little more than a dictionary of 500 E-Numbers. It is designed to enable you to translate the small print on soft drinks, sweeties in the corner store, and the great parade of processed foods in your supermarket. If it's a product of food scarism, it is by no means a scaring book, yet a million people said: 'The situation is disturbing – I'd better buy a copy just in case.'

And it pays off, because you wonder why your son goes absolutely crazy after school when you let him have a packet of chewing gum or a soft drink, and you identify on the label the Number E102. And you read: *Tartrazine: Synthetic, azo dye ... appears to be most reactive of all the azo dyes.*

In a study of eighty-eight children with severe frequent migraine headaches, tartrazine caused symptoms in twelve of them. It provokes a response in some asthmatics, worsens nettle rash, and in susceptible people causes itching, runny noses, blurred vision, purple patches on the skin, and may keep small children awake at night. The Hyperactive Children's Support Group recommends it should be eliminated from the diets of children. It is banned in Norway and Austria. And Hanssen advises that you can find it in:

> fruit squash and cordial
> coloured fizzy drinks
> instant puddings
> packet convenience foods
> cake mixes
> custard powder
> soups (packets and tins)
> bottle sauces
> pickles
> salad creams and salad dressings
> ice cream and lollies
> sweets
> chewing gum
> marzipan
> jam
> marmalade
> jelly
> smoked cod and haddock
> mustard
> yogurt
> glycerin, lemon and honey products

shells of medicinal capsules

You compare notes with other parents. Then you hear the Minister of Agriculture, Fisheries and Food, confesses that one of his children has to be kept from food dyed with tartrazine because of hyperactivity. Should it therefore still be allowed to be used? The official answer continues to be that these are isolated cases, affecting a few 'intolerant' people.

Not a very reassuring position – which leaves many people jumping to the conclusion that the more E-Numbers listed on a product, the more dangerous it must be – a witch's cocktail perhaps.

E-Numbers are nothing more than convenient labels for the many chemicals used in the food industry, some natural, others synthetic. Some people think we overdose on chemicals to a degree which invites cancer, and next to heart disease, cancers are responsible for the largest number of deaths every year – statistics which do not get the same prominence as, for example, road deaths at holiday peaks. But as long ago as 1972 the Stamford Research Institute of California estimated that 80 per cent of all cancers were caused by chemicals which people encounter in their daily lives. The computation included the chemical agent in tobacco which causes lung cancer, which has been exhaustively researched, with the result that, although cigarettes are not banned, children are actively discouraged from smoking. In the case of additives, where research is inadequate, children are often the prime targets, especially in confectionery, soft drinks and snacks.

While the safety of certain additives is under suspicion, the great majority confuse the benefit of cheap and convenient food for housewives who no longer have the time or the talents to create satisfying, substantial or tasty meals for the family. As one supermarket executive put it: 'The housewife of the 1990s has become deskilled.' It's in those areas where food is 'instant' that the highest concentrations of additives are used, and that's the cost of the convenience of instant soup, salad dressings, dessert toppings, imitation fruit drinks, snack foods and pre-cooked dishes.

But food without any additives at all would be intolerable. At home we freely use salt, pepper, mustard, vinegar, and not just for taste. Salt is the oldest preservative known to man, withdrawing moisture from food which would otherwise oxidise and spoil. Vinegar is an acid which kills bacteria. Pepper and mustard contain

powerful chemicals which act on our bodies as irritants and generate
heat. Mustard has an emulsifying property, containing chemicals
which break up fat, holding the tiny droplets in suspension and
aiding digestion. What is a sausage, a ham sandwich, a plate of roast
beef without mustard? Herbs such as rosemary, sage and thyme have
bacteriocidal properties, which were appreciated in the Middle Ages
when the herbalist was a medic rather than a cook, and used his
skills to counter the effects of meat and poultry spoiling. And there's
no more effective additive than sugar, enabling us to preserve fruits,
and make 'conserves' of jam, and mixed with salt, all manner of
meat, fish, vegetables and pickles.

As additives they have specific working roles to play and it may
be that in our perversity we began to believe we enjoy the taste of
the additive itself, more than the food it's preserving or protecting,
the saltiness of a smoked ham, the smoky saltiness of kippers and
haddock, the salty sweetness of smoked salmon.

The use of additives increased tenfold in the post-War years, in tune
with the rise of the supermarket culture. Of 3,800 additives in general
use, 3,500 are flavours and are not specifically regulated. They run
the gamut of A to Z from allium sativum (garlic) and arbutus unedo
(strawberry) to zea mays (Indian maize) and zingiber officinale (root
ginger), embracing weird, wonderful and unlikely flavours such as
silver birch, blessed thistle, scurvy grass, oak moss, lemon-scented
spotted gum, German iris, dittany of Crete, garden radish, Chinese
rhubarb, dog violet, as well as stalwarts such as spearmint, licorice,
cardamon, cayenne, cassia, turmeric, allspice.

There are 330 additives which are specifically permitted and regulated by Government, and they fall into a very wide spectrum of
twenty-four different categories, from the more obvious preservatives and colours, to emulsifying agents to prevent mayonnaises
from separating, stabilisers and thickeners, anti-oxidants to stop oils
going rancid, sweeteners; cosmetics such as glazing agents to put a
shine on food such as dried fruit (mineral oils) and sweets (dextrin)
and bleaches to whiten flour; humectants to keep food moist, such
as sorbitol in pastries and cakes, and glycerol in sweets; buffers to
maintain an acid-alkali balance, when one or the other is added;
bulking agents used in slimming foods to give the impression you're
eating more than you think, such as alpha cellulose and polydextrose
which have no calories; excipients to make dry mixtures manageable

and carry flavourings (such as sorbitan monostearate); alkali bases (the hydroxides) to decrease the acidity in sweets; and acids (as a preservative, and to enhance other additives) such as acetic acid in pickles and phosphoric acid in colas to add a sour note against the sickly sweetness; firming and crisping agents in tinned fruit and vegetables (such as calcium chloride, calcium hydroxide, calcium malate); sequestrants which slow down decay in food by attaching themselves to trace metals; solvents, which help disperse other additives through food (and those used to extract fish oil, and the flavour agents in coffee and tea, such as Dichloromethane). Not to mention anti-caking agents which let table salt run freely (magnesium carbonate) and chemicals which prevent powdered milk and icing sugar from sticking into lumps; liquid freezants for food such as strawberries which must be rapidly frozen (liquid nitrogen quickly extracts warmth); propellants, used in aerosol containers; anti-foaming agents to stop beers and other liquids frothing when they are being bottled, and to stop liquids from boiling over in the cooking processes; release agents, which are powders or grease used to prevent food from sticking to moulds or factory machinery.

All these are carefully regulated, though there are others which are not, such as enzymes, catalysts which effect changes, such as rennet which curdles milk to make junket, paw-paw and pineapple juice which tenderises meat; and various dilutants, clarifying and fining agents (for alcohols), crystallisation inhibitors (for ice creams), whipping aids for creams and desserts.

The British food industry uses around a quarter of a million tons of additives a year; well on the way to £500 million worth of business. The preservatives are the most essential, and most useful, because they inhibit potential toxins and poisons; the flavourings are what the gourmets complain about; and apart from those just listed which aid production, the rest are largely cosmetic, providing colour and mouthfeel.

Flavour is a sore point. Professor Alan Holmes of the Leatherhead food research laboratories maintains that the natural flavours used in the food industry are more easily destroyed by the heat processes used than artificial flavours. He instances boiled sweets. Equally, Wall's food scientists have maintained that you can't taste any refinement of flavour in an ice cream when you lick it, because the sheer cold depresses the sensitivity of the taste buds, effectively anaesthetising them. There's no answer to that. Except that commonsense returns, and you know that natural fruit flavours taste better in ice creams, as they do in sweets, than artificial ones. Good flavour lingers on as pleasantly and surely as bad flavour, and it isn't boiled out or frozen out.

But food scientists are adamant, and the food industry agrees to prefer the artificial to the real for the sake of consistency and cheapness. Natural flavours aren't so intense, and they undergo seasonal changes. And there is a wider range of artificial flavours.

Colour is something else, and the customer is said to prefer cheese coloured with Day-glo orange, canned peas like a colour in a child's paintbox, kippers dyed reddish-brown with a coal-tar derivative, strawberries a strident red, where the natural products produce anaemic colours after processing: cheese is white, cooked peas turn grey-green, kippers are greyish, strawberries go pinkish-brown. Orange drinks are required to be poster-coloured and make a garish comparison with a glass of freshly-squeezed real juice.

The colours are used to imply freshness, and indeed the best butter comes from the best cream which is milked from cows eating the spring grass, rich in the carotene which provides a deeper shade of yellow.

Purists would say that using additives in this way is cheating, and to some extent the history of additives is also the history of adulteration. Dishonest traders and shopkeepers throughout history have seen a way to pass off bad as good. The consumers' fight against food adulteration has been long and difficult.

As long ago as Roman times unscrupulous cooks used soda when boiling green vegetables to give them the appearance of brilliant freshness (until recently a top London restaurant used copper pans to achieve the same effect with its cabbage). They put potash into dull wine to give it colour and clarity. We know from *The Canterbury Tales* that adulteration of food was common in Chaucer's day – and the Miller was the biggest cheat of all.

In the eighteenth century what was sold as wine might be any mixture of alcohols, spirit, cider and the juice of hedgerow sloes. By the nineteenth century British food was a scandal, especially in the cities and towns, now growing with the spread of the Industrial Revolution. Public anger, voiced in the first two decades of the century, reached a climax in 1820 when a German-born chemist, Frederick Accum, published a devastating account of food adulteration. The book, written before it was fashionable to have short titles, was entitled *A Treatise on Adulterations of Food and Culinary Poisons, exhibiting the Fraudulent Sophistications of Bread, Beer, Wine, Spiritous Liquors, Tea, Coffee, Cream, Confectionary, Vinegar, Mustard, Pepper, Cheese, Olive Oil, Pickles, and other articles employed in Domestic Economy and Methods of Detecting them.* Accum was one of the most highly regarded men in his field, a member of the Royal Irish Academy, Member of the Royal Academy of Sciences, of the Royal Society of Arts of Berlin. While others had complained, Accum named the names of the people practising the frauds.

His account of the adulteration of food includes flour of inferior quality mixed with alum, and sometimes potatoes for cheapness; he revealed that there had been almost one hundred convictions of traders and druggists in 1819 for using a poison called cocculus indicus, as well as dubious ingredients such as harts-horn shavings and mixed drugs and spices to give dilute beers and alcohols the impression of strength. The adulteration of tea was so widespread that an official report recorded that for six million pounds of real tea imported from India, four million tons of rubbish was sold; leaves picked from hawthorn bushes, leaves of the ash, elderberry, sloe bushes, boiled, baked and rubbed by hand to get them to curl like Indian tea. Green tea was made by pressing the leaves on copper and then colouring them with poisonous verdigris to achieve the required bloom, and sold to be mixed with real tea. Red lead was used to colour the rind of cheese. Copper provided the bright green colour which made pickles look so appetising.

Accum's Treatise ran to four editions within two years, the first exposé of its kind, and a bestseller. But he'd made enemies, and his popular success ended in ignominy when the Royal Institution charged him with defacing books in their library. It seems he'd removed endpapers to write notes on. Rather than defend himself against the charges he fled to Berlin and took up a professorship there.

Accum's book focussed attention on fraud, but didn't end it, and the practices grew rather than decreased, especially in respect of beer, flour and tea (old leaves were collected, dried, mixed with rose pink and blacklead to 'face' them). Coffee was adulterated with chicory and roast barley, and coloured with red ochre.

Fifteen people died from eating sweets bought in Bradford Market, as a result of a mistake when a sweetmaker tried to adulterate lozenges with plaster of paris and used arsenic by mistake. Twenty people died after a banquet in Nottingham after eating green blancmange which had been coloured with arsenite of copper. Children were made ill from mineral dyes used in sweets, and there were deaths of people drinking rum poisoned with cocculus indicus, and cases of paralysis due to lead chromate in cayenne pepper and mustard.

The people who suffered most were of course the poor, especially those in institutions, from hospitals and barracks to schools, prisons and the workhouse. But adulterations made food cheap, and cheap food is always in demand among the poor. The better-off and better-educated who'd read the exposés could afford to buy unadulterated food in better shops.

The social historian, John Burnett, comments that ignorance and poverty condemned the mass of people to an adulterated diet, but when they were financially able to exercise a choice, some continued to prefer the impure to the genuine. 'Eating habits are so highly conservative, and people had been so long conditioned to impure bread, tea, pickles and the rest that they did not always immediately like the flavour or the appearance of unadulterated foods. Early pioneers of pure food sometimes encountered strong consumer opposition. Co-operative societies, for example, experienced such difficulties in selling uncoloured teas that at least one was obliged to employ a lecturer to tell people what good tea looked like.'

He points out that the adulterators were practising their ill deeds when Christian morality was at its most ostentatious, but far from suffering self-reproach, the guilty traders sought to justify themselves. 'Faced with irrefutable evidence of their offence, adulterating traders put forward a number of justifications designed to prove that they were, in fact, performing a public service, that adulterations were only practised in response to public taste, that they constituted improvements and lowered the price of foods which would have otherwise been too expensive for the poor to buy. Needless to say it was not mentioned that adulteration was always for the profit of the seller and at the expense of the buyer, and that quite apart from the possible dangers to health, adulterated goods were dearest in the end.'

In 1875 these scandals were ended by the Food and Drugs Act which secured our right to safe food, and requires that what we buy should be of the nature, substance and quality we pay for.

Although there is still fierce dissatisfaction about the use of certain additives, especially coal-tar dyes, it is assumed the health risks are very, very small indeed, although not non-existent. The most vehement critics of additives are those who say they are used to defraud. And while they may not pass off tea with poisonous copper or lead, they conspire to sell air and water with the subtle assistance of additives.

It is additives which enable a cheap mixture of sugar syrup, powdered milk, colouring and flavouring, beaten into many times its volume, to be sold as expensive scoops of 'ice cream'. It is additives like polyphosphates which are injected into hams, bacon, chickens, sausages, and fish products to enable them to hold 10 per cent or more extra water, and increase profits, and in so doing produce an inferior, degraded product. Additives explain why the British loaf is moist and damp and spongy, compared with the dry, nutty finish of its Continental counterparts; it's baked for the minimum time to retain maximum weight, which means maximum water.

Above all, additives are used to disguise poor quality ingredients such as minced beef and pork products, burgers and sausages, which have been debased with fat, gristle, mechanically recovered meat (MRM) and colouring, used to disguise ground-up bone, offal and rusk.

The same goes for the use of cheese flavourings in snacks to suggest cheese is an ingredient, or tomato colouring when no tomato is included. Meat and fruit pies often give the illusion of being well filled, when in fact gelling additives and thickening agents have been used.

And what is extremely difficult for the untutored customer to detect are those additives, stabilisers, emulsifiers, and so on, which aid the inclusion of fat, sugar and salt, the most invasive 'additives' of all. While you are puzzling over the E-Number which is present in the anti-oxidant in a bag of crisps, it may escape your attention that the reason why the anti-oxidant is there is because it's needed to stop the fat oxidising and going rancid. Potatoes don't contain fat, but crisps do, and they soak up more than their own weight in the cooking process. So the hidden additive is really the fat! As much as 70 per cent of the calorific value of every crisp is the cooking oil. And oil is a prominent ingredient in fish fingers and crispbakes, being absorbed by the breadcrumb coating, the crumbs and the oil being cheaper ingredients than the fish or meat it covers. (Unwrap a crisp-batter coated scampi and weigh the fish and batter coating respectively and then see if you think the cost of the scampi is reasonable).

It is additives which persuade you to pay over the odds for sugared water, the squashes and carbonated drinks which mimic fresh fruit juices.

And it is additives, deployed with extraordinary skill, to work alchemy on flour, fat and sugar, which have turned Britain into the world's largest consumers of biscuits. One supermarket chain has almost 200 brands on sale.

Whole fresh foods are the least profitable lines for the shopkeeper; they require careful selection, there's the risk of damage in transit, a short shelf-life. Manufactured foods don't. They are simply paralysed with preservatives, propped up with bulking and thickening aids, injected with anti-oxidants, infused with phoney flavours, with a garish lick of paint to tart them all up. At their best, manufactured foods are an art form like glossy, classy, girlie magazines, and the pleasure they give is as brief.

Real food, like real life, is better if you give it a chance.

Of course, whole fresh food is subject to additives too: insecticides and herbicides used in the fields, sprays such as alar used on apples (implicated in cancer), colour sprayed on to oranges and other fruit to give an illusion of ripeness. Inert gases are used to store fruit and vegetables.

With so much alarming evidence to digest, you choose either to eat up, hope it will never happen to you and trust the scientists (remember that the scientists and their masters have been wilfully wrong about lung cancer, about thalidomide, about cancer from asbestos or from nuclear power), or you can buy organic foods.

The 1990s are likely to see a polarisation. Half the population will demand (and get) fewer additives in food, and the other half will take what's offered. But a small proportion, possibly 10 per cent, will form an elite of eaters, acutely well-informed about the sources of their food, with guarantees of safety as much as quality, and they will pay more for it.

SAFETY

The London Food Commission prepared this list of additives under suspicion, beginning with the coal-tar dyes, which are derivatives from the petro-chemical industry, and are suspected of causing birth defects, mutations, cancer and acute illness; two of them, Tartrazine (E 102) and Sunset Yellow (E 110) have been dropped from baby foods, but are freely used in products advertised for children, from fish fingers to soft drinks.

colours

E102, E104, 107, E110, E122, E123, E124, E127, 128, E131, E132, 133, E142, E151, 154, 155, E180	coal-tar dyes	may cause asthma, rashes, hyperactivity; some have been linked to cancer in test animals
E120	cochineal (insect extract)	suspected of causing food intolerance
E150	chemically treated burnt sugar	some forms may damage genes; may reduce white blood cells and destroy vitamin B6
E160b	annatto (tree-seed extract)	may cause asthma, rashes; poorly tested for safety

preservatives

E210, E211, E212, E213, E214, E215, E216, E217, E218, E219	benzoates	may cause asthma, rashes, hyperactivity
E220, E221, E222, E223, E224, E226, E227	sulphites	may provoke asthma; destroy vitamin B1
E249, E250, E251, E252	nitrates/nitrites	can produce nitrosamines which are linked to cancers;

		can reduce blood oxygen levels

antioxidants

E310, E311, E312	gallates	may cause intolerance and liver damage, and can irritate the intestine
E320, E321	BHA and BHT	may cause rashes and hyperactivity; linked to cancer in test animals

emulisifiers, thickeners etc.

E385	calcium disodium EDTA	possible link to liver damage in test animals
E407	carageenan (seaweed extract)	linked to ulcers in colon and foetal
E413	tragacanth gum	may cause intolerance, and linked to liver damage in test animals
416	karaya gum	may cause intolerance; is a laxative, so might reduce nutrient intake
430, 431, 432, 433, 434, 435, 436	stearates and polysorbates	possible link to skin and intestinal inflammation, diarrhoea and possibly cancer
E450a, E450b, E450c	di-, tri- and polyphosphates	possible link to kidney damage in test animals; can have laxative effect

flavour enhancers

620, 621, 622, 623	glutamates	may cause dizziness

		and palpitations; reproductive damage in test animals
627, 631, 635	other enhancers	may aggravate gout

improvers and bleaches

924, 925, 926	flour treating agents	may irritate stomach; bleaches destroy natural vitamin E

sweeteners

–	saccharin	linked to bladder cancer in test animals
–	aspartame	possible link to neural problems

(Table reprinted by permission of The Food Commission.)

11

HEALTH FOODS

In these times of deep suspicion towards all the aspects of food production – from cruelty to crop spraying; from additives to health scares – the health food and wholefood shops are enjoying a tremendous boom.

If Big is seen as Bad, then Small is Beautiful. These stores represent a huge range of hopes and beliefs, many conflicting. Between them they cater for vegetarians – running into millions in the 1990s; for wholefooders – who can't get such fresh grain and pulses elsewhere; for supporters of organic foods – from fields where crops are grown without insecticides and artificial fertilisers; for people who seek foods without coal tar colouring dyes and benzoate preservatives; for an enduring band of believers, inspired by the claims of royal jelly from queen bees and the oil of evening primrose; and finally for those who are prey to anything in a pillbox which makes a salesman's pitch – on the grounds that everything else has failed, and this might not do any good, but it probably won't do any harm.

It's easy to suggest gullibility – but if health foods do for the customer what Eastern faith healers achieve, their claims may not be entirely wasted. Who doesn't know of someone, who has despaired of orthodox medicine, seeking a remedy for agonising back pain or debilitating migraine? Or racked with burning pains in joints due to arthritis? Or suffering from sleeplessness, anxiety and fatigue?

When Maurice Hanssen's daughter was five or six years old she was afflicted by warts on the back of her hand. 'She was distraught. Other children at school shunned her,' he says. 'I told her I would get rid of them. I went out and got an organically grown potato, cut it in half, and rubbed it on her warts. I told her I would bury the potato in the garden, and that as it rotted the warts would disappear. It worked. Now, I know that warts are caused by a virus, and there's no conventional remedy, and I had no reason to believe that it would work, but it did. It's based on an old myth.'

Maurice Hanssen is a great believer in health food shops on the grounds that they give people faith, and faith's a great healer. 'You tell a child when it hurts itself: "I can kiss it better." And it works. The most powerful healing force in the old days was the doctor's bedside manner – it was the best drug in his armoury. What do busy doctors offer today?'

Maurice Hanssen has been professionally involved in health foods all his life, though he is best known as the author of *E for Additives*, which was first published in 1987 and has run through several editions to top the million mark. His own background is in food technology, in producing foods for people on special diets. As long ago as the 1950s he observed that the food industry in general gave no thought to the nutritional consequences of what they were producing, and it's for this reason that he cheers the role of the health food shop in providing many of the vitamin supplements that may be lost to people who are reliant on mass-produced food.

'If you look up food composition tables in a nutritional textbook, they will say – under *Apples – 30 mg of Vitamin C per 100 g of fruit*. That would be enough per day to stop you getting scurvy! But in fact these tables don't reveal the whole truth. 100 g of apple can contain as little as 6 mg or as much as 60 mg depending on the type of apple and how it has been stored.

'The Golden Delicious, for example, has been cultivated because it is wrinkle and blemish free, but no consideration at all was given to its nutritional value. The idea of a combination of taste and nutrition has been absolutely ignored, it isn't on the agenda. The Golden Delicious is on the low edge. So it is difficult to know you are eating a balanced diet.'

For this reason he has his own top-up list, and every day he consumes regular vitamin and mineral supplements: Vitamins A, C and E, which play a key role in the functioning of the immune system, and selenium and beta carotene.

Scientists and nutritionists who rather scoff at health food shops for pandering to hypochondriacs don't quarrel with his choice, though many would argue that you should get sufficient of these vitamins from a varied and balanced diet – fruit, vegetables, dairy foods and bread.

'Bread *should* have enough Selenium but it's lacking in a lot of British-grown flour,' says Hanssen. He feels comfortable in health food shops in spite of what some people might consider bizarre products – ginseng, royal jelly, pollen, essence of green-lipped mussels. 'I'd rather walk round a health food shop than a sweet shop or a cigarette and tobacco shop,' he retorts. 'Most of the best medicines are psychosomatic. Most of the products do something which is harmless. Isn't it better to take possibly cranky but mostly innocent health products than to go to a doctor who tells you to bugger off and take a Valium? The people who run the shops are nice (well, some can be appalling) but most of them are very caring. I remember the case of a health food shop running an incentive scheme for staff, and when the winner was announced, he said he didn't want it – "Give it to Charity". People who staff these shops are usually very concerned for their customers, they have time for them.'

Millions of happy customers prove the satisfaction these stores give, and there's no more shining example than the irrepressible and bouncy musical star, Toyah Wilcox, in her thirties but as spirited as a teenager. The Heath and Heather health store chain published an interview with her in their house magazine, *Health Today*, in which she detailed a shopping spree in a local health store.

She is a vegan, with a great dependence on organic produce, which her gardener grows, and she enjoys cauliflower and spinach. Carrots with lemon juice are late-night snacks, followed by fresh fruit, nuts, and dried fruit, unsulphured of course.

She takes vitamin supplements, stressing that what's beneficial for her might not be for others: she trusts Cantamega 2000, and Healthcrafts Mega B Complex, and Efamol evening primrose oil capsules (she finds they help with pre-menstrual tension), and to counteract constipation during her periods she takes Ortisan which is 'fabulously gentle'.

She has a sweet tooth, so she snacks on Food Watch's dairy-free chocolate beans, and a couple of Panda licorice bars.

Toyah gave up a daily ration of eight strong cups of coffee a day because they made her shaky, cut down to one, and drinks herbal or fruit tea every half-hour, such as Heath and Heather's lemon verbena, Salus Haus' Sunrise, and Pompadour's peppermint tea.

She gave up alcohol several years ago (she says she enjoys conversation too much to want it to be clouded by drink), and turns to Aqua Libra, the non-alcoholic sparkling herbal fruit drink, which she merely sips as it is very sweet and irritates her teeth.

To counter stress, which is a considerable problem in her line of work, she uses homeopathic remedies. Stress led to regular colds, which have more or less gone since she started taking Gelsemium, which she has with a Vitamin C tablet every hour when she does get a cold, 'until the body's immune system returns to normal'. She takes Lane's Intacept supplement which she says controls apathy, the result of her frequent tiredness.

For three weeks in the year Toyah cuts out processed foods to eat only, raw, organic food, accompanied by a spoonful of Psyllium Husks (herbal bran), a quarter of a teaspoon of Probion (intestinal gut flora supplement), a tumbler of water with a colonite tablet (a herbal cleansing prepartion) which 'gently scrapes the intestines clean'.

That, in a nutshell, is what makes the teasingly tempestuous Toyah tick.

As we look back, we find that food's mystical and magical qualities have always had quasi-religious significance, from bread, the staff of life, in Western society, to maize as a corn god among Central American Indians, and rice in Buddhist and Eastern cultures.

American Indians regarded maize as central to their understanding of the world, and the six colours of the main varieties of the grain represented the six points of the compass: North was red maize, South black, West yellow, East Blue; 'Up' was white, while 'Down', the nether world, was variegated corn.

In Japan rice was considered 'the most sacred thing on earth' next to the Emperor. It is a fertility symbol (which is why it is thrown at weddings – confetti is its shoddy technological replacement) and the subject of numerous religious myths.

And, of course, as well as myth, foods have been the stuff of black magic, and the casting of spells, none more memorable than the brew prepared by the three witches in *Macbeth*, a stew of dog's tongue, frog's toes, lizard's leg, owl's wing, shark's maw, goat's liver, newt's eye, bat's wool, grass snake, blind-worm, adder's fangs, yew and hemlock. (Do not exceed the stated dose).

In mediaeval times, the basis of medicine was the study of 'Humours'. Following the teachings of Hippocrates, 500 years before Christ, Greek, Roman and later mediaeval doctors attributed to food characteristics which could influence equally the body and the mind. The Doctrine of Humours was based on the four elements, Fire, Earth, Water and Air which were represented as Hot, Dry, Moist and Cold. A combination of two elements represented a Complexion, which had its own Humour. So a Sanguine Complexion (red-faced, robust, hearty, quick-tempered) was due to Hot and Moist qualities (Fire and Water). Phlegm was the Humour for those of Phlegmatic Complexion (Cold and Moist), bile for Choleric Complexion (Hot and Dry), black bile for the Melancholic (Cold and Dry). Much was left to the interpretation and intuition of the doctor who would decide if one Humour was affecting another, in which case the appropriate foodstuffs would be recommended or discouraged. Foods were classed by the same four elements. Lamb was Moist and unsuited to old people who were considered too Phlegmatic already. Cabbage was Hot in the first degree, Cold in the second. Lettuce was Cold and Moist.

Laughable? The theories were based on a mixture of experience and intuition, and in that respect no sillier than many of our nutritional beliefs today, equally based on applied science and imaginative interpretation.

By the seventeenth century Nicholas Culpeper was able to amass a compendium of medicinal remedies derived from his Complete Herbal listing – 400-odd herbs and plants and their medicinal properties. His appendix included an alphabetical list of 'all human diseases' with the names of the herbs that will cure them. Cures are offered for baldness (Walnut, Yarrow), mad dog bites (Angelica, Gentian, Mint), blood in urine (Comfrey), cramp (Camomile, Mustard, Penny Royal), dandruff (Beets, Willow-tree), drowsiness (Rosemary), fainting (Honeysuckle, Lavender), forgetfulness (Water Lily), freckles (Cucumber), Haemorrhoids (Privet, Tamarisk tree), King's Evil (Golden Rod, Mistletoe, Tansy, Sage), melancholy (Cabbage, Feverfew, Herb Robert), swooning (Lavender, Penny Royal), toothache (Hyssop, Mulberry tree, Wild poppy), warts (Black poplar, Buckthorn, Celandine), wind-breaking (Bay, Dill, Angelica, Rosemary), worms (Mustard, Peach tree, Hemp, Walnuts).

These may seem no more strange than the ingredients of remedies offered in today's health foods and tisanes. We shouldn't scoff at the claims of magical and mystical properties in these herbs, as many of them have been subsumed into the modern pharmacist's craft. Indeed the Foxglove and Deadly Nightshade provide two very important drugs which have had a significant role in the treatment of heart disease, though they are deadly in large doses.

The early nineteenth century welcomed the arrival of nutrition as a modern science, and from this time on the twin religions of wholefoodism and healthfoodism have travelled parallel, but contrary, paths.

A French chemist, Antoine Lavoisier, was first to establish that life was a chemical function and he invented the word 'oxidation' to describe the body's process of burning up the chemicals in the food we consume. Until this time the essence of food was simply understood to be 'nutrament'.

The German chemist, Justus von Liebig, set up the foundation of our present understanding and with his students eventually established the three main components of nutrition we know today: proteins, initially named albuminosa (we still speak of the albumen in egg, the white of egg which is protein); carbohydrates, first called saccharina, acknowledging that they convert to sugars in the body; and fats, which they categorised as oleosa. Liebig and his pupils went on to determine the different roles of each of these basic substances, and their experiments isolated the building blocks in proteins, some sixteen amino acids, and eventually the Vita Amines of life itself, vitamins.

Among other things, Liebig applied his scientific discoveries to evolving a beef extract, and from this moment the modern food industry was on its way. Louis Pasteur had already established the principle of heat treatment to sterilise. As science lent its strength to the Industrial Revolution in Europe, a strong reaction developed among those who saw old values being swept away. The writer William Cobbett in his famous social study of England's cottage economy in 1821 was dismayed at the way the basic cornerstones of country life were being destroyed as new, inferior factory produce started to replace good, home-grown food. He deplored the widespread introduction of tea, an unnecessary drug, which, unlike beer, contained nothing nutritious and produced want of sleep and weakened the nerves. Industrial beer, with its additives and adulterations had replaced home-brewed beer which had been killed off by punitive taxes on malt, the basic ingredient. And bread baked at home was beginning to be replaced by commercial bread from town and city bakers, who gave in to the irresistible temptation to increase profits by dropping standards, taking short cuts and, indeed, simply cheating. It angered Cobbett that the labourer should be reduced to spending his wages on bread from a baker's shop. He evoked a picture, as beautifully as any Victorian painter, of the wholesome sight of a pretty woman heating her oven and setting in her bread. And if the effort 'does make the sign of labour glisten on her brow, where is the man that would not kiss that off, rather than lick the plaster from the cheek of a duchess?'

The poet Percy Bysshe Shelley embraced vegetarianism as an expression of the Natural Life, and pointed out that the Bible and French mythology suggested that man was a herbivore. He claimed that there was 'no disease, bodily or mental, which adoption of a vegetable diet and pure water has not infallibly mitigated.'

It was in America in the middle of the nineteenth century that food reform assumed the evangelistic fervour we know today, starting with a Presbyterian preacher, Dr Sylvester Graham, who gives his name to Graham flour (wholemeal flour). He managed to convey the notion that white flour was evil and wholegrain Godly. He said that those who removed the bran from the grain during milling were pulling asunder what God had joined together. But his personal view that wholemeal bread was able to remove disorders and prevent disease is a theory that continues to excite a certain band of scientists and gave us the dietary fibre revolution of the 1970s and 1980s.

Graham inspired the invention by James C. Jackson of the first modern breakfast cereal, Granula, which was made by baking wholemeal flour and water paste until it went hard, breaking it up and baking it again, crushing the pieces into even smaller bits. It needed to be soaked overnight in milk before you could eat it.

In England Dr Thomas Allinson, the Victorian pioneer of medicine and nutrition, took the extraordinary step in 1895 of buying his own flour mills to mill stoneground flour, founding the Natural Food Company, which was later named Allinson's. (It is now the largest millers of stoneground flour in Europe.) He gave social as well as health reasons for eating wholemeal bread: 'The rich should eat it so that it may carry off some of their superfluous foods and drinks. And the poor must eat it, then they will not need to buy so much fresh foods and other expensive articles of diet. If a law could be passed forbidding the separation of the bran from the fine flour it would add very greatly to the health and wealth of our nation, and lessen considerably the receipts of the publican, tobacconist, chemist, dentist, doctor or undertaker.' He added zealously: 'To banish the white flour loaf from his home is the duty of every good citizen.'

Then came the Kellogg brothers, expounding further religious, wholefood theories, and making their name synonymous with breakfast cereal. They came from a Seventh Day Adventist family who ran a sanatorium in Michigan. Dr John Harvey Kellogg was the director – and the inventor of cornflakes, an idea which apparently came to him in a dream. His brother Will saw the invention through the development stage, producing the flattened flake by accident, after boiling the grain too long, but liking the result when it was rolled out. Will broke up with his brother, and decided to promote the product through advertising – and the rest is as much a story of American advertising as it is of a novel foodstuff.

John Harvey Kellogg was remembered instead for his passionate devotion to the cause of the wholegrain and its importance in the diet as 'roughage'. It would prompt three bowel movements a day, accelerating the processes of the digestive system and speeding up the elimination of toxic elements. He put a strong case for vegetarianism, regarding meat as a second- or third-hand product in that animals have already processed the vegetable matter. He stated that there was nothing of nutritional significance in meat or fish that couldn't be derived from vegetable products.

But cereals weren't the only foods invested with special powers. In the Balkans, yogurt enjoyed the reputation of contributing to beaming good health and long life. This piece of folklore was given credence in 1904 by the Russian Nobel prize winner, Ilya Metchnikoff, of the Pasteur Institute in Paris, who declared that the live bacteria in yogurt drive out harmful 'putrefactive' bacteria which weaken the higher elements in the body. Metchnikoff believed it illustrated the perversity and imperfection of Nature, and that our colon, designed to handle bulky plant foods, was useful for animals but useless in man, making a home for millions of bacteria which have nothing to do but produce toxins, which gradually poison us. He argued that yogurt's acidity (from the lactic acid) would kill off unwelcome bacteria (as would the acidity of sauerkraut, pickles and sour milk). It became an enormously popular theory – creating the momentum which eventually launched sweetened fruit yogurts as an everyday children's food, tasty, nutritious – but incapable of colonising the colon with user-friendly bacteria, as it's now known that Lactobacillus bulgaricus do not survive in the gut!

The search to identify the secret of long life was on, and the focus swung to Switzerland in the 1920s where Dr Max Bircher-Benner laid down his famous dietary principles which advocated that at least half the daily diet should be raw food. He threw in cereals and yogurt but the eating of meat was discouraged. Fresh, vital, raw foods, he argued, restore the conditions essential to life. 'It may be because such nutrition is the ancient and original food of man, for the absorption of which our organism was primarily constructed.' Like others before him he deplored the 'devitalisation' of over-processed foods on the grounds that they were far from their natural state, and also blamed over-rich foods, which between them over-stimulated the nervous system with the help of toxins such as tea and coffee, cocoa and chocolate, cola drinks, alcohol and tobacco.

The central tenet of Dr Bircher-Benner's religion was muesli – his own invention. It was adapted in part from basic traditional gruels (Scottish porridge made with oats, Old English frumenty made with wheat) with the essential addition of freshly grated raw fruit; (it was an article of faith that raw food should be consumed at the beginning of every meal). He regarded muesli as a prescription rather than a recipe, to give the best balance of nutrients, and at his clinic above Zurich it was referred to as 'The Dish'.

Its fame spread far and wide and it became known as 'the epitome' of nutrition. People in France would ask for 'Un Birche'; Henry Ford became a devotee; and in England it became known as a Swiss Breakfast.

Like yogurt, it has become a fashionable mass-produced item, far, far from its honest intentions.

Godliness (not the consumption of dried grass) was also behind the Hay diet. Dr William Howard Hay's diet, first produced in 1927, doesn't mix acids with starches at the same meal, his theory being that the digestion process is alkaline and the consumption of acid fruit will immediately stop the process, causing fermentation of undigested starches and internal poisoning. It's supported by few nutritionists today, but it carried weight with some of Dr Hay's readers of a Biblical disposition. He advised them not to buy food which hadn't been 'outlined by God to Adam and Eve in the Garden of Eden'.

The 1920s were of great significance in nutrition, bringing the discovery of the functions of almost all the vitamins, and the understanding of deficiency in each of them, in various kinds of illness, from vitamin C (whose lack is responsible for scurvy, a disease which turns the lips and mouth purple and sore. It could kill from malnutrition, and afflicted sailors far from fresh foods: the practice of giving sailors lemons and limes gave the Englishmen his sobriquet 'Limey'.

Deficiency of vitamins B (now referred to as a complex as there are a group associated with the same dietary factors) was found to be responsible for illness and death in the Dutch East Indies from pellagra and beri-beri. Vitamin B is present in the skin of rice, which was being lost in the rice polishing process, in other words, in the production of a more cosmetic and pleasing product, as with white flour, where B vitamins are lost during the refining process. But no need to worry. The B vitamin family is readily available in meat, fish, milk, cheese and vegetables.

Vitamin A deficiency affects sight, and blindness occurs in India where there's a lack of milk, liver and green vegetables in the diet.

Vitamin D deficiency affects the growth of bones – but fortunately it's generated by sunlight (in a good year) as well as being available in margarine, eggs and oily fish.

Vitamin E deficiency leads to anaemia but we get enough from cereals and egg, and vitamin K is involved in blood clotting (but it's in most vegetables and cereals).

The horror of what happens if you have a deficiency in vitamins gradually led to the development in vitamin supplements – and along with these studies followed research into the many minerals and trace elements, into their composition and what role they might play. Accordingly the understanding of what happens if there is a deficiency of minerals such as iron, calcium, magnesium, phosphorous, potassium, or trace elements such as zinc, selenium, manganese, iodine, fluorine, copper, cobalt and chromium, prompts a vast commercial enterprise selling you 'insurance' cover that you don't want, but that salesmen convince you that you do.

Post-War food fads have been changing steadily, perhaps not as quickly as designer fashion, but there's a parallel, because every new fashion reflects an old one. The pendulum swings backwards and forwards. Today we look with suspicion on 'convenience food', and believe in the merits of 'inconvenience food', which we have to buy freshly and often, and take trouble to prepare ourselves. But this enthusiasm was just as passionate in the last century.

Today we are concerned, as we were in the past, about the conditions in which animals and poultry are reared, and we worry about the safety aspects of taking food on the long road down the 'food chain', from farm to factory, from supermarket to home.

For much of this century it has been the vegetarians who have used moral force to promote healthier eating. For this, they have been frequently held up to ridicule by the meat-eating establishment – from the Bloomsbury set, who frequented the first vegetarian restaurant in London (Shearns in Tottenham Court Road, a former greengrocers), to George Bernard Shaw and Stafford Cripps. Many a writer had cheap fun at their expense, as George Orwell did when he poured scorn on the Fabians, sneering at these sandal-wearing socialists who had forsaken red meat for vegetables. Even today Prince Charles can expect to get some stick from carnivorous columnists in the press because of his fondness for organic vegetables.

If British vegetarians come over as weak-kneed and lily-livered, the Americans in contrast manage themselves vigorously and robustly. One star of the day was the charismatic Dr Gayelord Hauser, beautician and dietitian, whose evangelistic philosophy was summed up by the title of his famous book, *Look Younger, Live Longer*. 'The Gayelord Hauser notion of Vitality Foods described some foods, often vegetarian ones, with a particular oomph in them.' Gayelord Hauser's faith was founded on Five Wonder Foods: Brewer's yeast, powdered skimmed milk, yogurt, wheatgerm and black treacle. They contributed to your well-being by providing essential proteins, all the B vitamins, calcium, iron and ample other minerals. He offered a Live Longer Reducing Ritual, a daily boost when you are slimming. One fish liver oil capsule, one vitamin C tablet, one wheatgerm capsule, six standard yeast tablets.

Hauser was superseded by Adelle Davis who became the American queen of diet, author of many bestsellers, awesome in their comprehensive range and detail, pursuing the story of vitamins and minerals as the key to the healthy life. She promoted offal energetically as a valuable dietary source – known unfashionably in the States as 'organ meats'.

In Britain, the vegetarian movement became self-consciously fashionable at the beginning of the 1960s when David and Kay Canter and Daphne Swann opened one of the first vegetarian restaurants in London, Cranks, defiantly intellectual middle class, with menus elaborated in elegant italic script, plates and pottery bowls hand-thrown by middle class country craftsmen, the materials likewise woven on middle class looms. But the rough country food (as was never eaten in the rough country) was an appealing alternative to industrial food which had sunk to an unthinkable low – plastic white bread, sausages with no real meat, beer which was being made by machines and very badly.

In America the health food movement gathered force when the 1960s embraced macrobiotic food as a way of life along with Flower Power. It was brought to Britain by two Americans, Craig and Greg Sams, who started Seed, a wholefood restaurant, in London in 1967, the hippies' Summer of Love. It led in 1970 to them setting up Harmony Foods, the first wholesale wholefood business; and following that the Ceres Bakery to sell wholemeal bread. Their view that bread should be pure was monastic, depending on a Holy Trinity of flour, yeast and salt.

The macrobiotic diet is based on the yin-yang principles in Zen Buddhism, made famous in a diet book by George Ohsawa, which suggest the body's alkali-acid balance can be achieved by a diet which is essentially grain, and specifically brown rice. (Among extreme practitioners, this led to illness such as scurvy and anaemia because grains are not complete protein, and are deficient in some essential vitamins and minerals.)

At the same time Jordan's, independent millers who'd refused to sell out to the big three companies which had a virtual monopoly of milling and baking, joined the wholefood battle, adding to their wholemeal flour range a new alternative cereal from whole grain, Original Crunchy, achieving national recognition for this kind of lifestyle, by removing the idea that it was 'alternative'.

Behind the continuing story of health foods and wholefoods, there's usually a common thread, the changing attitude towards meat. In a country where every soul has considered 'Meat and Two Veg' as the definition of a sound, nutritional meal and is affluent enough to be able to afford it, it's surprising to find that the

vegetarians are gaining ground. All the traditional stances are shift-
ing, on health grounds, ethical, religious, even on aesthetic grounds.
A recent figure puts the number of vegetarians at three million. Less
meat is being bought from butchers, although more meat products
are being eaten in the form of processed meat, such as burgers.

The 1990s will see the continuing growth of the ethical vegetarian,
represented by figures such as Colin Spencer, who became a vegetarian in 1974 because of famine in the Third World. He is author
of many books on vegetarian eating, and a past chairman of the
Guild of Food Writers. He also voices a repugnance towards the
killing of animals, and especially the horrors of factory farming.

He promotes the pragmatic view that we could help the Third
World more if we were to feed the world's grain directly to those
who need it, instead of processing it first, uneconomically, through
the agency of cows, pigs and chickens. 'Producing meat is an
inefficient method of feeding a population. One acre of soya beans
will enable one person to live for five years, while the same acre of
barley fed to a beef steer would enable one person to live for only
four months.'

His view that world hunger stems from the self-interest of
multinational companies is gaining ground; he describes it as a
'wasteful and selfish system to the detriment of the poor and the
benefit of their own profits.'

It's a measure of the public's approval of ecological policies that
Colin Spencer, unlike many vegetarians who have gone before him,
is in no way seen as a crank. In fact, it's those who don't think we
should move towards the Greening of the Planet who are regarded
as the cranks. 'I still believe, against much evidence to the contrary,'
he says, 'that homo sapiens grows a little more civilised as the human
race becomes older. There can be no doubt that the vegetable way
of life is the most civilised today. It is also the most inexpensive and
practical for today's needs.'

HEALTH FOOD GUIDE

Although wholefood and health food shops cater largely for vegetarians, nutritionists wholeheartedly praise the benefits of the freshness and quality of many of their goods – even if they doubt the

need to buy vitamin preparations as health insurance. Indeed an excess of some vitamins can lead to toxicity.

When the shouting dies down, and all the advertisers of vitamin and mineral supplements have had their say, what is the serious nutritionist's view? Simply, that fresh food is the best health food.

In a balanced diet, largely unrefined carbohydrates such as wholemeal bread, pasta, rice, porridge and potatoes, supported by sparing amounts of meat, fish, cheese and eggs, bulked out by plenty of vegetables and fruit – all the vitamins and minerals we need will be supplied.

But, first, how much protein, carbohydrates and fat do we need for a balanced diet?

PROTEIN. Most of us in Britain eat two or three times as much as we need, although growing children and expectant mothers need more because of their special demands. Our body is made up of protein, our muscles, blood cells, even our skin, teeth and bones. As they are worn away we need more protein to replace the losses. When we eat more protein than we need for this purpose it is converted in the body into fat. What a waste!

Protein consists of twenty amino acids, and the body can synthesise all but eight, which are therefore known as the 'Eight Essential amino acids' and we have to provide them via our diet. They are – for the record: isoleucine, leucine, lysine, methionine, phenylalanine, threonine, tryptophan, valine. Foodstuffs vary in their volume of useful amino acids. Meat, eggs, milk products are complete proteins, and the soybean is nearly complete. Most plant protein lacks a full range of amino acids, but pulses, wholegrains and nuts have a reasonable amount. Vegetarians can only avoid a deficiency by balancing foods which have different amino acids in their protein, like baked beans on toast (where the protein is in the pulses and the wheat) or macaroni and cheese. Small amounts of meat do the same for demi-vegetarians, like spaghetti Bolognese with its small contribution of meat or lasagne with its meat and cheese sauce.

The World Health Organisation suggests 40 grammes of protein is the adequate daily need. As the actual protein content is roughly a fifth of the weight of rump steak, chops or liver, about half a pound of meat protein will do. But wheat has protein and so does white bread (as much as wholemeal) so a one pound loaf yields as much protein as the half-pound steak, although not of such good quality. Six ounces of cheese on its own provides our dietary need – or twelve ounces of fish; or three eight-ounce cans of baked beans; or two pints of milk; or six eggs; or five pounds of new potatoes (old ones have less protein).

It's easy to work out what modest quantities of each of these familiar daily foods should give us all we need. For example forty grams of protein is acquired from a combination of, say: two ounces fish, one ounce meat, two ounces bread, three ounces beans, and one egg, and one quarter pint of milk.

CARBOHYDRATES. Potatoes, wholemeal bread, breakfast cereals, pasta and rice are our main sources of unrefined carbohydrate, as well as fruit and vegetables. Processed carbohydrates include white bread and cakes and biscuits, and everything which has sugar in it, or sugar syrup, such as desserts, ice creams, sweets, sweet drinks such as squashes and colas, and sweetened foods such as yogurts and mueslis.

In the Western world carbohydrate represents about 40 per cent of the daily diet, but in the rest of the world it's around twice as much.

Advertisers claim that sugar provides energy but they are not alone in this. All carbohydrates provide energy and so do proteins and fats. But carbohydrate happens to be the principle source of the energy which makes our cells function.

Carbohydrates are divided into starches and sugars. (Starches convert to sugars when they are cooked, which is why raw onion becomes sweet when it is fried, and why barley can be made into sweet wort which can then be fermented into ale). The sugars in fruits and vegetables are glucose, dextrose and fructose (table sugar is sucrose). But starch or sugar, it doesn't matter to the human digestion, which immediately converts them all to glucose which is rushed round the bloodstream to service the cells, and particularly to supply the brain and nervous system which can only run on glucose.

If the body can't get enough carbohydrate it begins to metabolise fats which can unbalance the acid balance. And when the body doesn't have fat reserves, as in the case of about 1,000 million people in the Third World, severe malnutrition ensues, and tissues begin to waste. In the Western world, when sufficient carbohydrates have been consumed to put the system in running order, the remainder are stored – as fat.

A small amount of excess carbohydrate is stored as glycogen, which has prompted athletes to feast on carbohydrates the day before an event to build up an excess to burn off in the race. This will delay the moment when the body starts to burn up other resources which impair the body when they are used up. (Pure sugar, refined carbohydrate, gives us energy devoid of nutrients, and overloads the body's regulatory system because it goes into the blood system at once.)

How much carbohydrate suits your needs depends on age, size, sex, rate of activity, energetic or sedentary lifestyle: say 2,500 calories for a man, 2,000 for a woman, rising to 5,000 and more for athletes and energetic manual workers. But excess will show on the scales.

The amount of energy you use, or burn up, can be measured in calories. Any that are not used are stored as fat, so the aim is to average out at a preferred regular weight. Carbohydrate gives you a satisfying amount of bulk, and less calories weight-for-weight than fats.

For example, four ounces of most cereals, rice, pasta are around 400 calories, more than meat or fish, but less than butter, which is nearly 900 calories for four ounces.

FAT. Fat is *the* problem in western diets, and we eat too much saturated fat, beef and lamb fat, lard, butter, cream, eggs and some vegetable oils (the ones that solidify such as palm oil and coconut oil). Fats contribute two-fifths of our daily calorie intake in the Western world, compared with one-tenth in the rest of the world.

Saturated fats are linked to heart disease but, whether saturated or unsaturated, they make the heartiest contribution to obesity, especially as they are usually enormously pleasing to gourmets and gourmands alike, delicious, smooth, comforting, filling. Think only of foie gras, sauce Bearnaise, Belgian chocolates. All the fat we eat which is excess to daily calorie needs is stored as fat which is undesirable today, but in pre-civilisation the fat man and woman would have had a better chance of survival.

A pound of butter or dripping provides a colossal 3,600 calories. Affluent man takes aboard about 1,000 calories in fat daily, five ounces, while the recommended amount would be 150 calories, the equivalent of three quarters of an ounce. This sounds easier to follow than it is, because much of the fat in our food is 'hidden' in pastry, cakes, ice cream and processed meats.

The good news is that some fats and acids contain essential fatty acids, such as linoleic, which convert into phospholipids. The body cannot synthesise them but they are essential to our diet, servicing brain cells, our nervous system, and the liver. They are present in olive oil, sunflower oil, and oily fish in particular.

CHOLESTEROL. Not a fat, though it leaves deposits on the walls of our blood vessels, and therefore causes circulation problems. It is a substance made in our own bodies which manages our sex hormones and bile salts. Unfortunately we consume foods which contain cholesterol and the body finds it difficult to secrete the excess. We also manufacture extra cholesterol when we are under stress – but it's thought it can only contribute to heart disease if there is a history of it in the family. Your doctor can advise.

High cholesterol foods include lobster and other shell-fish, foie gras and other liver, and eggs.

VITAMINS

Vitamin A (Retinol). You definitely shouldn't overdose on this one. It is a fat-soluble vitamin, like vitamins D, E and K, which build up in body tissue and eventually reach toxic levels, causing giddiness and headaches, aches in the bones, and loss of hair.

In the normal quantities it promotes a healthy skin and good eyesight in poor light. British fighter pilots credited their early successes in the last War to eating carrots, a propaganda device to conceal the fact that we had evolved radar.

Best sources are liver, eggs, cheese and vegetables. The darkest green leaves contain the most carotenoids, more than carrots, the most cited source. Everyone who trains as a nutritionist learns of Basil Brown, who in 1974 drank a gallon of carrot juice a day for ten days, turned yellow, and died of liver damage.

Vitamin B1 (Thiamine). A key vitamin which services the body by harnessing the energy in protein, carbohydrate and fat. Without adequate amounts, muscle and tissue run down, leading to fatigue and loss of weight, and emotional strain. Serious deficiency leads to muscular degeneration and emaciation as in the case of beri-beri, a disease which became widespread in South East Asia in the nineteenth century with the introduction of refined, polished rice. The B vitamins which are close to the husk were being milled away. Fortunately we get plenty in a balanced diet, as good sources of thiamine include pork, liver, cereals, peas, beans, peanuts and skimmed milk.

Vitamin B2 (Riboflavin). Deficiency of vitamin B is as common among the very poor of the Western world as those of the Third World. Signs are tiredness in the eyes and skin problems such as dermatitis.

The average family gets sufficient from a daily milk ration (it's in skimmed milk so you don't need the cream), from cheese, eggs, liver and meat.

Vitamin B3 (Nicotinic acid – abbreviated to niacin). This vitamin is absolutely necessary for the good function of every cell in the body, and a deficiency causes pellagra which can be a fatal disease. This occurs in Third World countries where maize is a staple food because, although the corn contains niacin, it doesn't release it for human digestion. The disease was pervasive in the cotton-picking fields of the Southern States, where its debilitating effects of mental confusion and degeneration were blamed on the weak character of the slaves. The physical manifestation is rough skin (pellagra is the Italian word for it because North Italians whose diet was mostly maize flour, polenta, were the first Europeans to suffer from it).

Fortunately a varied diet supplies ample niacin, from meat, chicken, fish (the best source), milk, cheese, eggs, bread, and even vegetables.

Vitamin B6 (Pyridoxine). Immensely important role in metabolising protein and converting glycogen as a short term reserve. As we need only two milligrams a day, deficiency is not a problem, and it's freely available in meat, fish, eggs, cereals and green vegetables.

Vitamin B12 (Cobalamin). Although only a few millionths of a gramme are required daily some macrobiotics don't get enough, which leads to problems with the digestive tract and spinal column.

In special cases where a person has a defect in their mechanism, and can't absorb this vitamin, it causes anaemia.

The macrobiotic who includes eggs in their diet can overcome this: yeast extract is a good source, as well as meat and liver.

Vitamin B family – Folic Acid. This aids the synthesis of haemoglobin in red blood cells. Serious deficiency leads to mild anaemia. A deficiency can also be responsible for digestion problems and in expectant mothers it can cause abnormality in the foetus.

The name folic comes from the Latin word for a leaf, indicating that green vegetables are the richest source of the vitamin. Also present in a varied diet of peas and beans, bread, offal and bananas.

Vitamin B family – Pantothenic Acid. It effects the release of energy from carbohydrates and fats but is unknown to be deficient in anyone's diet as it's freely available from meat and vegetables and cereals.

Vitamin B family – Biotin. This vitamin metabolises fat and carbohydrate and deficiencies have not been observed. Egg yolks and offal are particularly rich sources.

Vitamin C (Ascorbic Acid). The best known vitamin, partly due to the efforts of Dr Linus Pauling, the Nobel Prize winner, who championed it as a contender to prevent the common cold; it is bought in vast quantities in this belief, but twenty years after he made the claim there is little scientific evidence to support it. However, it is a desperately important vitamin, and deficiency leads to scurvy, and indeed damage to the whole body. It's important in sustaining the body's connective tissue, and acts as an anti-oxidant in the body, a function it also enjoys as an additive in food processing. Dr Pauling insists there is no such thing as an overdose, as the body secretes it freely, but pregnant mothers are advised not to take vitamin C supplements because it can affect new-born children who start life with an unrealistically high need for the vitamin and can get scurvy if that level isn't maintained.

Vitamin D. A key vitamin in giving strength to bones by mobilising calcium. A deficiency can cause rickets, which can deform young children when they are learning to walk. It is fat-soluble and cannot be secreted by the body. It's important to guard against an overdose, which can lead to damage of the kidney, stomach and blood vessels.

As well as from dietary sources (oily fish, mackerel, herring, sardines, eggs, margarine and liver) the body can make its own vitamin D from sunlight, the ultra-violet light activating a substance in our skins. People who don't see the sun in wintry northern cities and have a bad diet are at the same risk, the old as much as the young.

Vitamin E (Tocopherol). Experiments with rats have suggested this vitamin is important in the reproduction process, but this hasn't proved to be so in research into humans, so it's not the Virility Vitamin which is one claim made for it. A deficiency can lead to anaemia, but an excess can affect the body's hormonal system and produce tiredness.

Vitamin K. This has an important role in blood-clotting, but deficiency is rare except in new-born babies. Green vegetables are a ready source, but vitamin K is also a product of certain bacteria in the gut, so it's just possible temporarily to wipe out these friendly germs with a blast of antibiotics.

MINERALS

There are six which are essential to our health.

Potassium. Helps to balance fluids in the body. A deficiency can make the heart weak but is extremely rare as we have more than enough in meat, cereals, potatoes, vegetables and especially in citrus fruit and bananas.

Magnesium. Important for our bones and muscles, and readily available in most items of diet – dairy foods, cereals, green vegetables, peas, beans, and nuts.

Phosphorous. Active in all our cells, and especially important for teeth and bones. It is obtained from proteins such as meat and milk, as well as cereals.

Sulphur. A vital constituent in the amino acids in hair, nails, skin and connective tissues, as well as being an ingredient in insulin which controls blood sugar levels. Meat and pulses are rich in sulphur.

Calcium. Hugely important in maintaining strength of bones and teeth, which might seem permanent enough, but this is not the case and calcium levels have to be maintained or our whole framework is weakened. This is why some older people are vulnerable to broken bones. Calcium aids blood clotting, and keeps the muscle cells in good shape. It's especially important for growing children and expectant mothers.

Milk is a key source of calcium, along with cheese, yogurt, bread, sardines, and watercress. So is hard water from the tap.

Iron. Important for good condition of blood cells and muscle, and a deficiency leads to anaemia and tiredness.

Although our bodies can store iron for future use, we are less efficient at absorbing this mineral than the other key ones, and many people are victims of this condition without being aware of it. We get iron from meats and offal, leafy vegetables, grain, pulses, eggs, bread, and curry powder. And, surprisingly, we can get a huge source of dietary iron from cooking in old fashioned pots and pans. In one experiment with a meat and tomato sauce, cooking it in an iron pot yielded up to a hundred times more iron, dissolved by the acid from the tomato.

Wholemeal enthusiasts may know that phytic acid in the outer skin of their beloved grain binds the calcium and prevents it being absorbed in the body. And spinach, claimed to put iron into Popeye's muscles, denies him calcium for his bones because the oxalic acid in the leaves combines with it to make it unavailable.

Salt (Sodium Chloride). Without salt we die, but it's in every food in its natural state without us needing to add any from the salt cellar. It's essential in controlling the fluids in our body. Our problem is not getting enough, but having too much because we like the taste so much. Too much salt leads to hypertension and high blood pressure.

TRACE MINERALS

There are eight which are essential:

Zinc. A key mineral, aiding the function of enzymes, and con-centrated in the liver, kidney, pancreas and brain. Zinc is in most foods, especially meat.

Fluorine. Strengthens the enamel on teeth and slows the loss of calcium from the bones. Extremely large consumption can cause the teeth to become mottled, inflaming the debate of whether it should be compulsorily added to drinking water and toothpaste in order to protect children's teeth. In low doses it is satisfactory. So fluorine is in tapwater, but fish-bones and tea-leaves are other sources.

Copper. Vital function in the liver and brain, but deficiency is rare because it is in most foods. An excess of copper can cause damage to the liver, kidney and brain, so cooking acidic food like fruit in unlined or damaged copper utensils is dangerous.

Iodine. Controls the production of energy in all our cells and influ-ences the whole of our well-being. A deficiency of iodine leads to an enlarged thyroid gland, a disease called goitre. A serious deficiency in pregnancy can lead to mental and physical disabilities in the new-born child. Iodine is in fish, fruit and vegetables. It is only in some mountainous inland areas of the world that there isn't sufficient iodine available for dietary needs, and serious deficiencies occur.

Cobalt. Is allied to the function of vitamin B12, and is available in meat and yeast extracts.

Chromium. Helps the metabolism of fats and sugars. Cereals and fruits are the main sourse.

Selenium. Aids the function of vitamin E. It is found in most foods.

Manganese. Helps the function of the enzymes which break down fats, carbohydrates and proteins. Found in cereals and nuts.

12

IRRADIATION

In countries which have permitted the sale of irradiated foods, they have used a jolly green symbol, indicating an emerging green plant, radiating sunshine, labelled RADURA, the emblem of quality. In Britain critics of the process, who are numerous, think the Skull and Crossbones would be a more appropriate emblem.

We are the first children of the nuclear age, and many of us still don't feel we've tamed nuclear energy; we think not only of the horror of the bombs which destroyed Hiroshima and Nagasaki in 1945, but accidents at nuclear plants such as Three Mile Island in the United States and Chernobyl in Russia, which poisoned crops and made animal grazing unsafe for months. We think of safety anxieties about cancer among workers at British plants.

Radioactivity is the potent force in X-rays and is used in cancer treatments. Hence the suggestion that foodstuffs should be irradiated, to knock the living daylights out of anything in them that might breed on them and in them, beneficial organisms perishing with the potentially harmful. Doses are not high enough for radio-activity to be retained in the foods – they fade away after twenty-four hours – so there is no suggestion that irradiated food is going to make you light up and glow, or that people who've eaten irradiated food can be detected with geiger counters.

The process was actually evolved at the beginning of the century, and was permitted for use in 1916. Strawberries which had been irradiated lasted for several weeks without deteriorating, and not only was the texture not impaired, they tasted sweeter: if one ignored possible harmful effects, it seemed to be magical indeed, both preserving and improving, and conferring the added benefit that unseen germs and bacteria acquired in the food-handling processes, or by air-borne or water-borne flies, bluebottles, bugs and insects, would be destroyed into the bargain.

Given that other forms of food processing – cooking, preserving, canning and freezing – can alter flavour, colour and texture for the worse, modern science seemed to have achieved a miracle, of benefit to the consumer every bit as much as to the food industry.

But acceptance has been a long time coming, largely due to conflicting interpretations of the scientific evidence establishing its safety. The whole process still meets with tremendous consumer resistance, from the hostility of respected food authorities to the weight of influential and large organisations such as the Consumers' Associations and the Women's Institutes, The British Medical Association and others.

It is in this climate that the Government has legalised the process in the UK – bringing it into line with some thirty other countries.

The vociferous opposition comes on many fronts. There are those, such as Dr Richard Pugh, technical director of the second largest food chain, Tesco, who is not satisfied that testing is complete, and he should know as his doctorate was on the subject of gamma rays. Others, such as Dr Tim Lang and Dr Tony Webb, have written books and conducted campaigns to show that the process could be unsafe and open to abuse, and is anyway unnecessary at a time when we have too much 'technological' food, and should be eating more fresh food. And on taste grounds, as well as safety grounds, restaurant critics Egon Ronay and Drew Smith (formerly rivals as editors of the *Egon Ronay Hotel and Restaurant Guide* and *The Good Food Guide* respectively) joined forces to oppose it.

The process is a twentieth-century food manufacturer's dream. It can extend the shelf-life of berries such as strawberries and costly exotic tropical fruit such as mango by killing the enzymes which hasten the ripening process. It kills micro-organisms such as salmonella, listeria and camplylobacter in chicken and shellfish, and the bugs in spices, grain and pulses. It inhibits potatoes and onions from sprouting in storage, saving huge commercial losses. And, particularly attractive to the retail trade, it can be used to sterilise products after they have been packaged, protecting them from internal spoilage in the display cabinets, although it can't make them immune to subsequent contamination.

It can't be used to kill off salmonella and listeria in eggs or pâtés or soft cheeses, where the risk has been greatest in recent years. It can't stop botulism, the most dangerous poison that occurs in the food chain.

The biggest question about irradiation has to be on short- and long-term safety grounds. Radiation is part of our everyday lives, and we are exposed to low doses all the time, from power lines and display units on computers and televisions. High-powered radiation is represented by radio waves and micro-waves, infra-red rays, and ultra-violet light, but the most powerful forms at the upper end of the spectrum are X-rays and gamma rays from radioactive material. Radioactive bombardment generates great heat, and the energy knocks out the electrons in the foodstuff it is treating. When a molecule is broken it leaves positive and negatively charged particles called ions. At this intensity the process is called ionising irradiation, and it can make food radioactive.

When you consider the anxiety with which your dentist or hospital staff back off when they take an X-ray of your teeth or bones for fear that radioactivity might build up in them, you may wince to learn that the dose given to food is fifty million times as powerful.

Irradiation has had a bumpy passage. After making its bow in 1916, it was more or less shelved until 1953 when Dwight Eisenhower, the American President, endorsed a programme to extend the peaceful uses of nuclear power, the *Atoms for Peace Programme*.

Germany adopted irradiation for sausages and spices in 1957, but dropped it the following year, when the Soviet Union started to use it on a large scale to conserve potatoes and, a year later, their vast grain harvest. In the United States, where testing for food additives is extremely stringent, they permitted irradiation in 1963 for grain, potatoes and tinned bacon, but banned it in 1968. But now, because they have redefined irradiation as a process rather than an additive, it is escaping full scrutiny and is the subject of furious debate.

If irradiation is not defined as an additive, then it should be, say the critics, because it causes changes in foods. Some of these changes are known and have been tested. But some, like pesticide residues, have not been properly explored.

Dr Richard Pugh, chief scientist who advises Tesco, points out that there is as yet no research into the effect of these residues and he has concerns about the applications of irradiation and its potential for abuse. He explains with great clarity the complicated science involved:

'Whereas cooking is a heat-induced process which starts with physics and ends with chemistry, gamma irradiation *induces* chemistry. It is not a physical process. It is chemistry from the start and that is one of the fundamental differences between irradiation, the application of gamma irradiation, from the application of other forms of radiation, which you are more familiar with, thermal radiation, conventional cooking, infra-red grill types of convection heaters and so forth through to your microwave ovens and to radio frequency drying which is used in certain commercial processes for drying things like cereals and biscuits.

'Gamma irradiation causes chemistry by effectively splitting water molecules into very highly reactive species and, once you have generated these species, what happens next is in some way determined by the presence or absence of things *around* these highly reactive species.

'I liken it to throwing a piece of meat into a dog kennel. You are not sure which dog is going to get the meat first because there is competition for it. Depending on the presence or absence of certain compounds, materials, chemicals – call them what you will – the end result is very much determined by competition between molecules adjacent to the reactive species. So to predict the outcome is very difficult.

'Another analogy is to try to predict the outcome of a break in a snooker table – where sometimes there might be six pockets on the table, sometimes none, sometimes the cue ball might be slightly off-centre. Whatever. It is not a predictable process of chemistry. It is not easily characterised.

'In foods, the main mechanism will be by the ionisation of water and the subsequent reaction of free radicals. The food substrates or additives which may be present, the oxygen that may be adjacent to the surface of the food, they all come into play – and it is that complexity that leads me to some uncertainty about the widespread application of irradiation.'

Free radicals weren't even in the biology books a generation ago but now they are identified as starting cancers. Dr Pugh defines the free radical in this way:

'If you take a stable molecule, like the oxygen in the air wandering around, it's inactive, it's inert. One of its properties derives from the fact that the chemical structure of that molecule has not been disturbed, and it has electrons. Electrons, like people, tend to walk around in pairs. If, however, by some means you knock one of those electrons away you have left what we call an unpaired electron. A molecule with an unpaired electron is a radical, and it will desperately try to get paired again. It has this urge, an uncontrollable, overriding urge, to get this electron paired off. It will pair it off by attaching on to another molecule, creating another radical. It's a highly reactive species.

'If you have two radicals that are unpaired they will produce a stable molecule because all the radicals are paired off.

'Because they are so highly reactive, the reactions that you get depend on the environment in which they are generated. My own research was water-based systems and most of the major reactions are in the water itself, first of all to give these highly reactive species. But then they will attach themselves to anything that is dissolved in the water and initiate a whole string of chemistry. It is very easy to sidetrack it. If you have around an impurity that the radical gets to, rather than what you want it to get to, you've suddenly got a whole piece of new chemistry and a new product has been formed. You say hang on ... I don't want those. It's very easy to disturb what you think is a predictable mechanism by the presence of impurities.

'Think of fruit and vegetables. There are residues on fruit and vegetables and they are permitted to be there. But because you can't predict exactly what residues will be there, you can't predict the chemistry.

'There's no data available that takes account of the presence of pesticides on fruit and vegetables going into a radiation process. I'm not saying there is a health risk, I'm pointing out that to date no-one has addressed that aspect.'

Dr Pugh is responsible for the welfare of eight million customers who visit the company's 370 stores every week, and needs to be confident. White-coated laboratory technicians may work to impeccable standards, but ordinary supermarket staff won't know if there has been any abuse. But what if it smells and looks OK, but the spoilage is not obvious? Micro-organisms can leave behind residues which cause illness – in other words it's not the micro-organisms we have to identify and deal with, but their unnoticed residues.

'I am concerned that, as a retailer bringing in goods from all over the world, we deal at any one time with over 2,000 suppliers. I am not happy about passing control to others. Currently, I am able to verify what I need to know about food through my own resources, my own laboratories, or by contracting out work to third party organisations, research associations, public analytical laboratories. Whatever.

'But we retailers have no such means of verifying what we are told by a producer. If we had so much confidence and faith in what we are told by producers, then I would probably halve my technical resource overnight: and I don't employ 110 people because I am a philanthropist. I am in business to make money.

'I am concerned about controls. How we are going to assure ourselves that, if food is irradiated, it is done properly and well? And that the advantages supposedly accruing from that treatment are going to manifest themselves in the product?

'People have promised me extra shelf-life, so that I can keep food in ambient conditions instead of chilled conditions. It's no good me finding out later on, after a customer has been made ill, that the product wasn't correctly treated.

'So how do I know that the product has been effectively treated by ionising radiation? And how do I know that the recommended dose hasn't been exceeded? Or that someone hasn't been tempted to say "Well, if the first time wasn't enough, then let's pass it through again just to make sure"? The only way of having any control is by making good choices of suppliers.

'There are things irradiation can't do. Try to irradiate food which has high fat content! Meat products, for example, develop a wonderful odour which is generally known as 'wet-dog' .... Irradiation also accelerates rancidity in fats and can generate off-flavours. It's not, as widely believed, the panacea of all ills. It's not something that can be simply applied to all foods, the solver of all problems. There are major limitations to its potential.'

'Tesco's position is that we are not slamming the door on irradiation and saying "no" for ever more. Food irradiation could be a useful process. The benefits to manufacturers, retailers and customers could be enormous. But until we are satisfied that it can be done properly and controlled and independently monitored by a highly technical team and others, then we are saying we need to see some more work before we are able to move forward.'

Dr Pugh, forty, lives a hearty life, enjoying fresh food and plenty of exercise. His young son told schoolfriends his father was in charge of greens at Tesco, but in fact he's in charge of the Green issues, and over five years has instigated the most determined approaches to health, nutrition and lifestyle of any supermarket chain – bringing in a Healthy Eating range (of fifty dishes), devising healthplans, issuing nutritional information, in every way setting an example for the acceptable face of mass-marketing for the 1990s.

He eats no animal fat, no salt, and no table sugar. He and his wife are still using the same packet of sugar they bought eighteen months ago. He banished biscuits from the office (although his company sells no fewer than 192 brands) and replaced them with a fruit bowl. He cycles 150 miles a week, and pumps an exercise bike in his garage, which is fitted with a calorimeter. He nurses a dream of introducing a Health MOT for shoppers: they would bring their bodies in for overhaul, have weight, height and cholesterol checks, and compare performance with the previous check. The store, or perhaps the store's GP, could advise on performance and diet.

Idealists like Dr Pugh are evident in other major chains, such as Marks & Spencer (who put their emphasis on fresh food), Safeway, Waitrose, and he takes the view that a wind of change is blowing. 'I see myself as a quality controller rather than a morality controller, but in responding to what consumers need my work is beginning to take on moral overtones.'

Dr Pugh's is the voice of scientific caution. The gourmet and food critic Egon Ronay approached the subject in a spirit of gastronomic inquiry, hearing of reports that while some foods taste worse – 'wet-dog' meat, 'smelly nappies' prawns – others remained the same, and some such as fruits had extra sweetness.

Ronay commissioned Professor Alan Homes, director of the British Food Manufacturing Industries Research Association at Leatherhead, to organise the first, large-scale comparative tasting – tasting fresh fish, chicken, fruit, made-up dishes, against similar ones which had been irradiated. Far from being impressed by the achievement of the process, he found himself shocked and disturbed, and was prompted into launching a personal investigation.

'At once I detected something strange about the herring. One seemed to be wonderfully fresh, the other had a pungent smell. And it was the one that didn't smell which was the irradiated herring.

'We have our sense of smell and taste to warn us of foods that are not good. Most poisons, for example, have a bitter taste. It seemed to me that irradiation could be used to pass off bad food.'

He decided to investigate. He ran up a £400 telephone bill calling scientists as far apart as Thailand, Malaysia and the United States. He studied a now famous piece of research by an Indian scientist, Professor S.K. Srikantia, who'd indicated in 1975 that irradiated grain fed to children was responsible for cancer; and followed through a subsequent court case in America where the irradiation lobby was seeking to discredit the findings. (The Professor, former director of India's National Institute of Nutrition, claimed to have seen this grain fed to undernourished children. The effect on the wheat subsided after four weeks' storage.) Ronay spoke to forty experts including a professor in Alberta, the governors of three States, and the Food and Drugs Administration – getting their view that the likelihood of irradiation causing cancer was remote. 'It won't seem remote to the people who contract it,' observed Ronay.

In Japan he found it was diagnosed that irradiated food had effects on hormonal regulation; in Russia a report concluded that irradiated food caused cancer in the pituitary glands of animals.

He was persuaded, from another report, that a deadly poison called aflatoxin, which comes from mould on foods such as peanuts and is one of the most serious poisons we've experienced in Britain, is produced in greater quantities, not less, during irradiation. The international Atomic Energy Agency said this wouldn't occur in the doses they approve; Ronay didn't find that reassuring.

He also discovered that irradiated food was more susceptible to re-contamination to infection from moulds and fungi, suggesting that the foods would have to be treated with fungicides too. Another surprising discovery was that the process kills off friendly bacteria and bacilli like yeasts which fight Botulism – little friends, called pseudomonads, alcaligenes, lactobacilli and micrococci.

It also emerged that irradiating packaging had attendant risks. Paper and cardboard are unsuitable, and PVC when irradiated yields chemicals which convert to a powerful carcinogen.

As Ronay continued his inquiries round the world, a net of secrecy was tightening at home. No-one wanted to tell him anything. 'It reached an absurd point one day when I rang the research station at Leatherhead to check on the way it was funded, and I was told that they couldn't reveal the answer. In fact it is very well known that it is funded by the food industry, and I was able to look it up – there are 700 food companies who help fund it, in fact.

Drawn so far into the subject, Ronay found himself playing the detective in a who-dunnit. Given irradiation's unreliable perform-ance, why use it at all? Who wanted it? He found himself chasing a culprit, and came up with an irresistible theory. Who profits by the process? The Government! The principle sources of irradiation are Cobalt-60 and Caesium-137. In this country Cobalt-60 is used at the moment, but in the US they use Caesium-137 which is nuclear waste produced as a bi-product of civil nuclear power programmes and nuclear arms manufacture. 'This waste is handled by Nirex Ltd, a fully owned subsidiary of the British nuclear industry, whose key shares are in the Government's hands.'

Ronay's inquiries led him to Canada. 'A real heavyweight in the International field, Atomic Energy of Canada Ltd (AECL) is owned by the Canadian Government. The AECL goes to great lengths to set up irradiation plants in the developing world and elsewhere, one of its highly lucrative activities being to provide Cobalt-60 for such plants.'

He discovered that the Canadian Government which owns the Canadian International Development Agency (CIDA), had pro-vided about $4.6 million of equipment and training to establish an irradiator in Thailand, handling 41,000 tonnes of papayas, mangoes and shrimps a year. 'Controversy about the matter raged in the Canadian and Thai press because the irradiation of such foods are not permitted in Canada, yet the AECL assumed that their import will be allowed and petitioned the Government to this end.'

Inquiries now took him to China and South Korea, which had bought irradiators from the Canadian company, AECL, which is said to own sixty plants, and on to other countries where they were conducting feasibility studies (Brazil, Mexico, Chile, Egypt).

Meanwhile the huge International Atomic Energy Agency (IAEA), whose function is to promote the peaceful use of nuclear energy, spends a significant part of its budget trying to get food irradiation accepted. A huge bonanza awaits them if their global ambitions succeed. 'The prize is great, as 170 plants would be needed for irradiating all poultry consumed in the US alone and, according to the IAEA, it would take some 1,200 plants to deal with all foods consumed in the US. (The horrendous accident risks don't bear thinking about.)

'It comes down to this,' says Ronay, 'the American Food and Drugs Administration run by the US Government, classifies irradiation as a "process" and thus creates a market for enormous quantities of radioactive material; its trend-setting judgement is accepted the world over; the US Government has a problem to get rid of Caesium-137, the atomic waste, of which there are 3,000 mega-curies lying around world-wide.

'Meanwhile, one Canadian Government agency (CIDA) pushes irradiation and another (AECL) makes huge profits on it. Irradiation is heavily promoted internationally by the IAEA: an enormous number of irradiators will be needed as silent consumers acquiesce (if they do).'

The fight against irradiation is just beginning, Ronay believes, although most informed opinion, from the International Organisation of Consumer Unions with its 600 member organisations, who voted in Madrid for a world wide moratorium on the process (Australia has already done just that), to many people in Britain, including members of the British Medical Association, the Consumers' Association, the Women's Institute, the Farmers' Union of Wales.

The Government has promised that irradiation will be labelled as such. Ronay observes sarcastically: 'How will loosely sold fruit and vegetables in supermarkets be labelled? How will importers know whether mangoes and papaya from abroad have been irradiated, as tests haven't yet been devised to tell the difference? There is a famous case of a consignment of bad prawns arriving in Britain; they were sent to Holland to be irradiated – then they were reimported!'

In the trade, this practice already attracts the name 'dutching'. If you get some bad food you send it on 'a holiday to Holland'.

'The Government asserted that restaurants would have to declare if their food had been irradiated. This is naive. How would they know?'

Irradiation hasn't been proved safe and fails to satisfy modern safety standards, which insist that a risk, however small, is too great. The possibility for human error is evidently great; the prospects for abuse are tempting for unscrupulous parties all over the world. But, most of all, the process itself dismays all those who fight for the obvious health and nutritional benefits of fresh food.

Science has many, many good applications to improving our food supply. This isn't one of them. We shouldn't countenance a measure which is intended to be a substitute for clean, safe, fresh food.

13

KILLER BUGS

Food can kill you. Poisonous mushrooms. Poisons in fish – such as the fugu, a delicacy in Japan. Substances in food, in rhubarb leaves, in the green part of potatoes.

Food in storage can attract poisonous bacteria, the mould that invades damp rye grain and produces ergotism in humans, which induces a mad dance to death, or aflatoxin in peanuts, which got into the feeds of turkeys in Britain and resulted in the death of thousands in the 1950s.

Food spoils rapidly, the warmer and more humid it is. It generates its own poisons, picks up others from handling, from the movements of flies and insects.

These are perils we have fought for centuries to understand.

The peril of our own times – and our children's – is the danger of food poisoning when the food handling is beyond our control: the meal we eat in a restaurant, on an airline, on a hospital tray; the cook chill food from supermarkets; the efficiency of our freezer, refrigerators or microwave oven.

The peril is not only in processed foods, where disease may occur in canning, packaging, or simply by keeping in bad conditions at home or school or factory or hospital or canteen or restaurant, or by not cooking it properly. There may be deeper hidden dangers: disease in beef herds, in broiler chickens, in eggs, in shellfish from polluted waters.

Government Ministries seek to reassure the public that outbreaks of poisoning are not significant, but the anxiety about our food resources has reached scare levels at a time when almost any action planned by the food industry triggers alarm: its excessive use of additives, chemicals, colourings, flavourings, preservatives; and agribusiness's heavy use of insecticides and poisons in crops.

The Government says, put your trust in their scientific experts. We did, but they have been wrong again and again. So where can we find an independent expert we can believe?

The most insistent voice of authority on all issues which involve food is Professor Richard Lacey. He blew the whistle on Salmonella in chickens and in eggs and on BSE – Bovine Spongiform Encephalopathy, the 'Mad Cow Disease'. He has been a relentless critic of Government policies.

He is Professor of Microbiology at Leeds and one of the few completely independent scientists, and as such is consulted frequently by television and the press, a position which he relishes since resigning as a matter of principle from the Ministry of Agriculture's Veterinary Products Committee.

Efforts to dismiss him as a food scarist failed, when it turned out, unfortunately, that his warnings were coming true.

He is a highly principled man of fifty whose determined manner summons up the image of a Roman soothsayer, or a mediaeval prophet of doom – the former Junior Health Minister, Edwina Currie, describes him as author of 'a Doomsday scenario'.

The Government says that Mad Cow Disease can't be transmitted to humans. But no-one foresaw it could be transmitted from sheep (who have had the disease which is known as scrapie for 250 years) to cattle. But it was, because sheep's offal was processed and put in the feed of cows. Even so, the Government said, it couldn't be transmitted to humans. Then a cat died, Max the Siamese, in Bristol. Its owners had fed him not tinned petfood but straightforward butcher's meat. You're put in mind of the opening chapters of the Albert Camus novel, *The Plague*, where one remote incident after another is pooh-poohed by the authorities. When Max died, Humberside Education Council withdrew meat from school meals, and at once a Minister was pleading with people not to ban meat. 'Where will it all end? We will end up eating nothing in this country.'

If you ask Professor Lacey what can be done, the answer is appalling. Slaughter six million cattle, destroy our chicken flocks. Start again. The media, faced with such extreme solutions, hesitate to go all the way with him.

The producer of the BBC's *Food and Drink Programme*, Peter Bazalgette, takes the diplomatic view that both sides in any debate on health or safety overstate the case: 'I regard 30 per cent of what each side says as exaggeration.' Even if Professor Lacey accepted that, which he doesn't, 70 per cent of his case still presents us with the facts of terrible risks we may be taking with our food supply.

Take Mad Cow Disease, for example. 'The infectious agent is very, very small and very, very tough. It needs abnormally high heating to kill it. It will never be killed by normal cooking and no doubt it survives the temperature at food processing plants. If we are vulnerable, the danger is in sausages and burgers and brains and things. Cheap fillers.

'Suppose the worst did come to the worst, and 5 per cent of the population ended up demented in twenty years' time. That would be absolutely catastrophic because one demented person might require three other people to look after him.'

That's the blackest view he can extrapolate for meat eaters. But if – and nobody knows – if the disease is passed into milk by the oral route, everyone will be dead of brain damage in twenty to thirty years. 'That's a terribly pessimistic view,' he concedes. 'But it's just possible.'

'In South East Asia there's a disease called Kuru that cannibals used to get from eating other people's brains, which is very similar to BSE. It is also possible to infect rodents with the BSE. So we know it can go from sheep to cows by the oral route and we know it can go to rodents. What's more, we are not now sure that it came from sheep in the first place.

'I see no reason to think that human beings are necessarily resistant. We may or may not be. It's not known.'

What should we do? 'Get rid of our herds and start again. We can't identify the infectious agent. We can't isolate it. I think any research will be of limited value because it would take too long. The only thing is to get rid of it at the source.'

After denying the seriousness and significance of the outbreak, the Government was prompted into action by the refusal of West Germany to buy our meat – a grant of £12 million research into the disease, from the Ministry of Agriculture and the Department of Health.

But in Lacey's view the Government has always done too little, too late. And he's not one of the Reds-under-the bed or left-wingloonies the Conservatives like to ridicule. He's a conservative (with a small c) who sends his children to private schools and reads the *Daily Telegraph*, who would support any Government which realised money that spent on planning ahead is a saving in the long run.

How is it that a fifty-year-old professor of Microbiology in a Yorkshire university of whom few non-medical people had heard a few years ago should become the Nation's conscience in these matters?

A man who'd become increasingly disillusioned by the way Government funding was being withdrawn from research and education – where universities were being told to go and find money from industry to sponsor them, where managers were being put into hospitals to run the doctors – a man who'd never spoken out in public, chose suddenly to do so – and with dramatic effect. 'As microbiologists we were being threatened in all directions. If you're threatened, you tend to react. It wasn't calculated – these events have led to a great deal of anger among people like myself, and caused us to *do* things, where we might have been more restrained.'

'This department has a long interest in food microbiology and, when it was clear to me three years ago that everything was going wrong about food, I virtually changed over from working on antibiotics to working on food and listeria.'

Being responsible for West Riding Hospitals in his capacity of Control of Infection Officer he was appalled by the way cook chill processes were being imposed by managers on hospitals in order to privatise catering. 'This is the wrong thing to do. You privatise a system after showing it is safe. You do not introduce a system in order to privatise it.

It was during this undercurrent of anger he was feeling that the famous Salmonella story broke. It started in 1988 and raged throughout 1989, with the resignation or one Minister, and another moving out of his job, and resulted in the slaughter of many thousands of birds.

In the summer of 1988 in both the US and Britain notices went out from health departments warning of the dangers of eating soft-boiled eggs or raw eggs (as in mayonnaises). A paragraph appeared in *The Times*, another in the London *Standard*. Three months later it was the lead item on the BBC's *Food and Drink Programme*, supported by research in the US and with help from Environmental

Health Officers in Britain. It was explosive. 'There's something wrong with our eggs,' said Peter Bazalgette, the producer of the programme. 'What's the Government up to?' The following day he was called to do radio interviews on the main networks, and the fox was in the henhouse. 'We were accused overnight of being scaremongers. But we were eventually proved right.'

Pressure was building up. John MacGregor, then Minister of Agriculture, was scheduled to address the Guild of Food Writers, and was knocked back on his heels by a blast from Jane Grigson, the formidable cookery writer, who demanded assurances about the safety of our eggs, and told the 120 assembled food writers she would not mention eggs in her articles until they could be declared free of Salmonella.

Ten days later the BBC's programme *Watchdog* picked up the theme, introducing into the debate, for the first time, Professor Lacey. He appeared on the Monday, and there was massive publicity. On the Friday in another TV programme – on Central TV – he appeared with another participant who was an egg farmer who said he had a Salmonella-free flock. He asked what I thought the incidence was and I said: 'One in 7,000'.

To his astonishment, on the Saturday, Edwina Currie, the Junior Health Minister, made a statement admitting that there was a Salmonella risk in our chicken flocks.

On Monday the media were nothing short of hysterical. Professor Lacey made a series of statements about Edwina Currie. 'I said she was right; and, since she was right, she couldn't retract. She couldn't apologise, couldn't say, "I didn't mean it." This put her in a corner. She had to resign because she was right. There was no way out. You can't say something unpopular and correct. You can say something popular and wrong. No minister is ever going to say anything that's courageous or true again.'

One of the criticisms of the Government was that even when they knew the truth they were putting out misleading statements. 'They said some things which are incredible. They advised everyone to avoid eating raw eggs, which of course is correct, but implied, in advertisements, that normal cooked eggs are safe. This just isn't true. If you cook an egg normally – poaching or frying – the yolk temperature does not get high enough. The fried egg is the most difficult of all to cook so that the yolk is free of Salmonella. If there is any Salmonella inside the egg, it's more likely to be in the yolk than in the white, because the white contains quite a lot of inhibitory substances.'

The Department of Health also told everyone to put eggs in the fridge, as if to imply that the consumer is at fault. 'But eggs should not be stored in the fridge. They never should be, despite fridges having egg spaces in them. If you take a cold egg, it's even more difficult to cook the centre so that it's free of Salmonella – unless of course you take it out of the fridge four hours before you boil it.'

That's not all. The resistance of the egg to outside contamination is based on the pores in the egg shell, which are plugged. Those plugs can come out if water dissolves them, and that lets bacteria in. Condensation in the fridge can let bacteria in. The lesson is: keep eggs dry, but don't warm them. The supermarkets store them at room temperature. They should be stored at room temperature at home.

'If you use refrigeration to try to stop bacterial growth, you have to refrigerate the item in question immediately after it has been produced. By the time you actually buy eggs, you know they have been around for perhaps a week, two weeks or three weeks. It's too late. You would not cook a joint of beef and put that in room temperature for two weeks and *then* put it in the fridge, thinking it would be safe.'

Government scientists must know such things. What puzzles Professor Lacey is why they are not allowed to say them.

Once he had spoken out, he felt he had burned his boats and, as there was no going back, he drove forward. By no means a self-publicist, he became a publicist for the cause of food safety. He threw open lines of communication to the press, giving any amount of time to inquiries and facts, and none at all to frivolity or gossip.

As a moderately sheltered academic for most of his career, he wondered at first what he'd done. 'A few weeks afterwards I felt worried and insecure. Some of my colleagues, who were trying to be helpful, said that MI5 were after me and my phone was tapped. But I have the tacit support of my colleagues – who are not as free as I am to say what they know to be true – and I don't any longer imagine that I am threatened.' One thing led to another. The planned introduction of cook chill meals to the hospitals in his area prompted him to test them in the microbiology laboratory, and suddenly he was on to Listeria.

From being a local problem, he suddenly recognised it as a national problem, since we are the only country in the world developing cook chill for sale in supermarkets on such a large scale. Unlike other food products, this one introduces risks at stage after stage. There are many links in the food chain: from grower or farmer, factory, chilled delivery lorries, chill store at supermarkets, display shelves (have you noticed the drop in temperature when you step into a Marks & Spencer food hall?), to the customer's shopping bag or car boot, the kitchen, the fridge (is it at the necessary temperature?), the microwave (is it efficient? Some don't cook all-through at recommended times). There are so many points in the chain, that one weak link could spell disaster.

Listeria is one of the infections that arrives by the cook chill route. It also surfaces in cheeses. Although a lot of food contains it, it is rare to get the infection. But of those that do, one in three die. It's a risk we might not want to take.

'The danger area is the surface of food. That's where the warmth is. If you get Listeria on wrapped poultry, it is just on the surface.

'It is no surprise to me, now, that 30 per cent of our supermarket cooked and chilled chicken contains listeria. But that's not good enough and, if this had been the USA, the whole lot would have been confiscated, the shops would have been virtually closed down and so would the central production factory.

'Every supermarket in the country has got shelves which have got cold air, ventilating down, on products which are open to environmental warmth. Every one of these is unsatisfactory as a refrigerator, and sooner or later the whole lot will have to be cleared out and replaced. The supermarkets are going to resist this like anything, but they are going to have to do it.

'The problem is that you have radiant heat from lighting, people, fingers, hot bodies from the other side of the shelves; and, as so many items are wrapped in cellophane and related products, you get greenhouse effects.

'We have done surveys, (so have numerous other people), that show that, despite the ventilating air, the shelves being perhaps two or three degrees centigrade, the actual temperature on the surface of the food is anything between eight and fifteen degrees centigrade.

'The supermarkets contravene the Government's own advice about safe operations. Department of Health guidelines published in 1989 imposed three absolutely essential components:

1 There should only be three clear days between first cooking and reheating. A five day cycle maximum.
2 The storage temperature must be below three degrees centigrade.
3 Reheating is required for safety because, if you do get bacteria like Listeria growing, you have to use reheating to make it safe.

'The shelf life can be up to five or six days. The time before getting it on the shelves is anything between one and four days. So we're talking of between six and ten days – plus you've got the length of time in the home. You're talking of up to twelve days' cycle, way beyond three days.

'Temperature is out of control. The temperature of a lorry is often five degrees. The refrigerator shelves get radiant heat under the wrapping. A typical shelf temperature is six degrees or seven degrees. And many of these products are stated to be ready to eat hot or cold.

'These three criteria are Department of Health guidelines which I actually support: I was involved in putting a fair amount of pressure on them to produce these. But the Ministry of Agriculture will not impose these on the retail trade.'

Foods which pose the Listeria threat are pâtés and sausages, many of which are imported. 'Because of Listeria, the Germans are trying to do their utmost to look at their salamis to make sure they are free of Listeria because they are refrigerated for weeks. Salamis are made by bacteria-fermentation, so if they get Listeria in at the beginning it could actually multiply. Sometimes they include nitrites, sometimes not; more often not because they are unfashionable. We've tested them and they are perfectly safe.'

'Liver pâté is an even worse problem. Most of our pâté comes from Belgium and basically their system is not sound. The problem is very simple – it's a cook chill system. Canned pâté (treated at high temperature) is safe. Wrapped pâté is a problem. It is produced in production units, heated up to seventy degrees, chilled, wrapped, stored, transported for days or weeks, and the trouble is Listeria. It survives the first heating, to recover and then to multiply.'

The French probably have a Listeria problem but they never publish figures. 'Not suppression, just not organised very well. The French actually, I think, accept food poisoning as an acceptable risk in quality food. We, I think, have the worst of both worlds. We've got poor quality, dangerous food. The French have high quality, dangerous food. Other countries have medium quality, safe food. We've got the worst: bad food, which is unsafe.'

The Lacey solution is logical, but tough. Ban cook chill food.

'It is an important issue. If they impose regulations but people can't comply, I make only one inference: we ought to abandon cook chill. If we abandon it, there are two alternatives. When people want convenience meals they can have either sterilised food, and that means the canning process, or deep frozen things. There is no problem.

'It is a purist view. It's always been our view in microbiology. We always take a stand. Because we know human nature. We know risks. I'm the Control of Infections Officer for the whole of West Yorkshire. I am responsible for patients who might get infected in hospital. I'm involved with seeing that surgical instruments are clean and that there are proper isolation facilities. We have to take a line that always allows for lapses in human nature and lapses in equipment. We know that although you have a temperature of below three degrees, it may sometimes go up to six degrees; and if you've got a five day cycle, occasionally it will go to eight days, but if you have a twelve day cycle it may go to fifteen or twenty-four days. You see what I mean.'

Can cook chill be brought under control? He's doubtful. 'The mark-up on cook chill food is high. We've got to have laws which prevent risk taking. We've pioneered cook chill in Britain. This is why there has been such a row. We've got this combination of problems. Unsafe production system, unsafe storing, then the final cook unsatisfactory.'

The end of the food chain is the home. You might or might not succeed in killing the bugs in your food if you're using a microwave oven. It depends on the make.

Professor Lacey is explosive on the subject. 'Microwaves are fraudulent. They give the impression of being a satisfactory quick cooking device.

To render food safe, we've got to use cooking to kill the unwanted bacteria. There are three different factors which affect the killing of bacteria. One is the nature of the food that they are in. Secondly, the height of the temperature reached. Thirdly, the length of the temperature reached.

'With a microwave we have a number of problems. By their very nature they don't cook very long. Their whole *raison d'être* is speed.

'By definition a microwave oven doesn't kill bacteria such as Campylobacter, Salmonella and Listeria. If you've got bacterial toxins which cause food poisoning such as Botulism (whether it is decomposed or not), they are also governed by heat and length of cooking. So with contaminated food in a microwave you've got less chance of the toxins being destroyed.

'We've got the problem of penetration. Many people think micro-waves heat from inside out. That's what they've been saying for the last five years. I don't know how this propaganda was ever born. They heat *from the outside*.

'Apparently even the Government-approved microwave ovens still don't reliably penetrate the food. The science of microwave cooking isn't fully understood. Exactly how they generate heat is not known. They do something to the molecules, it is not exactly known why.

'Microwaves interact with ions and their energy is dissipated and don't penetrate, so that food that contains salt or monosodium glutamate gets even less heat in the centre. And all these convenience meals are full of monosodium glutamate. Lubec and his colleagues in Vienna report that microwaves change the stereo-asombric shape of amino acids, converting them into potentially toxic substances. We don't know how many are safe and how many are toxic.

'The reasons why you do not get penetration are many. Pieces of food are too large, there is a failure of rotation, the cooking time is too short. *Everything* is against the microwave working to *kill* bacteria.

'So I'm now adopting the stance that microwaves should only be used for food that you know is safe rather than as a primary cooking equipment.'

The most controversial microbiologist in Britain has always been a battler, but he'd never taken his foes in public before.

He came from a medical family. His father was a pathologist, and his uncle was a Professor of Microbiology in London. They lived in Essex and he was sent to prep and public schools.

He hated school and was always being reprimanded. 'I had the wrong attitude because I questioned the basis of an awful lot of the dogma. For example, the need to play games about three times a day and the need to have cold baths. The whole public school system did not appeal. My father, a middle-class professional doctor, had done the traditional thing. It was doing the best for me. I think my parents had several years of agony when they realised I wasn't happy.

'It was difficult having friends who were intelligent because one of the problems was that you were allowed only to talk to people in your particular age group in your House. It was a very intimidating environment. I quite enjoyed extra-curricular activities devoid from the sports obsession. I did quite well academically. I was one of the few to get to Cambridge.

He started to read Medicine at Jesus College. He immediately got into trouble with the syllabus because he couldn't stand anatomy. It wasn't the fear of dissecting corpses, but the discovery that it was a static subject. But the chemical side did interest him and he went to London Hospital for his chemical training. Typically he became irritated by the dogmatic approach, being told how he should do things without questioning them. But he won quite a few prizes.

His first experience after qualifying was in general surgery. The hours were unbelievably long. He had only two evenings off in six months. Then he turned to studying children who had problems with diseases of the metabolic state. He finally found his true interest when he moved to Bristol – to do pathology – and got involved in a microbiological project. 'I realised then how exciting it was to see bacteria grow overnight. It's a very rapid dynamic subject.'

He took up a research post in Bristol University, working on factors which kill bacteria on the skin. This was the basis of his doctorate for which he was awarded a degree in genetics. Some of his work involved using drugs, and it led to his first awareness of the politics behind medicine.

This was the beginning of a long-running battle with the drug companies. With colleagues, he identified a drug combination which included a totally unnecessary component. 'We got involved in the politics of this. This product had been given a product licence through recommendations from the Committee of Safety in Medicines without the single drugs being assessed. Astounding.' After ten years of his own research he organised the launch of a single drug, under contract from a Finnish company. 'Subsequently I had an awful lot of disputes with other drug companies who made combinations.' He moved to East Anglia where he developed this theme, prescribing no fewer than eight single drugs as antibiotics, cutting out the drug companies' profits and saving his hospital's money which could then be spent on care nursing.

In 1983 he accepted the post in Leeds as Professor of Clinical

Microbiology. 'I took a pay cut, but people listen to you more if you're a professor.' And, as he's responsible to his university, he's free to speak up. 'You're not, when your job's on the line. There are many frightened people and I see it as my job to keep the lines of communication open.'

The future? Professor Lacey's predictions are predictably glum. He says the politicians actually have no policy of their own, they accept a cheap food policy dictated to them by the supermarkets.

'We are under pressure from the supermarkets, things have gone wrong these last twenty years because we are not going in for quality. We've got no British-based anything. The supermarkets are getting the cheapest food they can from anywhere and it is not worth any farming group or breeding organisation developing its own system. That's why we haven't got any breeding egg-laying flocks. I believe the supermarkets are now so powerful they are going to control this Government, and they'll control the next.

'The average person is going to get out of the supermarket in the shortest possible time, dumping everything in the trolley once every two weeks, hating shopping, hating thinking about food. Buying convenience stuff, not really caring. That's my fear for the future.'

'Public confidence in food is now so low. What worries me is seeing young people with their trolleys picking out convenience meals, ogling the pictures. When I see them at the station eating this appalling food I think it's very, very sad that we accept what is so awful. We need to somehow get back to more local shops – more human contact.'

There will be one kind of food for the fussy, and another for the rest. There will be special stores with foods perceived to be healthy. 'My view is we'll become a nation of food faddists who will be suspicious. There'll be chaos. People will have their specialised diets. There will be an increase in specialised food shops pandering to people's views of what is good and safe, and the ideas will be perpetrated by magazines.'

How does the most demanding food expert in Britain manage his own diet?

By ordinary family standards, erratically.

Contrary to most nutritional advice he takes just two cups of tea but no breakfast. 'Never feel the need for it.'

Lunch. ('By this time I'm bloody hungry.') Usually a pasta-based meal in a restaurant, a pleasant walk, not far from the university.

Supper. A snack – because he arrives home after the rest of the family have eaten.

The weekends are reserved for serious eating, when he joins his wife Fiona and his two girls, Miranda and Gemma. The main meal on Saturdays and Sundays is between five p.m., and seven p.m., a proper three-course meal. ('If you make lunch the main meal, the rest of the day goes flat.') They like lamb or duck, with potatoes in many styles, and lots of vegetables, crisp and firm and spanking fresh. He eats a lot of good local Yorkshire cheese – too much, he thinks, but with margarine, not butter.

THE BUGS IN YOUR FOOD

BOTULISM. The most deadly of all bugs in food, has fortunately not occurred in the UK since 1978. But it could turn up with a vengeance, as it survives in temperatures as low as 3.3 degrees centigrade. Most home refrigerators are between zero centigrade and eight centigrade.

Symptoms: Nine to twenty-four hours after eating infected food, nausea and vomiting, dry mouth. Then dizziness and blurred vision. Paralysis.

The bacterium Clostridium botulinum is named after the Latin botulus, a sausage, but has usually surfaced in tins of vegetables which haven't been sufficiently heated. Eight died in Scotland after eating a tin of duck pâté in 1922.

One hundred millionth of a gram can kill a person, and the dormant spores are all around us (in some 5 per cent of any soil samples taken), but it needs special conditions for the spores to breed. When this happens no fewer than eight deadly toxins can be released. No bug so dramatically illustrates the importance of hygienic food handling, hand-washing, complete cooking, thorough chilling.

CLOSTRIDIUM PERFRINGENS. Less severe than Botulism but more common, contaminating stews left to cool slowly or kept in a warm kitchen overnight.

Symptoms: Twelve to eighteen hours after eating contaminated food, severe diarrhoea. (Don't let food remain at thirty to fifty degrees centigrade for more than one-and-a-half hours.)

STAPHYLOCOCCUS AUREUS. Thrives on foods such as chicken, creams and custards which are kept for a long time in a warm place.

Symptoms: Thirty minutes to twelve hours after eating infected food, vomiting, sometimes with blood. (Don't let food stand at warm temperatures.)

LISTERIA. A food poison which wasn't known twenty years ago, kills one in three people who get the infection. The very young, the sick, and pregnant mothers are most susceptible. (In the US over 400 a year die, from 1,600 reported cases). Far from diminishing the effect of Lysteria monocytogenes, refrigeration, if inadequate, may actually encourage it. Found in surfaces of soft cheeses, some salami, supermarket salads in dressing with low vinegar (eg coleslaw), and in cook chill foods.

Symptoms: Possibly five days to five weeks after eating the toxic food, sweating, fever, pains in the back; continuing seven to ten days – at the end of which a mother may have a stillbirth.

Still under-researched, but Listeria is present in 10 per cent of some salamis, soft cheeses, and up to 25 per cent of cook chill meals, according to Professor Lacey's research.

Subsequent cooking or the body's immune system can usually handle the levels which are present in food, but we may not always have control over high doses. At the moment, we do not know what dose is potentially dangerous for any person. The vulnerability of the patient may be an important factor – so pregnant mothers should not eat soft cheeses. We should thus endeavour to rid all cooked and processed food of Listeria completely.

SALMONELLA. There are some 2,000 strains, but *Salmonella enteriditis* is the newest strain of this bug which has been around for as long as records have been kept. It is noticeably different from *Salmonella typhymurium* which was common in the 1970s and 1980s. Most common in poultry and eggs but it can cross to cooked foods, which are in proximity in warm kitchens, and do its dirty work there.

Symptoms: Twelve to twenty-four hours after eating contaminated food, nausea and upset stomach, and spasms in the abdomen, followed by urgent diarrhoea, hot and cold sensations, profuse sweating, reaching its worst after about six hours.

Nineteen elderly patients at Stanley Road Hospital, Wakefield, died in 1984, when 450 patients contracted the poison from cooked beef which had been left out in the kitchen on a warm summer night. Two died the same year when 766 cases of Salmonella were identified on British Airways' planes apparently due to an aspic glaze used in a cook chill process. Professor Lacey believes there are upward of 14,000 cases a year.

Cooking kills the bug – which is why the Government urged people to cook eggs thoroughly. The microwave may have cold spots which don't kill the bacteria in cook chill recipe dishes. Salmonella may lurk in the cavity of birds, so the stuffed bird is more risky than one with an empty carcases (hence the bacteriocidal value of lemon juice put inside a bird).

Cross-contamination with other cooked meats is a danger – so hand-washing after handling poultry is essential. One million Salmonella bacteria can tuck themselves inside a finger-nail!

CAMPYLOBACTER. New recruit to the food poisoning scene, which joined the battle in 1980 with 30,000 cases upwards reported annually, particularly in summer months.

Symptoms: Approximately between three and ten days after eating, nausea, stomach ache, high temperature, fever, diarrhoea. Sometimes muscle pain, and headaches, rather like 'flu' symptoms. Lasts five to ten days.

Most common cause may be unpasteurised milk.

BACILLUS CEREUS. The Chinese takeaway bug, which most commonly occurs in fried rice.

Symptoms: Two or three hours after eating it, nausea and vomiting for up to a day. A feeling of exhaustion for days afterwards.

There are several kinds of this bug which survive several minutes boiling before being killed. Fried rice is made from cooked rice which has been allowed to cool. Slow cooling in the warm atmosphere of a kitchen is probably the ideal breeding ground for the bug, especially in takeaway kitchens where a large amount may hang around all evening. The rapid frying of the rice may not be thorough enough to kill the bacteria. At home you can protect yourself by cooking a small quantity and by putting it in the fridge as soon as it is cold.

VIBRIO PARAHAEMOLYTICUS. In Japan, where they eat a lot of sashimi, sliced raw fish, it's a common cause of food poisoning. It is water-borne and thrives in the summer in estuaries, mud, and shallow water, and can be present on crab, lobsters, oysters, mussels and fish in general.

Symptoms: Twelve to twenty-four hours after eating food, spasms and pains in the stomach, urgent diarrhoea, sometimes sweating and headaches, followed by weakness and tiredness for several days.

Acids kill the germs, which is another good reason for having lemon juice with seafood. Boiling effectively kills Vibrio, and it's very rare in Britain. Like all the other bugs, good hygiene will prevent cross contamination – so keep raw shellfish and fish separate from cooked foods.

14

REAL FOOD

Until Government recognises the vital role of food in our lives and appoints a Minister of Food independent of the Minister of Agriculture, we will continue to stumble on from crisis to crisis.

A Minister of Food would evolve policy on health, nutrition, safety, standards, quality. He would be responsible for expanding the scope of the subject, giving it due importance at the highest level in universities and research establishments, in technical colleges, schools, hospitals and especially in the medical profession.

A Minister of Food would establish priorities in our food supply, quality, taste, safety, health and nutrition. It would not be left to market forces.

No-one addresses this issue more passionately than Derek Cooper, President of the Guild of Food Writers, and presenter of Radio 4's prestigious Food Programme, and a constant thorn in the side of the food industry.

At one end of the scale he would immediately establish a University Chair of Food and at the other, he would establish cookery on the National Curriculum.

The love and understanding of food begins at home, he insists, and should continue at school. 'Cookery is not part of the National Curriculum. But even if you teach the value of fresh food at school, however, the child would still go back home, sit in front of the television set and see the latest pot noodle or Batman crisps with monster shapes. Commercials sell the subversive myth that tinned, packaged or frozen food is better than anything mother can make. "How did you make this Mum?" "Oh, I went to the supermarket

and bought a packet and added water." "Oh, scrumptious Mum!"
The pressures are to stop Mum doing any cooking whatsoever.'

'Why isn't food studied at the highest level? It is impossible to
get a British university degree in Food Studies. You can get a
degree in Agriculture, or in Food Processing, Food Chemistry, Food
Science, but not in Food. There's no Food Faculty. There's not
even a Ministry of Food. It's lumped in with Agriculture.'

Derek Cooper holds the food industry responsible for much of
the quality of life in this country, and if you look at that quality of
life you'll find it's 'palatally retarded' as far as food is concerned.

Generations of people have been conditioned to believe that all
food should be heavily processed, numbingly bland and as cheap as
possible. The prime criteria are that it has to look pretty and be easy
to swallow. 'Nothing chewy, you don't have to chew anything. It's
zombie food!'

People no longer recognise the taste of real things. 'There is a
strong possibility that if you squeezed juice from oranges for children
they will not like it because they have been brought up on orange
squash which has been loaded with sugar and bright artificial colouring. There is a whole generation of children being reared on the
Hebridean islands of Barra for whom the real taste of milk is actually
UHT, because it's a six-hour journey to bring them fresh milk from
the mainland. A hundred years ago my grandparents and every other
crofter kept a cow, so they had fresh milk to go with their herrings
and potatoes. UHT milk is very unpleasant. It has a metallic 'cooked'
taste. It could be possible that, if you introduced fresh milk to a Barra
schoolchild, he might not like it, in the way that my grandchildren are
being brought up in America on real ice cream and might not like
cheapened British 'ice cream' which is made of oil. The food industry
is shaping the taste of a generation, or to be more accurate, mis-
shaping it in the direction of the ersatz and the second rate.'

People in the food industry say that Cooper is constantly rubbishing them. 'I am not. I'm rubbishing their rubbish. There are
two kinds of food; there's the food of which the industry can be
rightly proud (which I'm happy to say I have sufficient money to
live on) and there's the crap food, the junk food. I have a great
respect for food science. It can be anything. But it has been degraded
in the interest of commercial expediency.'

In the last fifty years more and more food has been heavily
processed, he points out. Now, there is a consensus of medical

opinion urging that we should eat more fresh fruit and vegetables and wholefood. 'But there is very little money to be made out of selling oats or potatoes or carrots. The way you make money is by adding value. You get a great sack of potatoes, take out two good looking ones which have been rendered spotless by fungicides and insecticides and you put them on a polypropylene tray, having scrubbed them very carefully, and then you enrobe them in clingfilm and label them "Ideal for Baking". You charge ninety-eight pence. The potatoes have probably only cost you two pence or four pence. I don't care if they cost eight pence. The mark-up is remarkable.'

The profit is even greater, he says, if you process them down to a powder, extrude them, and mix them with lots of salt and artificial colourings and flavourings, to make snacks with a disgusting smell which overwhelms your tastebuds.

British supermarkets make three times the profit of their US counterparts, on sales of food, 7 per cent on turnover. Supermarkets in the US make 2 or less per cent. 'We have more multimillionaires in food than any other Western country. The ten top richest men in America and Japan are not food manufacturers or retailers, and yet some of the wealthiest people in this country have made their fortunes out of food.

There are two standards for food in Britain, he says: There's Sunday Supplement food and there's mass-produced food. On the one hand, Loseley ice cream which is quite expensive, and on the other hand commercial ice cream. 'I wrote to one manufacturer and asked them why it was that every time I eat their choc-ices I get a back blast of soap. The technical director wrote back to me and said he'd never encountered this problem before and couldn't think why. (I think because both soap and ice cream is made with palm oil.) I once addressed a coven of ice cream manufacturers and complained that there was often no cream in them at all. I said that their slogan ought to be: 'Our ice cream comes from contented palm trees.' It didn't go down very well.'

It's the same with bread, even Marks & Spencer sell white factory bread with its blown-up balloon effect, which isn't very nice; or you can buy their very expensive bread, the olive oil bread such as Ciabbata, which sells at a premium. 'You can, if you're lucky, go to the small and dwindling band of craftsmen who are still actually making batch bread, which takes six hours to rise, compared with the Chorleywood factory process of half an hour.'

The aim of the food industry, he says, is to eliminate the workforce by the processes of mechanisation and automation. The result is that bakers who are trying to reproduce the food we remember from childhood are a dying band. 'The taste of bread is all in the crust. Starch converts to sugar in the crust and generates an appetising smell. But factory bread is steamed to a minimum cooking time, to retain the maximum volume of water, and flavour never has the opportunity to develop.'

Meat is another example of two-tier standards. 'You can either buy a bit of cling-wrapped topside from the supermarket which even heavy stewing wouldn't redeem, or you can seek out a rib of Old Devon Longhorn cut from a rare beast fed solely on natural lucerne and hung properly for six weeks, meat as meat used to be before the agribusiness industry moved in.'

There are two kinds of burger. 'A splendidly healthy lean burger, if you regard red meat as healthy; or you can get a cheap burger which is full of MRM, mechanically recovered meat, which is arsehole and nostril and an excessive amount of fat and additives to give it the flavour and taste it naturally lacks.'

There are two kinds of sausage, too. You can either go to a very expensive real meat shop and have a succulent sausage made without any artificial ingredients, or you can buy an adulterated sausage by paying very little and you'll get very little.

Derek Cooper recalls an invitation to talk to the members of a farmers' club in Kent, and sitting down to a meal of bangers and chips. 'Nothing wrong with that but the bangers were really grotty, made from meat slurry. They had very little taste but that was all right because there were lots of bottles of ketchup and Daddy sauce to pep them up. I thought at the time how sad this was. Here was a group of farmers whose business was to feed the nation and they were giving themselves these awful cut-price bangers. It was as if food had no importance and anything would do. A few weeks earlier I'd been with a group of winegrowers in Burgundy and they put on a meal, nothing special, for us journalists. Everything was freshly cooked; the quality, the flavour, the taste were superb. There's a moral here. The farmers I'd been to see in England obviously didn't care what they ate. It was food, grub if you like, regarded as something filling at the end of the day. No care for quality, no thought put into it. The French, probably much poorer in income than the English farmers, had a different attitude – to them, food mattered. Unless food matters, standards fall – it doesn't have to be good it just has to *look* good. What I find very cynical is that quite often the people producing cheap food know exactly what they're doing. They wouldn't dream of eating it themselves – it's for Them, not Us.'

In the course of presenting The Food Programme he has frequently visited factories which produce rubbish, but the managers have taken him out to expensive restaurants to eat. 'I once went to a complex producing British wine and for lunch we had very good Spanish fino sherry and very good German wine. When I was leaving I said I hadn't tasted theirs and they said: "We'll send you some!" The implication was that the wine they were making was not the kind of thing they would happily drink themselves or offer to anyone they were anxious to impress.'

Beer is another example of double standards. There's carbonated, additive-rich beer and there is real ale. 'I went once to the directors' bar at the London headquarters of Whitbread's and I had a marvellous pint of bitter. I asked them why I couldn't get beer like that in my local Whitbread pub and they told me that this beer was very special. It came from their brewery in Henley.

'It's like going round an art gallery and suddenly realising that you are actually looking at mass produced reproductions of Titian and El Greco and Rubens: the colour's not quite right, it's all a bit blurred. You have a product which looks like a roast chicken and it isn't. It's steamed chicken and it has a sprayed on brown covering that looks as if it's roasted. You spray the corpse with caramel. The process is designed to make people think they're eating a genuinely roasted farmhouse fowl.

'If you're going to take the cheapest possible raw materials and bulk them out with additives and extenders, you're not going to produce terribly good food,' he says. 'I had a long argument even with Marks & Spencer once about a piece of boiling bacon we bought in Inverness to take to Skye. When we got there we had to throw it in the dustbin. It was actually reformed tumbled meat massaged with water-retentive sodium polyphosphate. It was like a piece of pink rubber. Appalling. I thought it was rubbish food and, as I don't eat rubbish, I threw it away. Marks & Spencer wrote to me and said that's what their customers liked.'

Another cause of his discontent is the way modern processing frequently knocks out real flavour. The frozen pea is often held up as the supreme achievement of agricultural research. It comes out of its pack really fresher than any you can buy in a greengrocers. But has it got any taste at all?

Food geneticists bred the frozen pea for the fields of Lincoln and Humberside so it contains all the parameters that agribusiness needs. 'I've been to the pea fields. If need be, they pick at four o'clock in the morning and within the hour this pea has been separated from the pod and is frozen. It's got this authentic pea green colour and tender texture. It looks like a million dollars, but has no taste. A few years ago we bought some of these peas in a greengrocers. We shelled them and we thought how marvellous they looked. We cooked them – and they were tasteless. They were surplus peas from the freezer fields. This is a problem with breeding for the freezer.'

The Americans have been trying to perfect a strawberry that will not disintegrate when it thaws, he says. If they could also build into that strawberry the flavour of a Royal Sovereign or the flavour of a traditional strawberry, that would be a major breakthrough. Cooper feels that what they are aiming for is a strawberry that looks good when it thaws regardless of what it is going to taste like.

Derek Cooper's complaint is that because the food doesn't taste of very much the food industry employs wordsmiths and advertising men to suggest artfully that it does. What really matters to them is whether it's going to *look* good; are people going to grab it off the shelf? Is the packaging right? And so people are tricked into falling for the cosmetic appeal of the food and not necessarily the taste. 'Everything has to fit into marketing concepts and I'm not sure that marketing concepts encourage the production of good honest food.'

Real food costs real money. 'You have to pay large sums of money for what purports to be real. Wild salmon, if you can be sure of getting it, costs a fishmonger's ransom. Organic wine made without chemicals, carrots grown in fields unsprayed with herbicides, hormone-free chickens and ham not bulked out with polyphosphates ... it all costs more.

'Hence the emergence of the small farmer in the Welsh hills, who was formerly chief cellist with the Hallé orchestra, or the painter who is now making bread. It's a kind of rearguard guerilla action being fought by people who are fed up with factory food.

'Up and down the country dedicated enthusiasts are producing alternative foods in sheer desperation – strange mustards, honeys of great rarity, unusual fermented goats' milk, smoked haunch of seaweed-fed Soay sheep, free-range quails' eggs untouched by *Salmonella enteriditis*, shingle-gathered samphire, stoneground flours, jams from copper pans and pre-pesticide apples from trees manured with old-fashioned dung.'

But why should we have to pay over the odds for special beer, bread, water, cheese and beef? Is it because the mass-produced alternative is so debased, adulterated and potentially dangerous that its hardly worth wrapping up? 'You've got this disturbing social divide. On the one hand a small number of people who are wealthy enough through the Thatcherite revolution to buy organic food and vegetables; and then you have the lumpen poor, who are living on debased degraded adulterated food, heavily hyped on television and often totally non-nutritious.'

Derek Cooper is a jolly man in his sixties. He divides his time between London and an island retreat in Skye. His middle name is Macdonald, after his mother, and a good part of his time is devoted to extolling the land of his maternal forebears in all its forms. He writes a weekly column in *Scotland on Sunday* and his books about the Highlands and Islands and in particular the Hebrides command universal respect.

His passion for real food goes back to his childhood in Raynes Park, Surrey, and summer holidays in the Hebrides. 'My father was working on the railways and was earning about five pounds a week. I was brought up in a very frugal house. We ate well because my mother knew how to cook good honest food, soups, stews, things of great nourishment, and because she'd been brought up in India we had dhal – lentils – and rice every Friday. Then there was the Scottish tradition of baking, and the taste of fresh salmon. So early on, I knew there were two sorts of food – fresh and canned.'

He worked his way to University College, Cardiff, and Wadham College, Oxford, where he became editor of *Isis*. His first job was as a broadcaster in Singapore. 'I suddenly found all this fresh food – you'd look down into the street and you'd see your whole meal cooked before your very eyes. You'd have marvellous Chinese food, Indian food, Malay food, Indonesian food. I began to realise that food and a people's culture were indissoluble. We'd lost a lot of our heritage to the food processors – Asians were still in control of what they ate.'

In 1967 he wrote his first book, *The Bad Food Guide*, an angry

satirical outburst against attitudes to food in Britain which many
deplored but most took for granted. It was in the bestseller list in
the *Sunday Times* for six weeks. 'The book was not only about bad
food in hotels and restaurants; it was about filth and malpractice and
the adulteration and debasement of food. It was also about fraud,
pesticides, and excessive amounts of nitrates in baby food. Very
polemic.'

In 1970 he wrote *The Beverage Report*, and then *The Gullibility
Gap* in 1974. For *Catering Times* he invented a character called Ray
Gunge, who was always ready with a quote, advising other caterers
how to exploit the customer even more creatively, inspired greatly
by the advertisements for convenience products which filled the
pages of *Catering Times*.

As President of the Guild of Food Writers he fulfilled an ambition
to pool the resources of all those who write or broadcast on food in
all its manifold aspects, inviting as members food scientists as freely
as cookery writers. As a pressure group they provide a welcome
antidote to the numerous lobbies acting for the food industry. The
most important of these may be the Food and Drink Federation,
and Derek Cooper has a respect for them and their uninhibited
aim of defending the interests of their members against excessive
Government regulation in the fine old tradition of unfettered private
enterprise.

Derek Cooper's most scathing humour is reserved for those who
appear to be consumer-biased organisations which they are not.
'Consider the name, British Nutrition Foundation. British: sounds
like the British Legion; Nutrition: good; Foundation: the Peace
Foundation, the Charity Foundation – is it a Foundation? I regard
the BNF as a damage limitation organisation funded by the food
industry.

'The BNF is also sponsored by the people who make the heaviest
saturated fat used in food processing, which is the Palm Oil Research
Institute of Malaysia. And by Proctor and Gamble who are about
to bring you Olestra, the polyester sucrose fat that does not fatten.
It is an incredible list. It even includes Slimming Magazines Hold-
ings Ltd. So you have all the people who make you fat and all the
people who make you thin, all supporting this splendid organisation
which campaigns tirelessly for good food and good health!'

So where can you go for impartial information? The food industry
employs a large number of verbally skilled people to hype what are

very often nutritionally undesirable products, and then you have an
enormous number of people on hand to spread the good news about
food. 'They have names like the Chicken Information Bureau, the
Breakfast Advisory Bureau, the British Egg Information Service. If
there were a Snack Food Foundation it would of course be financed
by the snack food industry solely to promote the ever increasing
consumption of snacks. This is why we needed the Guild of Food
Writers.'

The mythical 'housewife' is the target of the food industry. But
it's men, he says, who decide what they want, in a very patronising
way. 'The late Caroline Walker made the profound remark that the
food industry is dominated by middle-aged men from the middle
classes. There are very few women farmers. So this is a very male-
orientated society. Most of the farmers, the primary producers, the
food processors, the retailers, and the politicians are male. Yet most
men seldom go shopping, seldom cook and have little knowledge
about the close relationship between diet and health.

Considering the state of British food when Derek Cooper started
his great crusade, surely much has been for the better? Yes, it has,
but he mourns the loss of the small shopkeeper. 'I remember from
my childhood there was a choice of four butchers and six grocers in
the high street. Now we all go to the big hypermarket out of town.
I went into the new Tesco in Malden in Essex, it seemed as if Florida
had come to Britain. The family could spend a day there happily
grazing.

He's not against supermarkets. 'I think the quality control of an
organisation like Tesco's or Sainsbury's is fantastically high. Marks
& Spencer have a lot of excellent products. What you are buying is
convenience, image, trust and quality.'

The death of the small shopkeeper is being hastened by the
Uniform Business Rate, limiting choice still further. First of all we
lost the high street grocer and fishmonger, then the greengrocers
and butchers have been going, and now the delicatessens are selling
up in the face of supermarket competition. Cooper finds it saddening.
'I have this depressing nightmare of a Britain at the end of the
century where there will be no small shops left, only these giant
supermarkets where you can buy the same meals and the same sachet
of salad leaves from one end of the country to another. Gradually
choice will be eliminated and you will either eat according to Tesco's
idea of what food should be or Sainsbury's. And when competition

has finally been eliminated there'll just be this one giant superstore selling food from one giant factory.'

And he sees no lead coming from politicians. One party, the Conservatives, want to deregulate. 'They will do everything in their power to eradicate Salmonella or Botulism but they don't care a damn if the food which might harbour bacteria is in itself a bad nutritional bargain. They take the view that it's a free society. You don't have to eat cream buns and beer-flavoured crisps. You can eat plenty of fresh food, apples and vegetables, skimmed milk, it's all there. They would like to deregulate everything as much as possible, and hand everything back to the food industry, which obeys market forces and gives the consumer only what will sell. They food industry can also do the research. They don't want to pay for anything any more unless it makes economic sense and increases material prosperity, because that's all they are interested in.'

For the opposition party, food has never been an issue in the past. 'If the Labour Party were returned to power and were inclined to implement a radical change in the way we eat in keeping with the recommendations made by people such as Professor Philip James, that would be very interesting.'

It seems unlikely that any political party will move until it has been pushed hard, very hard indeed. And in this, Derek Cooper reflects, Britain has to go a long, long way. 'Our tradition is that food is something "to be got over". We'll have an early tea and get it over, and then we're free to mow the lawn or go for a walk or watch television. I remember going to Corsica with a party of journalists. The food was very interesting. There were two cookery editors and for a lot of the time we were talking about what we were eating. Eventually, a young girl in the party said: "What's the matter with you people? All you do is talk about food!"'

Food and cookery writers can raise the level of debate, he believes, and they must not relax their vigilance.

Until we create a Food Ministry, he would settle for an Omfoodsman. 'An Omfoodsman will do for food what the Ombudsman does for citizens aggrieved in other ways. The Omfoodsman will arbitrate in all matters relating to food and drink from common adulteration and misrepresentation to the broader issues of food policy. He will have a hardworking staff of food scientists, nutritionists, medical men and lawyers to advise him and his office will be funded by a levy on the food industry. His staff will be searching for pesticide residues in baby food, misleading claims on health products, substandard meat pies, food that presents a long-term health risk to the nation. He will of course have his work cut out initially, the Omfoodsman, but when everyone sees he means business there should be a remarkable overnight improvement in our food chain. Then there would be no need for a resistance movement for real ale or real bread. Everything would be good to eat and drink. Everything would be real.'

And who might one look to, to serve as the first Omfoodsman? Who indeed.

15

TASTE

Unless they happened to be Greek-Cypriot, how many greengrocers have any real knowledge or understanding of what they handle, save its price, and the name of the country of origin of the box? Many of those who sell meat, fish, vegetables and fruit take the view that the customers want the cheapest, so that's what they sell. When it's not deliberate, it's out of ignorance, for the people who serve in shops come from families who've never experienced the taste of good food, and nor have their parents before them. The people who cook food in canteens, schools, hospitals and many restaurants come from families where the taste of good food is not known. They are good souls who have gone into catering. Ignorance breeds ignorance. The exceptions to this rule are so few that they stand out like beacons in the dark.

I once asked Professor Brian Spencer, the charming, witty and intelligent head of the British Flour Milling and Baking Research Association at Chorleywood in Hertfordshire, which was responsible for bringing the white, sliced loaf into the world, why they didn't get someone of the stature of the food writer and historian, Elizabeth David, to sit on taste panels in assessing quality. Not only is she the most admired arbiter of taste in Britain, the person who led us out of the gastronomic desert of post-war Britain, but she is also author of the most considerable book on bread ever written.

His reply was interesting: 'Elizabeth David represents perhaps 0.1 per cent of the population. We're not concerned with such a small minority. Our job is not to cater for tastes which are too bland or too tasty. We try to aim at a middle spectrum. The vast majority of people don't have highly educated, highly sophisticated, very delicately tuned tastes like Elizabeth David. She's not representative of the bulk of people. She's at the gourmet end.'

Over lunch at the Association's headquarters they served rolls that were light in volume, airy, springy, fluffy, and had no taste at all. As a guest it seemed rude to comment, as if it were a reflection of their hospitality. But frankly, it was indeed a reflection on their hospitality. Here was a distinguished biochemist, a world authority on enzymes, which are the key to the behaviour of yeasts, who was directly responsible for providing most of the bread that goes on our table in Britain, and the bread on his table had no taste.

The taste of the future has to combine the fine skill of the craftsman baker with brilliant technology. What they did to bread, which had been going for about 3,000 years along the same sweet road, was as dramatic as putting a man on the moon. They removed at a stroke the laborious effort of making dough rise, by putting it through a high speed mixer, reducing the first bulk fermentation period from three hours to a few minutes. This technology produces superficial variety, but the end result is the same, moist loaves designed to have a spongy texture and long-keeping quality. If you had a good loaf you wouldn't want to keep it, you'd want to eat it.

The bread roll at Chorleywood was such a technological achievement: it was like a dog that could sing, but not like Pavarotti. When you go to Germany, the baker's is a craftsman's shop, with ready-to-eat sculptures of bread of every size, consistency, texture, colour and flavour. Every bite is appetising and fulfilling. In Italy and Spain it is a matter of pride to sell good bread. In France there are thirty or forty types of individual and different regional breads still being made. Two of their most famous breads, made and sold in Britain, ought to make the stores liable for prosecution under the Trade Description Act: the baguette and the pain de campagne. Both bear a cosmetic resemblance to the originals but, once cut open, the texture is shown to be – that old Chorleywood sponge.

I asked Professor Spencer why, with his team of the best bread and flour scientists, couldn't he get authentic bread on to our shelves.

'The hole is the great virtue of French bread. You cut your lip on the crust but underneath it's full of holes which can take a pound of butter. Superb stuff. We sent a researcher to Paris one year to the Grand Moulin of Paris to discover the secret. The critical thing is to end up with large bubbles. When you're handling the dough you

mustn't abuse it or knock air out of it. After you've mixed your
dough, long or slow fermentation, you must mould it into a ball and
leave it for ten minutes. Then it's carefully rolled into long batons,
and exact cuts are made on the top. The cuts are superfine, made at
a diagonal, almost horizontally, overlapping by no more than two
centimetres. The ratio of crust to crumb is of utmost importance.
For the first ten munutes it must be baked with moisture, then
finished with a dry bake. The object of the baguette is to finish with
a large area of crust. And large bubbles inside.'

A poster record of their research into French bread and photo-
graphs of experiments are pinned on a lab wall. 'It was wonderful
to have the bread around while we were making it,' says Spencer
wistfully. But he says the British will never buy French bread
seriously. French bread is made with soft flour and stales quickly.
'The English housewife doesn't want to buy bread twice a day, even
supposing there were enough bakers to make it.' It's been tried. A
few years ago a French baker came over and baked French bread
with French wheat and everyone said how wonderful. 'But it only
lasted three months.'

So they *can* bake it, but they blame the customers. And what
happens is a British compromise – we sell a baton made of Chorleywood fluff and *call* it a baguette.

Even Marks & Spencer sell a pain de campagne aimed at customers
with bigger French vocabularies. It would make a nice cushion, it's
so springy and bouncy. In France these huge circular two kilo loaves
are brought back from Paris by weekenders who've been in the
South or the Midi – and they are so irresistible you start picking at
them at once. They're made from dough which has been fermenting
for a week, larger and larger batches of flour being added daily, until
eventually it's slowly baked, sometimes in wood-fired ovens, with
the result that the crust is the thickness of suede shoe leather and
the inside is a waxy, holey, chewy texture, which is delicious fresh
and even better toasted the next day. While the pain de campagne
is in the house, everybody tucks into it as they might tuck into
the parma ham in the fridge, until it has all gone, and even when
it has gone it stays on as a memory. Can you say that of our pre-
tenders? How would people know if they were never served the real
thing?

People who know nothing about the prized traditions of France,
China, India, and the rest of the world appropriate their national

dishes, have a tasting panel (Elizabeth David not invited) and solemnly send the product out into the world. A soggy chicken stew with artificial colourings and flavourings and a pronounced taste of monosodium glutamate and preservatives is gravely named Coq au Vin, and passed on to the innocent public. Any mixture of carrots and onions with a vinegary sweet-sour flavour is – Chinese. A spot of curry powder and it's – Indian. Put rice into it and it's – Italian, a risotto. Rice with a prawn or two and it's – Spanish. Beans with some token blobs of meat has to be Chilli con Carne – Mexican, olé. Who do they think they are fooling?

The French serve Coq au Vin in most country restaurants every weekend. It's truly a national dish, and texture and flavour depend on the maturity of the bird and the plentiful red wine which tenderises and flavours it, with the unctuous addition of flavoursome home-cured bacon (not supermarket rashers full of polyphosphates and water) and some baby onions and baby mushrooms. If you've never tasted the real thing, or achieved it by proxy from Elizabeth David's books, you wouldn't know that what was often offered in Britain was not the real thing.

As every Italian knows, risotto is not a plate of pre-fluffed rice, but a dish made with the absorbent, fat rice of the Po Valley. Arborio is one style: cooked in oil with a little gently sweated chopped onion until it takes on a transparent colour, and then cooked with chicken stock made from a real chicken's carcass, for twenty to thirty minutes, stirring carefully, until it's *al dente*, when a generous quantity of best butter is stirred in, and finally a spoonful of parmesan, freshly grated from a block. Thirty minutes of patient attention, allied to perfect ingredients achieves this. The taste is dizzyingly delightful, nicely satisfying and filling, and it may just be lifted into gourmet class with slivers and the juice of truffles, or porcini, the richly smelling Italian dried mushrooms. This is about taste. And yet people in the food industry will offer us dishes borrowing this name, but in no way matching its simple beauty.

And how dare they appropriate the name paella? The Spanish version of risotto, nourished with big pieces of seafood, chicken, rabbit, snails, a veritable Christmas pudding of every morsel that is choice, excellent and tasty, flavoured with the royal scent of true saffron stamens, pound for pound the most expensive foodstuff in the world. Every stage in the cooking of a paella is a time-honoured ritual as careful as a Japanese tea ceremony. It isn't a bag of cooked rice with peas and frozen prawns.

When complaining about the present, we're apt to remember the Good Old Days. But for every good moment recalled, there were many miserable experiences we must be glad to have forgotten: gallons and gallons of beer stinking, sour and out of condition; or blocks and blocks of cheddar in the village greengrocer's going green with mould. There was much that went bad, in the Good Old Days. Today we enjoy the half-way house of having food in good condition all the time but lacking in character and flavour, for the flavour that food technologists put in are essentially crude to withstand the heat processing. When a *Sunday Express* reader won the paper's cookery competition, one of the prizes was to have his winning fish soup canned by Baxter's, the excellent Scottish canned food company. A good soup was made – and even at a comparative price by economising on some of the ingredients. The original soup and Baxter's soup were tasted side by side at The Belfry, the Mayfair restaurant club of Anton Mosimann, one of the country's most celebrated chefs. Well, the tinned soup was fine, but the exercise was embarrassing. Who wants tinned soup when the real thing beckons? When our waters are teeming with superb fish that make the great fish soups of France and Spain? To take that lovely soup and put it in a can where the heat treatment does to fish what you should never do to fish – cook it too long – is as cruel as putting a song-bird in a cage. And if people did buy the winning soup out of curiosity when they saw it on the supermarket shelves, I hope that some of them would have known that they could make better at home.

An inspiring example of what food technology could be doing comes from an exercise I carried out on the *Sunday Times* with Graham Rose, their imaginative gardening correspondent. In the late 1970s British apple growers were being rocked back on their heels by the French whose season starts earlier than ours, and they were getting their Golden Delicious to our markets before any of our apples had ripened.

British apples, it is no exaggeration to claim, probably because of our impossible climate, have been the best in the world for centuries, and the range of varieties actually runs into thousands. But what British growers decided to do was to grub up existing varieties and plant our own Golden Delicious. Now Golden Delicious from my garden are gold *and* delicious, but that's because I let them ripen on the tree. The appeal to the grower is not its taste, but its uniformity, its cosmetic appeal, and 'le crunch', its undoubted texture, but especially its capacity for being stored for long life, for cropping well, and for being able to be bred for disease resistance – in other words, a big little earner.

What we did was to engage Jack Matthews, one of the country's three leading apple growers, to revive six vanishing varieties of great British apples on his orchards near Bury St Edmunds in Suffolk – apples which were no longer in the shops and had disappeared from the nursery lists: Ashmead's Kernel, Orleans Reinette, Rosemary Russet, Ribston Pippin, James Grieve and the cooker Early Victoria (which bakes to a fluff like a soufflé). All were tasty, sturdy apples with character and pronounced flavour. But instead of being purely an exercise in nostalgia for the Good Old Days, Jack Matthews applied a touch of modern technology.

Had any of these been grown in the average garden, they would have quickly become unmanageable. He grafted the buds therefore onto dwarf stock, which meant that it would be possible to grow all six of them in a line a yard apart, occupying the smallest space, yet promising yields of ten to fifteen pounds per tree, ample for home consumption. Such was the appeal of this scheme, when they were offered to readers, every one of the collection of 2,000 orders was taken up in the first post. Apples doomed to extinction were saved for the ordinary garden.

Now the Battle for the British Apple is truly on, for the Government withdrew support for the National Collection at Brogdale in Kent, and it looks as if it may be able to survive on the nation's goodwill. It would be hopeful to think it is not the end – but the beginning of taste and quality fighting back.

The way we eat tomorrow depends very much on the way we eat today. Every experience shows that common sense, nutrition and health are not the chief factors in dictating our food, or certainly not as important as fashion at one extreme and cheapness at the other. Modern food technology has largely ignored the upmarket end of food, because it has represented such a small volume of business compared with mass markets. But the profit in the mass market becomes eroded by serious competition, and to make things even cheaper they have to make them worse, using cheaper and cheaper ingredients, forcing farmers to produce cheaper animals, which means cheaper feeding stuffs, and that means inferior materials such as the waste products of chickens, sheep, cows, until inevitably something goes wrong, and the food technologist is called in, not to engineer a superior product, but to use the cosmetic skill of his art to mask a bad one, drawing on a palette of garish colours and flavours, emulsifiers to give 'mouth feel' and bulking agents or air or water to give substance where none existed. This insubstantial wonder is then tested by the marketing people, and if enough taste panels of 'ordinary housewives' find it acceptable, cheap enough and convenient enough, it is handed over to the advertising agents.

People are astonished that Van Gogh's paintings sell for millions today, while the great artist died in poverty, and assume that the reward for great art is posthumous. This is not so. The great art of the twentieth century is advertising and its reward is immediate. Profits run into millions and millions and millions. From the historic campaigns for Guinness with its Toucan (*See What Toucan Do*) and the enduring *Guinness Gives You Strength* to Heineken's witty commercials (*Heineken Refreshes The Parts That Other Beers Don't Reach*); from Bisto the gravy thickener, whose Bisto kids sniffed the aroma from every poster hoarding in the country in the 1930s, to the sophisticated soap opera of Katie and the Oxo family; and the noisy tub-thumping of Mars – the temptingly sweet, sticky, chewy, delicious chocolate and fudge confection that helps you *Work, Rest and Play* – a sublimely nonsensical idea which you can forgive because it does give the sense of a treat. Advertising makes food and drink so much fun, invests it with glamour it wouldn't ordinarily have, something more than being necessary, nourishing, satisfying, tasty – it has to be glamorous. The advertisements, the packaging, the excitement of the Superstore, the equivalent of 1930s Picture Palace, offering all the fun of the fair: music, colour, children's rides. Anything and everything you want is there to be plucked off the shelves and taken home.

It's almost impossible to think of certain products without the glamour which the great modern artists of advertising have painted on, and it's not a cosmetic job they do, it's much more than that. Expert psychologists dig deep into the national unconscious to extract elements of need, of insecurity, of the desire to be loved, of inadequacy, of loneliness, of social inferiority, and create a message on the canvas of the product which satisfies these needs. To the teenager, they address his longing for excitement and adventure, selfishness and rebellion, with snacks that don't need to be shared in the home, that make a noisy, explosive crunch and crackle in the mouth, that are daringly bright and ostentatious, or drinks that are a badge of the identity of their age group, that create a sense of belonging – to the global world of Coca Cola, for example.

The advertising artists brilliantly manipulate the products – but for lasting star quality, the product, in the end, has to deliver something of the promise. Maybe it's cheap. Maybe it's tasty. Maybe it's fashionable. The advertising artist – with the help of millions of pounds of help, can edge his product ahead of a close rival, he can give the illusion of a better product. The application of his art applies mostly to cheaper products.

Classical music endures for centuries, and Mozart, Mahler and Mendelsohn can be as satisfying to the attuned ear as anything composed today; pop music is the wallpaper of our time, with a short sell-by date. Thus classical food might be described as the cuisine of the great French chefs, where a few spoonfuls of sauce may have been reduced from a stockpot of veal bones and vegetables which has been simmering for days to provide the essence and texture of a glutinous medium appropriate to the dish being served, its meat juices, herbs, spices, a touch of reduced cream carrying the flavours to the tongue and releasing them slowly and magically. Pop music might be the equivalent of the instant pleasure of a scoop of cold, sweet, smooth, refreshing, brightly coloured, sharply flavoured ice cream. It may however leave a nasty taste in the mouth, and for hours afterwards, as the ingredients become more apparent. You like the sensation, but the after effects were increasingly unpleasant, and you then feel angry or disappointed that you've wasted your time and money, and abused your palate.

A sauce made by the celebrated French chef Albert Roux at his restaurant, Le Gavroche, in London's Mayfair – probably the most expensive in the country – is Mozart ...

Bisto is something else. For all that the Van Goghs and Hockneys of the advertising world can do, Bisto is gravy thickening. It's not in fact wheat flour, or even cornflour, but potato flour, which is an excellent thickener, and is used as such in Poland and Russia. Bisto, claimed as the aromatic and secret ingredient that can turn around your Sunday joint, is potato flour and colouring, caramel colouring. And salt. Make some, taste it – where is its magic now? But add it to the meat juices in the cooking pan – and it will taste of the meat juices. Delicious. Of such stuff are dreams manufactured by the artists of the advertising world. Custard – ah, British custard, a stream which coats our memories of childhood, yellow as a new-born chick, the symbol of its eggy goodness, creamy, smooth. There is no egg, the yellow is colouring, and the creamy goodness is what you've just added – milk. What is custard powder? It's cornflour. The added value is the milk you put in, a lot of colouring, and a lot of advertising and window dressing. And it's brilliant because throughout life it will continue to evoke the happiness and warmth of childhood. It is pure pop, of no enduring quality – not like classic custard, which is a trembling, wobbly suspension of eggs, milk, cream, sugar, flavoured with real vanilla, which reaches a perfection when it's poured over a few slices of plain white bread and butter, and baked with sultanas – Chef Anton Mosimann's version of English bread and butter pudding.

Derek Cooper would argue that the nation's sense of taste, so unsophisticated after more than a century of neglect, is such that most people think gravy browning and cornflour custard and tinned fruit and coloured sugar water and fatty dyed sausage meat, and ham and bacon injected with water, are the real tastes of food. And until people do taste the real thing, they have no way of judging.

In the last few decades, many travel abroad and come back with a renewed excitement in the taste of fresh food and good cooking. Equally many do not. Many who cook for the millions of holi-daymakers who go to Spain, Greece and Italy have no special expert-ise in their country's specialities. Nor do they need to have, as the customers are so obviously pleased with burgers and chips and simple pizzas and pasta.

Antonio Mas Ripoll, acclaimed by a French restaurant guide as the best cook in Majorca, owns a place which welcomes a mixture of Germans and English, and a smaller mixture of French and other nationalities. He can cook the traditional island's specialities passed down by his family – Sopa de Mallorca (a cabbage and vegetable soup poured onto thick, dry slices of – it goes without saying – good bread) or Conejo con Cebollas – rabbit with onions, the soft sweet onions cooked for hours with tomato to the consistency of a thin jam, to make the medium for the final cooking of the tender, moist rabbit. His cooking is perfection – but neither the British or the Germans appreciate it. The British are suspicious of unfamiliar tastes. The Germans look down on cabbage and rabbit. So Antonio cooks steak for them, but he cooks it very well. He does everything well. A century of ignorance isolates us from his skills.

So impoverished is the British tradition of eating that the best value eating places for a half-century have been Chinese, Indian and Greek, thanks to the immigration of thousands from our former colonies in Hong Kong, India and Cyprus. The people who cook in them are seldom trained cooks – many were seamen originally who got their passage from Pakistan and Hong Kong by working in the ship's galleys.

In Britain we consider their dishes spicy, appetising, tasty, filling, fun and cheap. Supermarkets respond to what's perceived to be an area of appeal. The level of sophistication of these dishes compared with what is produced by home cooks in their own countries is low, and laughable compared with the traditions of the great restaurants of Hong Kong, where they draw on the tradition of thousands of years of high quality cooking by chefs who served the great emperors through the dynasties.

How can these truths be brought closer to home? We can't get to India and China, but we can sample their cooking in restaurants here, and we look to the restaurant guide books, the *Good Food Guide*, the *Michelin Guide* and the *Ronay Guide*, to set standards, praise and encourage and popularise the best. Egon Ronay, for his part, also engaged in campaigns to improve food in public places, in motorways, at airports, on airlines, in hospitals, schools, factory and works canteens, for the Forces.

Listening to Egon Ronay, you at first despair it's possible to raise the perception of taste in Britain to any standard at all. You'd be forgiven for thinking that we won't make it to the twenty-first century, that we are going down the plug with America, and gradually taking everyone else with us. But this will not be so, because, in spite of apathy and ignorance, every hard-won battle did in fact inch us further forward. Compared with a half-century ago, when Egon Ronay first came to Britain, we might be on another planet.

Egon Ronay is Hungarian-born, and fled to England after the War when the Communists took over, removing all those with power, affluence or intellect, like his own family – celebrated restaurateurs in Budapest, and prior to that in Transylvania. Ronay has such a lofty gastronomic viewpoint, you wonder why he bothered with us. His first visit to Britain was as a student when he stayed with friends in Cambridge and discovered mustard pickles. 'It wasn't that English food was inedible, it simply had no interest in it.'

The 1940s were grim, and he arrived as we were emerging from rationing. 'You could eat well in top class restaurants and hotels, where there were French chefs, but there was nothing in the medium range, apart from Lyons Corner Houses, where you could get a good breakfast; kippers, bacon and eggs. Some of the food was unbelievable, those strange tennis ball things, Scotch eggs, very badly done. The people who influenced food at this time had been to public school, where the food had been not just without interest, but horrifying. So you didn't discuss food.'

He started his famous guide in 1958, as a result of writing a restaurant column in the *Daily Telegraph*. The 1960s were times of great changes in the social order, and this influenced the state of eating out. 'For the first time people who had been to grammar schools, who'd eaten good food at home, started coming to restaurants. They were used to speaking their mind and complaining if they didn't like what they got, and stating preferences. They were professional people like fashion photographers, advertising people, journalists and so on.'

As he travelled the length and breadth of the country he was appalled to find that it wasn't just that the food didn't taste of anything. 'It was a gruelling experience, the food was so often dreadful.' Nobody realised how little they had to do to turn it around. 'Why not good coffee? You have the coffee, you have the water, and the heat. It puzzles me. Why shouldn't the simplest things be marvellous?'

He wasn't alone, fortunately. On television Philip Harben and Fanny Craddock, the one practical and confidential, the other grand and flamboyant like a musical comedy star, introduced the notion of better cookery on the first television cookery series in the late 1950s and early 1960s.

Elizabeth David had written *Mediterranean Cooking* immediately after the War, and it was eagerly devoured. The success of her following books was assured, *French Provincial Cooking* and *French Country Cooking*, followed by *Italian Food*. Her beautiful writing evokes the pleasures of eating as no other cookery writer of our time, as well as passing on the riches and wealth of these great cuisines, but many will remember, too, the impetus she gave to food writers with her regular critical articles in the *Spectator* and other periodicals, lashing complacency, exposing frauds and deceptions, and signposting the road to better food, signalling the stores (many of them Italian and in London's Soho) which set an example of providing unremittingly excellent basic produce, pasta, salami, olives and olive oil. For a generation every writer who wrote a cookery book noted their debt to her.

Soon, fortunately, she was no longer alone and writing about food became a serious and even profitable profession, which it had not been in the days of Ambrose Heath and Elizabeth Craig who each wrote over a hundred cookery books, and had little to show for it financially. (Ambrose Heath who loved the good life was actually made bankrupt twice.) Onto this scene stole Robert Carrier, a charismatic young American of Irish/German descent whose real name is MacMahon. With his great sense of showbusiness (a frustrated musical actor), he introduced the idea of glorious technicolour to selling food and capitalised on the birth of colour supplements to the Sunday newspapers.

Having lived in Paris and travelled in Italy, with the innocence of Americans and the bare-faced cheek of the Irish, he adopted the role of distinguished gastronomer, published what was probably the most expensive cookery book ever produced at the time – *Great Dishes of the World* – and went on to open not one, but two restaurants which each won Michelin Stars, Carrier's in Camden, North London, and Hintlesham Hall in Suffolk. The stage was set, a star was on it, and others followed a trail he showed to be lucrative (home in Eaton Square, London, a flat on the Rive Gauche, Paris, an apartment in Manhattan, an eighteenth-century country house in Suffolk, and a Moorish palace in Marrakesh).

If Robert Carrier influenced fashion in food, the most influential cookery writer was to be Jane Grigson, who gave twenty-five years of inspiration and leadership to others in the field through her writing in the *Observer*, and who wrote a shelf-full of definitive books, nine in all, which represent a potent monument to establishing new standards and levels of expectation for cooks in this country – starting with *Charcuterie and French Pork Cookery*. (Based on living in a summer holiday home near Touraine on the Loire, which was a cave she'd bought for £468 to the dismay of her father who assumed the money would be better spent. But he was so wrong.)

Jane Grigson brought to our understanding of food the history and social customs which were responsible for them, and not only did she bring us scholarly and practical insight into the food of France and Europe, but she also reached back into English history, and retrieved the style and elegance of cooks in the sixteenth, seventeenth and eighteenth centuries, before the nation became brutalised by the effects of the Industrial Revolution.

I last spoke to her in the cosy kitchen of her home in Broad Town, Wiltshire. She had cooked a meal enhanced by vegetables picked from the garden half an hour before. Her philosophy, she claimed, was simple: Cooking was not an art, like poetry, but a trade or a craft. 'You could compare the best to making Chippendale chairs.'

She said she wanted to show people that hope for the future lay in respect for the past. 'What bugs me about bad food is when you think of the millions of gardeners and farmers who have lived before one, and they've taken all that trouble to develop a crab apple into a Cox's Orange Pippin – to spoil that by treating it badly, it's blasphemous really.'

She wanted people to understand also that cooking for the family and friends demands respect. She quoted Marguerite Yourcenar on cooking. 'An operation which is performed two or three times a day, and the purpose of which is to sustain life, surely merits all our care.'

Jane Grigson was born in the North-East. Her father was Town Clerk of Sunderland and it was a matter of sadness to her that the North suffers the greatest impoverishment in eating. She observed that the social philosopher Engels worked out that the poorer you are the higher proportion of your income you spend on food. 'He compiled statistics among the working poor and the craftsmen in Germany or Switzerland and discovered that the craftsmen were spending a lower proportion of their income than the truly poor, which makes sense. The proportion of your income you spend on food has always been a measure of poverty. The middle class spend 20 per cent and the poor 48 per cent. England is the only country to break Engels' law. The poor in the North spend only 20 per cent of their income on food so the food they are eating must be diabolical – a really malnutritional diet.'

Jane Grigson said she deplored the national attitude to food. 'People like stuffing themselves. This is what I find hard. I can't bear looking at people in a restaurant where they can help themselves. They would rather stuff themselves with something not very good. My great quibble against the English is that everything has got to be cheap. That to me is the root of the problem. I doubt whether we can get past that obstacle.'

She resented, too, that people in public life in Britain tried to disguise the fact that they enjoyed good food and, if it was discovered that they did, they would become objects of derision in the press. 'People like Roy Jenkins or Roy Hattersley are criticised because they like good food. As if you ought to live on hamburgers and chips, stewed tea and buns. I took this up with French friends who are socialist, and they roared with laughter, because, of course, they like good food.'

Jane Grigson's commentary on eating in her lifetime is revealing and shows that, even if it's a field full of weeds, there are flowers, too, which can be protected and nourished.

In her childhood in the 1930s, there was food for the middle class and food for the poor. 'For the middle class household, tea was the great entertaining meal. Family tea on Sunday with millions of cakes, all home made, and sandwiches. We used to long for bought cake. In fact there were three wonderful patisseries in the town, with Swiss and Austrian backgrounds, and when my mother had Bridge parties she would buy all their cakes and sausage rolls. When we had children's parties we used to have lobster pâtés. This was marvellous but around the wonderful patisseries and full upper middle class food we were surrounded by slums where people were living on bread, tea and marge and the children had rickets. I've never seen children looking like that since. The Depression was a very depressed time with a very inadequate diet. The great treat in the elementary schools at Christmas would be to give each child an orange and a bar of chocolate. I don't think they ever saw fruit otherwise.

'In the 1930s it was very surprising how many people down to a very low social level had a servant. The lower middle classes would have poor little girls who did everything and in very homely cir-cumstances. They cooked, although this would be basic and pretty grim. Even our cooks were always miners' daughters and all they could really do was a roast. They all resented my mother going into the kitchen. She was allowed to make puddings occasionally.'

The 1940s changed everyone's lives. 'With the War all these girls went into the munitions factories and suddenly my mother was allowed into the kitchen – this was very typical – and she was delighted. We ate extremely well through the War: not through the black market because my father was a food controller in the town, so if any shopkeepers saw us coming they were never going to give her anything extra in case it got back to my father's notice and he would prosecute. But my mother was very resourceful and we would walk out and pick nettles. She was really marvellous over the food and understood how to make wonderful stews and vegetables. She just had a gift for it.

'Because of rationing, suddenly everybody had to eat certain things. The bread was much improved – you had the National loaf which was much better bread. The only trouble was that perhaps the poor couldn't afford to buy butter and they had to have marge. But they did have to have cheese. All these things were on rations and a lot of things were on points. People were encouraged to dig out their flowers and plants and grow things to eat. In the North we always had root vegetables which were very dull and we didn't have much fruit really.'

The 1950s? 'People were much more alert to the possibilities of what could be done.' She had the opportunity to travel to Italy, thanks to being left a hundred pounds by an aunt, and was astonished to find that a defeated nation could have such wonderful food. She was suddenly introduced to vegetables and olive oil. 'It was spaghetti with raw eggs broken into it or eggs baked in the oven. The food tasted so good and then I came back and Elizabeth David's book on Mediterranean cookery came out; suddenly there were lots of things one could do. None of the writers so far had hit the imagination like Elizabeth did. The 1950s were totally dominated by her. She opened us up to Europe culturally. The 1950s was a time of discovery, when you recognised kindred spirits. I always remember people walking around with those blue packets of Neopolitan spaghetti under their arms. They'd found shops where you could buy decent pasta. When you went out to dinner everybody was excitedly trying all the Elizabeth David recipes – Coq au Vin, chicken liver pâté, Boeuf Bourguignonne, and courgettes of course. Cream was then the sign of revolution. To us, cream and butter were the great liberators. We'd been deprived of them for a century and a half – since Elizabeth Acton. Suddenly it became fun.'

By the 1960s people had more money, and there was a better standard in some shops. 'There were more interesting shops and good restaurants starting to open. The Hole in the Wall, Bath, was open in 1947. There was Francis Coulson's Sharrow Bay in the Lake District, and The Elizabeth in Oxford. These three restaurants were the only decent restaurants outside London. They were meccas. The Hole in the Wall was doing three sittings a night in the 1960s and this was so exciting. George Perry-Smith was cooking from Elizabeth David's books and his great thing was that wonderful cold table from which you ate for your first course. I've never seen a cold table like it anywhere else and somehow one had the feeling that Elizabeth and George between them created the English idea of what French cooking was; because I've never found it in France. This great lavish spread – the French would serve the food quite differently.'

By the 1970s Jane Grigson was well into becoming *the* established cookery writer – having married the poet and critic Geoffrey Grigson with whom she'd bought the home in France, and being very much encouraged by him in her career. The 1970s, with her help, saw the emergence of small food producers, such as cheesemakers, a yearning for better bread than factory bread, better beer than keg beer, and the launch of the very effective Campaign for Real Ale.

The 1980s saw greater acceptance of the small food producers by a much larger proportion of the population. Henrietta Green compiled an important book of food producers, which was adapted for the motorist as *R.A.C. Food Routes.* Jane Grigson saw off the decade, leading an attack on food minister, John MacGregor, claiming she never thought it would be her role as a cookery writer to have to accuse the Government of hiding the appalling truth about the level of Salmonella in eggs. She was an implacable enemy of food debased by food processing and full of additives and inferior ingredients which were no better than the bad foods the poor had to eat in her childhood. As an epitaph, it was suggested she should be remembered by a rousing call she had made, as far back as the 1960s, when people were demonstrating against the Bomb. 'Why,' she demanded, 'are we not on the streets demonstrating, when our foods are being stuffed full of very slow poison?'

Jane Grigson is a voice to inspire the next generation of writers and cooks, as Elizabeth David was before her.

Encouraged by writers of their stature, we ought to be optimistic about the future, but quality will only improve if we act in concert. We must look to television cooks, newspaper and magazine columnists, restaurant guide editors, to insist on high standards, seek out the excellent and condemn the second-rate.

We need allies among doctors and nutritionists and educationalists and hospital authorities to ensure the food is not only tasty, but of good nutritional value.

We need to shake our politicians, and make them take more responsibility for improving food quality. Why doesn't the Department of Health bring down its high National Health Service Bills by addressing the root cause of heart disease and breast cancer – diet? Why is the Ministry of Agriculture, Fisheries and Food incapable of giving a lead, or is it afraid of offending the food industry lobbies?

It is a paradox that we should live in times of great plenty and yet not eat well. It is inconceivable to me that a civilised country such as ours can continue to endure this. If we cannot move our leaders then we must act unilaterally, and start to choose the foods we want, and boycott those we don't.

We need to make the people who supply our food start to think about what they're doing. We need to prod them, not with a blunt stick, but with a sharp one. Then, perhaps, and then only, will the message get through.

SUPERMARKET SHOPPING BASKET

A guide to choosing the food that's best for you and your family

Eating well is an extremely easy habit to acquire. True, it may not seem so 'convenient' at first, but it's easier to adapt to at home where you control the food supply, and less easy in the workplace where you don't.

This guide is based on what to put in your everyday supermarket trolley. You'll find you can eat marvellously all the time without recourse to wholefood shops and organic farms.

As a rule of thumb, most fresh food is good for you and tasty into the bargain, and processed food is likely to be less so. Here are three checklists: Eat all you want; Steady how you go; and Watch it.

EAT ALL YOU WANT

These are the healthiest, most nutritional, tastiest foods, and you should eat them without any hesitancy all the time.

FISH. First class food of A1 priority, excellent nutrients, apparently good for the brain after all, marvellous for slimmers too. Mackerel, herring, sardines (fresh and canned) should be high on your list, because they also thin the blood. But treat yourself to everything going – salmon, white fish, squid, shellfish, scallops, mussels, crab. Tinned salmon and tuna, too.

MEATS. Turkey and chicken, free-range preferably, rabbit and game. Excellent quality protein, good flavours. Cut off surplus fat from chicken, or pour it off when cooked.

BREAD, PASTA, CEREALS. Buy wholegrain rather than refined white bread, as it has more goodness, and more flavour, too. Eat plenty of pasta, it's the ultimate fast food with attractive texture; it's filling; and with a sauce which isn't fatty is excellent for your diet. Brown rice is good, if you like the texture. Buy a muesli mix which doesn't have extra sugar added, or mix your own, with oats, barley and wheat grains, plain or toasted for flavour. Also buy unsugared cereal such as porridge oats, Shredded Wheat, Puffed Wheat, Grape Nuts. Include Ryvita and crispbreads.

POTATOES. Marvellous. Full of Vitamin C and other good things. Bake them and boil them and mash them, but easy on the butter. Use yogurt and herbs and spices instead.

PULSES. Dried beans and lentils and chick peas and so on. Excellent protein and goodness, high in fibre. Count in tins of baked beans; they are a good source of fibre and protein, even though many brands have added sugar and salt.

DAIRY. Skimmed milk is excellent protein, ideal to put on cereal. Cottage cheese may be good but it's dull. But fromage frais and ricotta and mozarella are excellent low-fat cheeses. Plain unsweetened yogurts, especially the best-quality, are healthy and enhance many dishes, especially Indian, made into a spicy dressing.

VEGETABLES. You can't eat enough (and the Scottish diet tends to be poor because they don't). World-wide research establishes that the beta-carotene (the precursor to Vitamin A) in cabbage, leafy greens and carrot is a vital element in the prevention of cancer. Vegetables yield most goodness uncooked, or lightly cooked, so use them often in grated salads, such as coleslaw, mixed with chopped onion, celery and apple. All contribute excellent Vitamin C as well. The French make a gastronomic virtue of serving grated vegetables as an hors d'oeuvre with a sharp dressing. Buy watercress and beetroot, green peppers, sweetcorn, broccoli, peas and beans, good sources of vitamins and fibre. Frozen vegetables are fine, and they do not suffer significant loss of nutrients.

FRUIT. All fruit is highly beneficial, both fresh and dried, providing a wide range of essential vitamins and minerals. The parents who can afford a cornucopia of fruit will find their children will become less insistent on sickly sweets and snacks and junk food. Fruit juice by the carton is a good bet.

STEADY HOW YOU GO

This checklist includes good nutritious foods, but they should be enjoyed in moderation.

MEAT. Lean meat such as beefburgers, or steak with fat removed before cooking. (Beef, lamb and pork still contain internal saturated fat after external fat has been removed.)

FISH. Highly salted fish such as smoked mackerel, kippers and smoked haddock are fine but not in excess.

DAIRY. Full-fat milk is excellent, a good source of calcium and B vitamins. It is fine as long as rest of diet is not high in fat. Buy cheese to eat in moderation. Cheddar has more fat than brie. Edam has a lot less.

Butter is nutritious, but it's high fat, and should be used in small quantities, as a tasty flavour enhancer. Sunflower margarines are the unsaturated alternatives, but still high in fat content. Use thinly.

Eggs are excellent food value, but the yolk is high in cholesterol. Nutritionists recommend you don't eat more than three a week.

OILS. Olive oil, peanut oil and sunflower oil are unsaturated oils, all very good if used in moderation, but remember that both saturated and unsaturated fats contribute excessive calories to the average Briton's diet.

NUTS. Splendid source of protein and good nutrients, and so is peanut butter, but don't eat to excess because of the high oil content. Avoid salted nuts, not only because of the salt, but because they encourage excessive consumption.

SAUCES AND PICKLES. Fine in moderation but they may be high in sugar and salt.

YEAST EXTRACTS. Yeast is excellent source of B vitamins, but it's heavy on the salt.

HONEY. A delicious treat, but it's nutritionally little different from pure sugar. Jams and jellies, too.

VEGETABLES. Avocado pears are fine, but note their high oil content.

WINE. Enjoy in moderation. Social rather than health benefits.

WATCH IT

All these foods have an established place in our culture, but they are the ones which eaten to excess lead to ill-health, high in fat and sugar and salt, low in fibre. Those we insist on enjoying should be regarded as occasional pleasures, not part of our day-to-day diet. Think of them with caution as you might think of that once-a-year Christmas treat, mince pies with rum butter; suet and sugar in the filling, fat in the pastry, fat and sugar and alcohol in the topping, and a heart-stopping combination.

MEAT. Fatty meats such as lamb chops, pork chops, bacon and sausages all have too much fat. The same goes for salami, which is 45 per cent fat, though it's not usually eaten in large quantities. Pork pie is doubly fat, with fat in the meat and lard in the pie crust.

DAIRY. Double cream is something to use in very modest amounts, perhaps whipped to an airy fluff as in French Chantilly cream. Eat cheese in modest amounts, since it's also made from cream. Stilton has a high fat content. So does parmesan cheese, but this is less important as it's usually used in very small amounts grated. Philadelphia and cream cheeses have 47 per cent fat.

SAUCES AND CREAMS. Mayonnaise. Caution. It contains 80 per cent fat. Tomato ketchup contains one-fifth sugar.

SOFT DRINKS. Colas and squashes may contain a very high level of sugar, and little real juice, expensive sugared water with no nutritional value. Have a look at the E numbers too, as some children are allergic to colourings.

SNACKS. Crisps are a great fun food, but they do have a high fat content (70 per cent of their calories are provided by the cooking oil) and salt. Many snacks are extruded cheap carbohydrate, absorbing low quality fat, dosed with sugar or salt, stabilised with additives. Not good value.

DESSERTS. Biscuits and cakes are high in sugar and fat, usually low in fibre. Pastries have a high fat content, and a lot of sugar. Black Forest Gateau is mainly fat and sugar, and so are toppings and whips. Confectionery is high in sugar, of course, and chocolates are high in fat too.

SPIRITS. Uplifting, of course, except when they have a detrimental effect. High in calories.

SELECT BIBLIOGRAPHY

Many books provided me with information and inspiration; I am particularly indebted to the following:

The Englishman's Food by J.C. Drummond and Anne Wilbraham, with Dorothy Hollingsworth (Jonathan Cape, 1958)
Plenty and Want by John Burnett (Routledge, 1989)
Food and Drink in Britain by C. Anne Wilson (Constable, 1973)
Food in England by Dorothy Hartley (Macdonald and Jane's, 1954)
Food in History by Reay Tannahill (Eyre Methuen, 1973)
English Bread and Yeast Cookery by Elizabeth David (Allen Lane, 1977)
English Food by Jane Grigson (Macmillan, 1974)
The Cook's Encyclopaedia by Tom Stobart (Cameron and Tayleur, 1980)
On Food and Cooking by Harold McGee (Allen and Unwin, 1986)
Much Depends on Dinner by Margaret Vissar (Penguin, 1989)
Safe Shopping, Safe Cooking, Safe Eating by Richard Lacey (Penguin, 1989)
The Food Scandal by Geoffrey Cannon and Caroline Walker (Century Hutchinson, 1984)
The Politics of Food by Geoffrey Cannon (Century Hutchinson, 1987)
Food Science by Magnus Pyke (John Murray, 1964)
Food and Society by Magnus Pyke (John Murray, 1968)
Synthetic Food by Magnus Pyke (John Murray, 1970)
Technological Eating by Magnus Pyke (John Murray, 1972)
Pure, White and Deadly by John Yudkin (Penguin, 1986)
What We Eat Today by Michael and Sheilagh Crawford (Neville Spearman, 1972)
The Driving Force by Professor Michael Crawford and David Marsh (Heinemann, 1989)

The Food Connection by Colin Tudge (BBC, 1985)

The Famine Business by Colin Tudge (Faber and Faber, 1977)

Future Cook by Colin Tudge (Mitchell Beazley, 1980)

The Sunday Times Book of Body Maintenance edited by Oliver Gillie and Derrik Mercer (Michael Joseph, 1978)

E for Additives by Maurice Hanssen (Thorsons, 1984)

Food Additives by Erik Millstone (Penguin, 1986)

Understanding Additives (Consumers' Association, 1988)

Food Irradiation, The Facts, by Tony Webb and Dr Tim Lang (Thorsons, 1987)

The Safe Food Handbook by Joan and Derek Taylor (Ebury Press, 1990)

The Eskimo Diet by Dr Reg Saynor and Dr Frank Ryan (Ebury Press, 1990)

Food Resources Conventional and Novel by N.W. Pirie (Pelican, 1969)

Tropical Legumes (National Academy of Sciences, 1979)

Human Nutrition and Dietetics by Davidson, Passmore, Brock and Truswell (Churchill Livingstone, 1975)

Scientific Tables (Geigy, 1970)

Diet, Nutrition and the Prevention of Chronic Disease (World Health Organistion, 1990)

INDEX